D1367577

# A SPANISH TAPESTRY

# A Spanish Tapestry

## TOWN AND COUNTRY
## IN CASTILE

—

### MICHAEL KENNY

—

INTRODUCTION BY
### E. E. EVANS-PRITCHARD

GLOUCESTER, MASS.

PETER SMITH

1969

# PREFACE TO THE PAPERBACK EDITION

IN THIS book I have tried to present two pictures of contemporary life in Spain—the rural and the urban. To some extent I have also traced the interwoven relationships between them.

Since both the village and the urban parish dealt with form part of Castile, the characters who appear are Castilian types and their behaviour is typically Castilian. Yet one shuns the word 'typical', too often outrageously misused by tourists and Spaniards alike. Moreover, the village I have called Ramosierra is not even typical of Castile as a whole, if only because its villagers are now a good deal more prosperous than most in other Castilian villages.

Again, though San Martín, the urban parish, may be generally representative of parishes in Madrid, the Spanish capital is by no means representative of Spanish cities. Hence this book does not purport to be a description of Spanish stereotypes. Its compass is always local, even when discussion of certain concepts has involved me in regional or national implications.

Knowledge of Spain gleaned from the classrooms of most English schools is often dismally inadequate. The ordinary tourist's limited range of interest and contact does little to change, let alone improve, his preconceived notions of the country. To some then this book may appear unduly long. Yet it does little more than review, with some analysis, a number of important social and economic institutions in Castile and the interactions of human behaviour arising from them. My comments on current political or religious issues in Spain are concerned solely with their effects on these deep-rooted institutions, and I have therefore made no attempt to evaluate the policies of Church and State on their own merits.

The distinctive cultural patterns found in Spain arise partly from the peculiar merging of the two area influences to which she has always been subject—the Mediterranean (in which I include North Africa) and the Northwest European. Side by side with these influences there seem to exist sets of interdependent, sometimes contrasted, dual institutions, values, and concepts such as those associated with bureaucracy and patronage, the masculine and the feminine, the urban and the rural—each pair apparently more sharply divisible than in most European countries to the north. The concepts that I call *immaculate motherhood* and *honourable manhood* are striking examples of these. There are always two Spains and I see nothing new in suggesting that there is an ideal as opposed to a real behaviour in every society. Herein lies the riddle of seemingly contradictory social attitudes. This is certainly true of Spain. Throughout Castile the most casual visitor can scarcely fail to notice evidence of a fine feeling of brotherhood. Yet he should not expect to find, as a result of this feeling, any highly developed sense of civic responsibility or more than a rare instance of concerted community action. Whatever their merits or failings there is nevertheless a certain grandeur and vital passion to both virtues and vices in Castile.

Since this book was written in 1958 some sweeping changes have taken place in Spain. I would describe these in general as an opening-up of the country and of the minds of the people to greater external influence, in a word—Europeanisation on a grander scale. Others might choose to regard these changes in terms of liberalization and reform especially in the economic and financial spheres and, to a much lesser extent, in the political and religious. Perhaps the most striking contemporary phenomenon is that of young and able Spaniards pouring out of the country as emigrants to other parts of Europe 'in order to better themselves' (not 'just to survive', a motivation characteristic of the nineteenth century waves to Latin America). At the same time vast and unprecedented numbers of foreign tourists are streaming into Spain. The immediate consequences are obvious, whatever the side-effects may be. There is a positive flood of rising aspirations. Madrid has finally become a truly cosmopolitan capital with a traffic problem, and with its traditional tiled-roof skyline broken by multiple television antennae. Even the village of Ramosierra has a modern school-building with central heating. Both town and country are being increasingly exposed to innovative ideas and material techniques whether brought back by the returned emigrant or introduced by the foreign visitor.

I would ask the reader to bear these changes in mind when he comes across a statistic or a fact which seems out of date. It is not possible in this edition—nor do I think it desirable—to make a major revision of the original text. That must stand on its own merits. Nevertheless I shall deal with the process, trend and effects of the above changes in a forthcoming book on Spanish emigration.

For one creates a composite picture of a society at a certain period in time and this picture has a unity and an integrated quality which would not be the case if one were to allow for every sort of change likely to occur. I lived, worked and studied for five years in Spain. I felt myself to be part of the society, lending my services and receiving services in return from it. But when I returned two years ago as a summer visitor it was as an outsider and I keenly felt the loss of a certain status that I could not easily recapture. In the city, this status had been achieved by becoming a working member of a markedly heterogeneous community. In the village, this status was an ascribed one accruing naturally to formal membership in a relatively homogeneous community. As a member of the men's sodality who returns at least to fulfil his minimal duties in the annual fiestas there is always a niche I can reoccupy in the village. Perhaps it is for reasons such as these that the material presented in this book reflects more on personalities in the village, more on situations and events in the city.

So much material cannot be collected without many difficulties, and without much help. The very size and complexity of the groups described, especially in the city, constitute formidable obstacles. Furthermore, the Castilian (except in his sporadic bursts of somewhat startling frankness) is naturally loath to discuss intimate details of his life with strangers, let alone foreigners. It would be an alarming task indeed for the investigator, armed with a long questionnaire, to knock at doors in Spain expecting to elicit the sort of information required for a study in depth of this complex society. A long and continuous period of residence in the society therefore pays many dividends. One develops the patience to absorb information without actively seeking it; a slow process but an immensely satisfying and rewarding one.

I can never repay the ineffable kindness and warmth of the many in Ramosierra and San Martín who, without always fully understanding my purpose, still gave most generously of their time to further it. The friends in Madrid who were patient with my ignorance and unstinting with their advice are too numerous to mention. The parish priests of both Ramosierra and San Martín graciously provided me with facilities and information which were at times invaluable. Señor D. Antonio Mingote kindly furnished me with original drawings of the evocative cartoons here reproduced with his permission. And finally, I owe much to the encouragement and criticism of Professor E. E. Evans-Pritchard, Dr. J. G. Peristiany, Dr. John Beattie, Dr. Robert Pring-Mill and Dr. Godfrey Lienhardt at Oxford; of Dr. Julio Caro-Baroja in Madrid; of Professor Regina Flannery Herzfeld and Dr. Gottfried O. Lang in Washington, D.C.; and, not least, to my wife.

None of these can of course be held responsible for the views and interpretations in this book, which are mine alone. In conclusion, it should be stated that I have changed the names of certain villages and people mentioned in these pages.

M. K.

*Washington D.C.*
March 1965

# CONTENTS

# ILLUSTRATIONS

# INTRODUCTION

THE IMAGE of a discipline as it once was continues to represent it long after its outlook, its methods, its techniques, and even the content of its research, have changed. Anthropology is still generally thought of as exclusively the study of primitive peoples, as barbarology; and this is understandable because till recently anthropologists did mostly study primitive peoples, and their main theoretical advances were made by such studies, which also shaped the terminology of the subject.

Slowly, and largely by force of circumstance, we have broken away from this exclusiveness of terrain and interest, and in doing so we have had to abandon our privilege of each having his own little private reserve, some primitive tribe in Central Africa or New Guinea, which no other anthropologist has visited or is ever likely to visit. How often has one heard an anthropologist speak of 'my people'. Also, now that we have begun to conduct research among civilized and literate peoples our studies overlap with those pursued by scholars in other branches of learning, the historian and the student of literature, for example. The anthropologist has much to gain from these associations. The study of a people's institutions is the more valuable if their development can be traced and if they are represented by the people themselves, as they see them, in a literature.

Some excellent studies of civilized peoples have already been made by anthropologists, in India, in the Arab lands, and elsewhere. It has been for them a more difficult task than might appear, for they had received their training for the most part in an anthropology that was based on research among primitive peoples, so they had to adjust methods of observation and inquiry, and also terminology, to meet a somewhat different situation.

Studies in Europe, almost all of village life, have also begun to take their place on the shelves of our anthropological libraries. There were, of course, studies of the kind before the professional anthropologist entered the field, and some were very good, like Edith Durham's account of the customs of the Balkans; but I think that the first study which persuaded anthropologists of the importance of research among European peoples, not only for its own sake, but also for its theoretical significance, was that made by Arensberg and Kimball in Southern Ireland. I should like to mention other pioneering studies which have since been made, but I must restrict myself to the mention of only one, the one which deals, as Mr Kenny's book does, with aspects of Spanish life, Dr Julian Pitt-Rivers' *The People of the Sierra* (1954). Dr Pitt-Rivers studied an Andalusian community and Mr Kenny has studied a rural Castilian parish and an urban parish in Madrid, and the contrast presented by regional differences is of great interest.

Mr Kenny's account of rural and urban life in Spain is a vivid and detailed piece of descriptive ethnographical writing. This is a fascinating book to read because it is a very personal account by a man who entered into every department of Spanish life and who saw something interesting everywhere – in flats, pitches, meals, daily budgets, maids, gossip; everything is included and commented on. 'Spanish Tapestry' is a good title for a book which presents so many characters and scenes.

Mr Kenny, who read anthropology at Oxford, could not have conducted his research in the manner he has done without anthropological training. He had further two great advantages. He spoke fluent Spanish before he began his research, having earlier spent several years in Spain. He was also a Catholic, an important qualification in a country where religion permeates the whole culture; for he could not have participated so easily and intimately in the life of the people had he not been of the same Church; though Spanish Catholicism has, of course, some distinctive features, particularly with regard to the cult of the Virgin. Indeed, perhaps the most important discussions in the book are of the part played by religion, through the influence of the Church on the women, and of patronage; though Mr Kenny's account of politics is also illuminating. He gives an excellent description of the fiestas in the rural parish and of the texture of village life in general, and of the changes taking place as villages lose their relative isolation – the one he describes was never entirely isolated – and are drawn more and more into the national life. His description of the town life of Madrid is of equal interest, and by contrasting the life of village and town the characteristic features of each are revealed more clearly than if a study had been made of only one of them.

I can highly commend Mr Kenny's book to anyone who wants to know what Spaniards are like, what it is in their way of life, their values and institutions, which makes Spaniards different from other peoples. Not that his book needs any commendation of mine. Its own merits are sufficient. I write a preface to it only because the author is a valued friend and in recognition that he is a pupil of our Institute of Social Anthropology at Oxford, which is as much to our credit as to his. If I may try a bit of Spanish myself: *el buen paño en el arca se vende*, good cloth sells itself in the box, good wine needs no bush.

E. E. EVANS-PRITCHARD

All Souls College,
    Oxford.

# Part I

# THE RURAL PARISH

# 1

## RAMOSIERRA: PUEBLO AND PARISH

THE SMOOTH arterial road from Madrid strikes north-east, passes through Alcalá de Henares, where Cervantes attended the university, leaves the new American air base on the left at Torrejón, and leads into the province of Guadalajara and its capital of the same name, where the Italians are reputed to have fled in the Civil War. Here one may drive due north through the Roman-arched gate of Medinaceli and the walled town of Almazán. From Almazán to Soria, 163 miles from Madrid, there is a steady climb through sabine forest where resin cups are clamped to almost every tree. It was in these cool reaches of the Duero, that runs through Soria in Old Castile—a sharp contrasting relief to the barren plains of the south—that Juan I fixed his court and residence for a year in the fourteenth century. His interest lay in the thick pine forests which surround Ramosierra and the neighbouring villages —in the hunting of wild boar, deer and bear.

To get to Ramosierra in the province of Soria[1] nowadays he would take the *exclusiva*, the daily coach from Soria which runs due north and, leaving the toasted-red table-top below, circles the foothills of the Sierra Cebollera and the Sierra de Urbión. Nestling among these foothills and camouflaged among the lofty pines are a number of villages of which Ramosierra is one. It is just one hour's twisting, jogging run from Soria in the ramshackle coach.

There are doubts about its origin, but Ptolemy referred to it as one of a group of Celtiberian villages in this area contemporary

---

[1] Soria is the second largest of eight provinces in the region of Old Castile. It has an area of 3,977 sq. m., but with a population of 159,824 has a density of only 40.2 per sq. m. Compare the province of Madrid, in New Castile, with 3,090 sq. m., a population of 1,579,793 in 1940, and a density of 511.3 per sq. m.

with the better-known Numancia (also a few miles from Soria) which was finally sacked by the Romans after a tragically heroic stand. Ramosierra boasted of a certain fame for its archers, and there existed a special unit under the orders of the *Comes Hispaniarum* which some believe was composed solely of natives of Ramosierra. During its history the village has acquired another more localized name, that of 'Corte de los Pinares' ('Court among the Pines'), probably because of the sixteenth-century palaces and mansions built there by the nobles of the king's court, who used it as a hunting lodge.

Ramosierra's present limits, encompassing about 10,500 acres, are defined by the borders of four other municipalities, of which the most important for our purposes is Arboleda, to the west. There seems to have been little change in these municipal limits since Ramosierra was granted the title of *villa* and permitted to have its own mayor and council in 1774 during the reign of Carlos III. The ecclesiastical limits of its one parish are almost exactly the same as they were then, and it is highly likely that the municipal ones were based on these. Perhaps the only alteration in the territory recently has been in the east, where the building of a huge reservoir and dam was undertaken before the Civil War, largely with transient Andalusian labour, and is now in the final stages of completion.

The word *pueblo* really has three distinct meanings. It is used loosely to describe any small town or village, in fact any inhabited place which does not merit the stricter use of the words *ciudad* (city) or *población* (population). It is used to define the sum total of inhabitants who live in that place, and in this sense takes on the overtones implied in the translation 'common people' or 'populace'. Finally, it may be applied to the nation as a people. Thus Ramosierra is a *pueblo*, Madrid is a *ciudad* or *población*; while at the same time the inhabitants of Madrid as a whole may be described as *el pueblo*, and Spain itself when compared to other nations is also a *pueblo*.

A fact little known outside the classroom is that the average altitude of Spain is some 2,000 feet, making it second only to Switzerland as the highest country in Europe. Inaccessibility is perhaps Spain's outstanding physical feature, and in the middle of this citadel of stone lies Castile on a flat tableland, itself split into two by the Sierra de Gredos and the Sierra de Guadarrama. According to tradition, these two central regions of Old and New Castile owe their names to the many castles built there during Moorish wars. Ramosierra lies in Old Castile, whose boundaries extend to the north beyond the Cantabrian mountains, and which is to some extent influenced culturally by such neighbouring provinces as Aragon and Leon. Madrid, on the other hand, lies in New Castile and, as the capital with its own special characteristics, influences rather than is influenced by other cultural areas. It is well known that Castile is the driving force behind the present unity of Spain, and every schoolgirl is familiar with the Castilian's character and personality through the pen of Cervantes.

In the very use of the word *pueblo* can be traced its underlying connotation of a sense of compactness: of groups of people drawn together and compressed into communities by external pressures. These pressures beget a mentality whereby 'everything of one's own is best, and everything of others' worse—particularly everything of others in neighbouring communities.'[1] Once a man is uprooted from ties of locality, this extreme parochialism becomes much less apparent, and it tends to disappear among peoples from central and southern Spain. Hence the paucity of clubs or associations formed by migrant Andalusians and Castilians who have gone to live in the big towns or abroad; whereas people from the more culturally compact northern regions, including such provinces as Asturias, Galicia, Catalonia and the Basque group, at once reform their ranks wherever they emigrate. Soria, as a province, fails to conform in this sense to the pattern of the north, to which—as part of Old Castile—it belongs. But Ramosierra's ties of local patriotism, while relaxing in Madrid and other big towns in Spain, do, as we shall see, reassert themselves in foreign lands.

Ramosierra, some 3,500 feet above sea-level, lies at the mouth of a lush valley which rises gradually to a mountain pass in the north at over 6,000 feet, part of the Sierra de Urbión range. On either side the foothills slope sharply and are clothed in a profusion of oak, beech and, above all, pine trees. These forests are the cherished common patrimony of the village. Though under the jurisdiction

[1] Cf. Julio Caro Baroja, *El Sociocentrismo de los Pueblos Españoles*, separata del homenaje a Fritz Kruger. U.N.C., Tomo 2, Mendoza, 1954, p. 459.

of Ramosierra, the northern limits which stretch away into the heart of the valley are in fact common ground owned mutually by 150 villages of the province. There, on the often snow-bound forest slopes, are two small villages, both little more than a group of less than a dozen homesteads. Wrapped almost continually in a cold grey mist in winter, and practically sealed off from the rest of the world, these tiny hamlets have a mayor appointed by Ramosierra to look after their administrative problems. Despite the severe winters, the people of this area are sturdy and healthy; they declare proudly: 'even the dust here is clean'.

One's first view of the village is (as is natural in Old Castile) the stork be-nested belfry of its one church, an imposing grey stone seventeenth-century structure on the banks of a minor tributary of the Duero. As the coach passes the cemetery on the left and crosses the bridge below the village, women can still be seen at the washing-place, framed in a chequered pattern of drying clothes on the grassy slopes. A few hundred yards farther on, a lonely shrine marks the sudden end of the pueblo.

The crowd awaiting the daily coach gives the impression that a great many people in Ramosierra have nothing to do. In fact, the people who line the road and gaze have at the moment nothing better to do, for to stroll and see who arrives on the coach fits in nicely with their evening promenade, and so becomes a local daily event. Strangers—foreigners even more so—are regarded with special interest. Since almost immediately my luggage was urinated on by two passing village dogs my presence could hardly have been more felt. Though they would not do anything to stop the dogs, neither would they be so rude as to laugh or comment before me. This lively curiosity in others, common to most parts of rural Spain, is like a great ever-watchful public eye boring into one's back. It is closely allied to the sanction of public opinion, and is obvious as soon as one crosses the border from France.

Although the main road cuts through the village, all but a few of the two-storied stone houses lie north of it so that the cobbled village high street, whose traditional name has been changed to 'Calle General Franco', rises steadily to the centre and then sharply to the church and town hall in the main square. Some of the twisting side streets passing between the half-timbered houses have also recently been paved with cobbles, on which the yoked oxen now slip with their loads. Vestiges of a past grandeur still haunt the main square (in this case not the central square) and the higher part of the town generally. Ruins of a Renaissance palace burnt by the French in 1810 during the Peninsular War recall, so they say, the heroic stand of 200 villagers against overwhelming odds; but pockmarks presumably left by French rifle fire on the church walls near by are sometimes attributed to the Civil War of 1936. The ruins are now used as a stockade for the bulls during the August fiestas.

Farther along from the square is the old palace of a former Archbishop of Palermo, a native of Ramosierra, which now houses an elementary school and is a gathering point for the whole village at fiestas. The present mayor lives in a fine sixteenth-century building opposite. It is reasonable to suppose that the dual *barrio* (quarter) system existed until about the end of the nineteenth century, and that residence in the higher part of the village conferred prestige. The housing shortage and the fact that wealthy emigrants returning from South America and Mexico have fixed their residences in the lower part of the village have cut across this status line.

New two-storey houses of fine red brick (from the tile kilns nearby) now straggle beyond the village along the main road towards Arboleda. But with all their advantages in interior decoration they are mere dwellings for families, whereas the older houses serve as dwelling, stable and barn combined; most of them have two separate entrances through stable-like doors with the top half swinging inwards and left open; half the house is given over almost entirely to chickens and pigs, or to store wood or fodder, or serves as a cattle shed in winter. Above is a loft. The other half of the house has a communicating door which leads to the kitchen, general living-room, and lavatory below, with three or four bedrooms and an attic above. Only modern houses, and some of those belonging to the rich, have running water, but the public fountain is still a surer source than the private tap. Most kitchens are distinguished by the old-type Castilian *chimenea* or fireplace with open hearth, huge cooking-pots and cone-shaped stack projecting through the russet tiles on the roof. Some of the better though not necessarily larger stone houses have railed iron balconies at the windows of the second storey. As one might expect, they are those which give on to either of the two squares or on to the main streets along which the processions pass. Balconies in Spain have a social function; they are used not only for courting, but for making a show at fiestas and for keeping a curious eye on passing neighbours. The balcony is not just an architectural nicety; it is a social adjunct.

Some three hundred houses provide crowded shelter for the 1,460 souls listed in the 1954 parish record, which includes the few families living in the two outlying hamlets. But the population is usually referred to in terms of the numbers of *vecinos*. This status-giving title legally means 'contribution-paying householder' (the family head) although its colloquial meaning is 'neighbour'. There were 324 of these in 1956. Municipal statutes define *vecino* as 'any male Spaniard *emancipado* [i.e. one who is over 18, living apart from and independent of his father] who habitually resides within the municipality and is included on the electoral register'. But this legal neighbourship may also be granted at the will of the municipal council to outsiders who have been living for at least two consecutive years within the municipality, or to those who marry into the village and claim neighbourhood rights in the seventh month after marriage. Moreover, a public official whose post demands permanent residence in the *pueblo* is usually given the legal status of *vecino*. That these distinctions are neither lightly made nor wholeheartedly accepted will be seen in the following chapter; for neighbourship carries rights and obligations.

Each *vecino* is entitled to the use of all public utilities such as fountains, streams and watering places for cattle; he has right of public way and access to common pasture land, and may, with further qualifications, participate in the important annual distribution of the products of this common land—the Pine Luck. He may vote and also be elected to municipal office. On being authorized and paying the appropriate tax he may engage in any industry or trade in the locality. If he falls foul of the town council he has a legal right of appeal. In return he must, if an immigrant, possess for himself and his family a certificate of good conduct from the local authority of his last place of residence. He must obey the council and its accredited agents; he must pay his State and (if he owns property) provincial taxes on time. In an emergency he may be required to lodge for three days in his own house members of the Army or Civil Guard, providing for each pair one bed, mattress, pillow and blanket, two sheets, light, vinegar, wood (or a place by the fire for cooking). Should the soldier be of the rank of sergeant or above a superior type of mattress is specified. Again, the parishioner's draught animals and vehicles may be impressed to transport armaments, troops, disabled jailbirds, nuns and wandering poor to other villages. Lastly he must be prepared to act as a sort of king's messenger for government mail when the postal service breaks down.

Every villager is fully aware of his rights; it is doubtful whether he realizes the extent of his obligations. But except in the most extreme circumstances it is highly unlikely either that he would regard them as obligations, or that any member of the town council would enforce them in his official capacity. The obligation often shades into favour, the official merges into friend or kinsman. We shall now see how vitally his rights affect the villager's standard and manner of living.

# 2

## THE PINE LUCK

IF YOU mention in Soria (capital of the province of the same name) that you are going up to Ramosierra, they will nod their heads knowingly and say: 'Ah yes! The pine trees!' as if to imply that not only is Ramosierra situated among pine forests but that there is some peculiar, beneficial aura surrounding them. True it is that the pines belong to the villagers by right—from time immemorial, they will say.[1] In fact the pine forests were donated to the village by King Juan II of Castile in the fifteenth century, not only as a royal gesture of gratitude for the many happy hours he and his father had spent hunting in the vicinity, but also because of the part played by former villagers, despite their wretched poverty, in the wars against the Moors. Arboleda, a larger village some nineteen miles across the mountains, was similarly endowed with a pine forest bordering on that of Ramosierra. Territorial disputes, later clothed by religious legend, increased the latent hostility between the two villages; it is still perpetuated in mock battle during the August fiestas in Ramosierra.

A study of the meagre written history about this area of Spain shows that rivalries still causing internal tensions today were operative as far back as 1537, when extensive forest fires were attributed to arson on the part of cattle-owners covetous of more abundant pasture land. A body of forest guards was instituted by provincial charter to prevent the illegal cutting of wood and the destruction of the fresh young pine shoots by intruding goats and cattle. Successive encroachments by farmers, combined with 'overcut-

[1] These are the *tierras comunes*, part of the provincial *mancomunidad*, one of the two types of land owned by communes in Spain. The other type, *bienes de propio*, were sold under the law of 1855. Only seven other villages in the province have similar, though less valuable, common patrimonies.

ting', mark the trail of continuous decay of what was once dense forest. 'The land is tired out,' they say. Erosion, leaving the ground stony and sterile, has played its part in the ruin of these juniperous sabine forests; straying goats have also done much damage; but human hands have wrought the chief havoc by felling trees and breaking up hitherto uncultivated ground. Some local murmurs attribute the drying up of the trees to the dying curses of Moors slain among them. But the Forestry Commission has other ideas and has begun an extensive campaign for reafforestation in Old Castile. By 1955 one million pine trees had been planted in the Agreda district of Soria alone.

It is the Forestry Commission which, in May, in order to prevent overcutting decides with its official mark which pines are to be cut in Ramosierra during the coming year. The pueblo accepts this service grudgingly. It is only to be expected that older men, wise in the ways of the woods for generations back, should regard it as an intrusion into purely village affairs, an encroachment on their rights over 'their' trees.

One must speak of 'luck' in relation to the pines for, though officially these constitute the common patrimony, shares are determined by lot—a neutral method dear to a Spaniard's heart. A junta of six men, elected by the town council from among those long skilled in forest work who can 'see' the timber in the trees, goes out to grade the trees into three qualities. These are then numbered and parcelled out in lots according to the number of *vecinos* on the list for the year. As each lot must contain an equitable distribution of grades, and as the number of trees to be felled varies according to the Forestry Commission's selection of areas, some trees in a lot may be far distant from others. It is this, as well as the junta's margin of error, that accounts for disparity in the value of the shares.

Although the *vecinos* grunt and grumble a good deal, it is the general opinion that no junta can be infallible, and in theory, each *vecino* is entitled to serve on it eventually. But as this task, though it confers prestige, is one of great responsibility, the junta's members are usually drawn from among the older men in the village whose status and experience render them comparatively impervious to criticism. The selection of the pines occurs in May; the tickets bearing the number of each lot are put in an urn and extracted at random as the names of the participating *vecinos* are bawled out at an extraordinary meeting of the town council.

The feeling that traditional rights are being slowly whittled away, and not only by the Forestry Commission, is very strong. In 1659 there were 110 *vecinos* entitled to the Pine Luck; in 1850 there were 180; in 1956 the number was 315. The rise in population would of itself account for this increase in Pine Luck shares, but the villagers tend to ignore this and to resent the admission of new shareholders.

Some ten years ago they rose in open revolt. This is not to suggest that everyone was up in arms, for in fact only sixty-five persons were directly involved. Nevertheless, one must distinguish between a family or a group of families acting as a unit and a village at large acting cohesively. When individual behavioural patterns are translated into community terms it is usually to meet some common external threat. Where there is subconscious antagonism between town and country the town may constitute the threat; war or the danger of war may strengthen pueblo ties, but it is to be noted that the Civil War of 1936-9 caused divisions in Ramosierra; finally, the threat may be to economic interests which concern everyone. This was the case in the village.

More than sixty villagers were arrested by the *Guardia Civil* after a protest demonstration outside the town hall in the snow on a bitingly cold winter's night, and were transported to the provincial jail twenty-five miles away. The reason given was that the *practicante* (a kind of practising male nurse) and the telegraphist, both public functionaries who lived and worked in the pueblo but had not been born there, had claimed the right to the Pine Luck. They had been refused it by the town council. They then engaged a lawyer and carried their case to the Supreme Court of Appeal in Madrid. After the usual lengthy proceedings judgement was given in their favour and an order made that they should be granted the right to the Pine Luck or, what was tantamount to it, a cash equivalent each year.

As the news of this decree spread and indignation grew the crowd outside the town hall swelled to numbers far exceeding the sixty-five ultimate victims of authority (and people do not lightheartedly or casually gather together in a temperature twenty degrees below zero—these parts annually record the lowest temperatures in Spain). Of those arrested a few were in the crowd by chance, and not fully aware of the facts of the case; twenty-five were women, and three or four sturdy septuagenarians—the province has quite a reputation for longevity. Ramosierra has only six stalwarts in the Civil Guard section posted to the village and room for only two miscreants in its jail. Extra police were therefore rushed from Soria to deal with the situation, their intervention being looked upon none too kindly by the mass of the village, for on occasions such as this the police brook no argument. 'They were whisked away just like that!' said one informant with an expressive wave of his hands. 'Like common prisoners!' he added contemptuously. Needless to say even the Soria jail was packed and, though the women were detained for only a nominal seventy-two hours, the men fumed behind bars for ten days. They were then released, primarily through the good offices of a sympathizer who petitioned influential friends in Madrid. Whilst in jail, however, 'the unfortunate ones' did not entirely lack home comforts, for spouses and relatives daily brought them special food and consolation. Some even slept soundly on their own mattresses brought from home. 'It was rather like an enforced stay in a disagreeable nursing home,' remarked one observer.

Apart from the ill-feeling aroused, a good deal of personal expense and inconvenience was caused. Lawyers' fees for the defence at the trial and the loss of work entailed ate up many a man's savings and put some in debt. But the economy of a small community often depends on subtle divisions of labour. One man may form part of a team cutting and loading pine, whose efficiency is seriously impaired by the absence of one of its members. Another may be a specialized operator in the sawmill, whose absence creates a hiatus in production. Farmland must be cared for and a daily business run. If their owners are away for any length of time the economy is disrupted. The economic link is part of a social chain and the individual is not easily replaceable, as in the more diversified economy of an industrial system.

Although those arrested were acquitted, since it was felt that the local judge in Soria who ordered their arrest had acted rashly, they were awarded no damages. But the repercussions of the case were far-reaching and it is said that Generalissimo Franco himself ordered a general revision throughout the country of old privileges

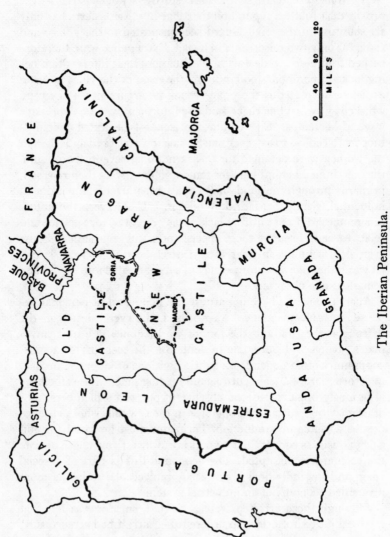

The Iberian Peninsula.

such as the Pine Luck. The villagers simply say that they were
defending their rights given to them by the Catholic Kings—
much seems to date rather vaguely from Ferdinand and Isabella
in their minds—since in such a hard climate[1] they could only survive through keeping a few cattle plus the benefits from the pines.
No doubt this is not the first time that such rights have been thus
defended, yet it is the first case within living memory, and no
similar incident is even hinted at in municipal archives.

Official reference to these rights in old parchments mentions
them cursorily in passing as 'of little value' and as existing 'from
time immemorial or by tradition'. But this is a hasty bureaucratic
view, for their value lies precisely in the important part they play
in the social structure at the local level. The constitution of the
common patrimony is now set down (since 1948) in ten articles
which make it clear that the legal title of *vecino* does not necessarily
qualify a man for the Pine Luck right unless he fulfils certain conditions which irrevocably bind him to the pueblo and ensure his
identity with it. Hence the discrepancy between the list of *vecinos*
and the list of Pine Luck participants. Before the 1948 troubles,
any family head who had been inscribed on the electoral register
for six months received the Pine Luck, so flexible had the ancient
unwritten constitution become. It was to regenerate the spirit of
this local privilege that the village revolted: to restrict the Pine
Luck to those who are direct descendants of native-born right-
holders.

In the Pine Luck system as it exists today the right descends
vertically down the generations, ceasing only when there are no
more children or when a holder loses his or her right by permanently leaving the locality. A *vecino* and a *vecina*, each holding
the right, may marry, but conjointly they will hold only one lot, in
the husband's name, with reversion to the widow after his death.
There is no instance in the village of such a widow's remarrying,
but in theory there is nothing to prevent an outsider's marrying
her and claiming the Pine Luck right seven months later. When
a widow dies without remarrying all her children share one lot

[1] The impassability of the roads between Ramosierra and Soria
because of heavy snow for as long as four months during winter was one
of the factors instrumental in granting Ramosierra autonomous civil and
criminal jurisdiction in the eighteenth century.

between them. There are cases in the village of joint holding by two or more brothers or two or more sisters; and each will continue to hold this part-right until either he or she marries (when, if one party at least is 25 or over, the full right can be claimed), or dies without issue, or leaves the neighbourhood for good. In all cases six months residence in each year is an essential condition.

The articles were not very clearly drawn up and provoked 128 written and legally stamped protests from indignant villagers. In the main the outcry was against arbitrary drafting on the part of the town council ('things should be settled in harmony, listening to everyone and judging communally, not just a decision by a few') and against the breaking with what they called tradition in the land, that is, the granting of the Pine Luck to those whose families did not own entailed landed property in the neighbourhood. The disgruntled 128 claimed in particular that the right should be based on three-generation residence in the village; that certain of the articles as drawn up opened the door to outsiders; and that the minimum period of residence each year should be nine months instead of six. It is curtly recorded that the dissentients' representatives were outvoted at an extraordinary meeting of the council.

Basically, then, the minimum qualifications are three: to be over 25, to be married, and to spend half the year in Ramosierra. The male reaches full maturity (and full status in the Pine Luck system) only on marrying, to become the head of a nuclear family functioning as an integral part of the village social structure. His children are living reminders of his stake in the village, for each child is a potential lot-holder and grows up conscious of the bounty that is his or hers by right. But the more children, the more lots there will be; the greater the population, the more *vecinos*; the more *vecinos*, the smaller the individual benefits. Thus a balance is set.

A woman with a Pine Luck right is a doubly attractive marriage partner for an 'outsider'. In the last century men from the larger village of Arboleda were only too anxious to marry into Ramosierra despite such obstacles as 'entrance fees' in kind. But even now such intermarriage between the two villages is regarded as rather *feo* (ugly). Yet outsiders attracted by the Pine Luck help to reduce the danger of endogamy within the smaller, prestige-conscious groups, acting as a regulating factor to supplement the laws of the Roman Catholic Church on the subject, which are flexible enough for dispensations to be frequent. (The mother of an ex-mayor needed and obtained a dispensation to marry her first cousin.) Cross-cousin marriage often provides a solution to problems of inheritance and, as Pitt-Rivers remarks, 'is a way to reinforce the disintegrating family unit'.[1] It was apparently quite common in the village before modern means of transport and military service outside the province widened the field of courtship, and before emigration became popular.

Rights lost by the few who marry and leave the village have been largely offset by rights acquired by 'outsider' spouses marrying into the village. Yet it is not uncommon to find emigrants who have returned in the twilight of their lives to settle down once more and claim their birthright—the Pine Luck. The majority indeed married local girls. Is the economic benefit in itself enough to bring them back? In 1958, before deductions by the town council for the cost of the fiestas, for public works, and for the labour involved in the marking and division of the pines, each *vecino* received approximately 2,250 pesetas as his maximum monthly share of the Pine Luck, or about £23 at the then rate of exchange. This is more than enough to keep a thrifty family and, if supplemented by a variety of activities to be discussed later, to provide an insurance against lean years.[2] Just before the Civil War, however, Pine Luck benefits were less than a fifth of their value today; then sheep and cattle were far more numerous, pasture land was precious, and wood was cheap. Shepherds and cattle owners were known to set fire deliberately to parts of the forest land, until the Ministry of Agriculture intervened and prison sentences stopped such practices. Since the value of the right can fluctuate so much within a generation, it is evident that the economic benefit has been of less importance than the more positive social benefit of binding a man to his pueblo and its social structure. Nevertheless this new post-war affluence is having an effect, as I hope to show.

---

[1] *The People of the Sierras*, 1954, p. 105.
[2] In practice it is not possible for *vecinos* to receive exactly equal shares. In 1957 they varied from a minimum of 11,000 pesetas to a maximum of 18,000.

# 3

## SUPPLEMENTING THE COMMON PATRIMONY

BESIDES the crowd of villagers who have gathered for the arrival of the daily coach, one of the first things you see in Ramosierra is stacks of freshly sawn planks on the hillock above the entrance to the village. From afar they look like carefully constructed heaps of matchsticks, so arranged as to allow a free air-flow between the planks and thus preserve the stack from excessive moisture. Even without the pine-topped hills they give an immediate clue to the main industry of the community. Down below the church on the banks of the river are more stacks, alternating with massive uncut trunks hauled there by teams of sweating oxen. By 8 o'clock each morning the whine of the sawmill and the thump-thumping of the old-fashioned turbine mix with the sound of the church bells calling to mass.

There are four sawmills, of which two are administered for the pueblo by the town council, another is run by two brothers, nephews of the mayor, and the fourth by a man rich both in material wealth and in the traditions of the village. This is the 'mother' industry of the region. The forests, the pines, provide employment for most of the younger men and essential fuel for the winter. It is not surprising to find each year the two tallest pines in the neighbourhood re-erected in the main square; the village fiestas take place round them in August.

Regular communication with the capital, Soria, was not established until 1923 and the industry, for other than domestic needs, is in its comparative infancy. People used to cut down and work the trees of their own particular lot won through the Pine Luck; but now many a *vecino* will contract with a younger man on a half-share basis to fell the trees for him, and then either await his turn at one of the municipal sawmills or, alternatively, sell the trunks or the standing trees on the hill to the private dealers in timber who in fact are the owners of the other two sawmills. He may even, if in urgent need of money, sell his trees as a speculation before the draw for the Pine Luck.

The hard labour of felling, shearing and hauling down the scattered pines to the sawmills begins in November and proceeds until the lots are exhausted or until the weather prevents further work. As much as possible must be done before the New Year in order to give the sawmills enough work throughout January, February and March, when outdoor work comes to a standstill and even the milk freezes. At the sawmills the trees are handed over to the cutting team. Difficult trunks are first sawn by hand. Better quality wood goes straight through the circular saw like cheese, and all timber is then planed by machine into planks of various widths before being stacked outside or in the various small warehouses, not all owned by the private dealers. One, for instance, belongs to a local grocer, a returned emigrant, who merely lets space. No precautions against fire seem to be taken, although warehouses may contain as much as a million pesetas' worth of wood; smoking is freely permitted and there is not a sign of a fire extinguisher. This casual attitude towards material objects of value is to be found throughout Spain. Fire insurance is, however, held by some of the wealthier people for their houses.

Perhaps the most efficient of the sawmills is that rented to one of Ramosierra's seven carpenters. 'El Mecanico' has a knack with machinery of all kinds, a reputation for being able to make or mend anything. He attributes his skill to the eight years he spent in the Air Force, and proudly shows off his band saw, circular saw, planing machine and automatic sharpener which, though none of them is modern and most would be roundly condemned by an industrial accidents inspector in this country, are held in high esteem in the village. He pays 1,500 pesetas a quarter rent, and electric power costs him from 1,500 to 2,000 pesetas a month. He employs his sixteen-year-old son and a man to help him with the carpentry and two men on the band saw, which he hires out to his neighbours at thirty pesetas an hour. Other hired labour is taken on as required for moving the cut timber. Wages vary from fifty to a hundred pesetas a day according to the degree of specialization, and are regulated by the National Falange Party vertical syndicates operating through the provincial capital branch in Soria.

Soria is twenty-five miles away; it might as well be 2,000. There is no known case of a wage dispute; indeed, it would be thought unfitting for the village to appeal to an authority in Soria, either as a community or in support of an individual—like washing one's dirty linen in public. Wages are still very much a matter of private concern between employer and employed; in fact, it is doubtful whether any one actually thinks of himself as an employee. A man rarely uses the word *trabajar* (to work); 'helping out' or 'giving a hand' much more accurately expresses his attitude, even when he is not working for recognized kin. There is no concept, as in Madrid, of 'the firm', though proper deference and respect are paid to the man who 'holds the reins' or 'has the word'. There is as yet lacking a sharp mental division between labour and capital in what is ostensibly a capitalist society. Christian names are used between employer and employee except where the employer merits the title *Don*, which in a sense automatically weakens his acceptance in the community, recognizing as it does his connections with the outside world. Nevertheless, since the standard of living surpasses that of many other villages in the area, daily wages are correspondingly higher and attract a certain number of outside workers. These, though they may have been introduced by friends or relations in Ramosierra, tend to address their employers with the prefix *Señor*.

Spasmodic attempts in the past to develop industry have met with small success. 'El Mecanico' admitted that some years ago and after some opposition he opened a small toy factory, but could not get capital to develop it, and one night, after he had left, the factory was burnt down. Asked about the opposition to his schemes, he talked in vague terms of *caciquismo*, the power wielded by the influential bosses who, he said, were against any expansion in the village which might tend to diminish their own patronage. All this was shouted above the whine of the saws while he stood ankle-deep in sawdust, sacks of which were stacked in one corner. How to put the sawdust to some commercial use had always been a problem. In Ramosierra it had been burnt for as long as he could remember, and when outside capitalists proposed to build a small factory for mixing it with resin and making boarding the town council refused its consent.

The two brothers who have modernized their mill claim that they alone work indoors throughout the winter. Gregorio, the younger, is regarded as something of an innovator with go-ahead ideas; and in an isolated and personalized community this attitude requires more courage and single-mindedness than in the more impersonal and semi-industrialized society of Madrid. It also easily leads to criticism and to a suspicion that Gregorio's ideas outrun his means of implementing them; in fact there is an underlying resentment towards any innovation for good or evil and an indefinable pleasure in the misfortune of others.

Public works provide a further source of employment for the younger men. The building of a ten-mile road through thick forests and up harsh mountain slopes (to heights as much as 6,000 feet above sea level) was begun more than thirty years ago and is still unfinished; it will link up two sizeable villages and eventually give access to the Soria-Logroño road. The Ramosierra labourers return home every night, but many of those from neighbouring villages and the migrant Andalusians live on the spot in rough shacks. In the construction of the new reservoir and dam to the east a large part of the labour force was transient, drawn from Andalusia and Extremadura, two of the poorest provinces in Spain. Living conditions on these public works projects are very rugged and during the Civil War such workers were regarded, at least by the parish priest and local authorities, as focal points for the spread of Communism. Men engaged from Ramosierra tend to fall into the foreman-supervisor class but, in general, work connected with these projects has a low prestige value in the village.

Another village industry is the tile-kiln beyond the new houses on the road to Arboleda. It uses the old-fashioned cone-shaped ovens, and the tiles to be baked are neatly laid out on the grass verge beside the road. Although owned by the town council, it is leased to a family which runs it as a joint concern. It produces enough for all building purposes in the village. *Carrasca*, or holm oak wood, is used as fuel instead of pine, which burns too quickly. Charcoal is also made in small quantities from holm oak and heather.

The conflict of interests between the agriculturists, herdsmen, and owners of forest land is a relic from the incessant intertribal feuds of the ancient Celtiberians—warrior herdsmen led by a 'prince' or a 'senate' (Soria retains vestiges of this in its 'twelve lineages'), living in jealously guarded territory and constantly at war with their neighbours for the possession of horses and extensive flocks of sheep and goats. More relevant to our purpose are the movements of flocks of sheep in this area during the winter. Flocks are either mobile, migratory (*trashumantes*) or remain grazing by river banks in the plains and lowlands (*estantes* or *riberiegos*). With the introduction of the merino by the Benimerines Berbers in or about 1146, producing a finer wool, transhumance was accentuated owing to the search for richer pasture towards the warm plains of Andalusia and Extremadura in winter, the flocks returning to the mountains of the *meseta* and the north in summer. Intervals of peace between Christian and Moor helped to enrich Castilian flocks with the merino, the hardy Spanish *churro* sheep being retained as an *estante* for the quality of its meat. Roast lamb is a common delicacy in this province.

Such importance was attached to this system of pasture that even in war contending sides respected the free movement of the flocks and the customary camping sites. Shepherds from Castile, Aragon and Navarre met three times a year in an assembly known as *La Mesta* to fix routes, allocate pasture land and request royal protection, since by this time sheep were fast becoming a great source of national wealth. Here shepherds and owners of flocks drew up contracts, imposed sanctions on 'pirate' shepherds, and decided upon distinctive branding marks. Shepherds from the Sierra de Urbión area in the province of Soria were the first to form a true corporative body. Expanded into a national body (in so far as the word 'national' had any meaning in those times), it was given the title of *Honorable Concejo de la Mesta* by Alfonso the Wise in 1272, and granted privileges which conflicted with the interests of the farmers. Thus began a rivalry which lasted (indeed, in some form still persists today) until the eighteenth century, when physiocratic economic theories favoured agriculture.[1] *La Mesta* was succeeded by the *Asociación General de Ganaderos*

[1] In 1795 La Mesta lost its separate jurisdiction and farmers were allowed to fence their lands.

*del Reino*, which dealt with the many problems arising from the sheepwalks, known as *cañadas* in Castile, of which the most important started from Leon and Castile and ended in Extremadura and Andalusia, traversing Madrid by the streets now called Alcalá and Castellana, where one may still occasionally see small flocks passing early in the morning. The walk had an average width of eighty yards, and it was calculated that on the southern route the flocks moved some 550 miles in a little over a month. The *cañada soriana* follows the river and just skirts Ramosierra.

The significance of these sheepwalks, in the economic sense and as channels of communication for culture traits, can hardly be overstressed. Their users, the owners of the flocks and their servants, were exempted by *fueros* or privileges from payment of tolls, from arrest and from military service. They rapidly grew prosperous; their frequent contact with the rich pastures of the southern provinces encouraged them to acquire land there. It was not uncommon for kings to grant noble rank to the more prosperous, as is shown by the coats of arms over the iron-studded doorways of mansions in villages like Ramosierra, Yanguas and San Pedro Manrique. These mansions were often both home and farmhouse, with lambing and shearing sheds, wool-washing troughs and the living quarters of the foreman shepherd on the far side of the courtyard. Verses from folk songs still heard catch the romanticism of these September migrations with their 1,000-strong flocks each under the care of an overseer, a head shepherd, two swains and their dogs and, finally, an intendant armed with plans and documents for dealing with the numerous mayors *en route*.

> *Ya se van los pastores a la Extremadura,*
> *ya se queda la sierra triste y oscura.*
> *Ya se van los pastores, ya se van marchando;*
> *más de cuatro zagalas quedan llorando.*[1]

A number of villagers have kin living in Seville and round about, most of them property owners now. Some have inherited property gradually acquired by generations of transhumant shep-

---

[1] Now the shepherds are going to Extremadura,
and already the mountains are sad and sombre.
Now the shepherds are leaving, already they are on the march;
more than four shepherdesses are left weeping.

herds. Others began as labourers on relatives' or friends' farms and built up capital through moneylending; their best clients, more often than not, were the *señoritos*, or sons of rich farmers, who had run through their allowances in the towns. Most of these migrants married locally and occasionally come up to Ramosierra for the annual festivals. The mayor, the biggest landowner in the village, derives most of his considerable wealth from vast estates in Andalusia inherited from his aunts. He describes himself, however, as a *ganadero* (cattle-owner or sheep-owner), though he is listed for official purposes as *vecino-labrador* (neighbour-husband-man).

Either description would fit most of the heads of families, except some of the craftsmen and traders, and even they usually own an acre or two of land and keep some kind of food-producing animal. A typical example of this plurality of occupation is the local innkeeper who is also a carpenter, keeps poultry at the back of the inn and sells eggs, keeps bees and sells honey, and runs an allotment; and the grocer and general-storekeeper, already mentioned, who is also a warehouseman, owns a plot of land where his family grows potatoes, and grazes two or three head of cattle on the common fields. Neither man is considered specially prosperous or at all unusual in his choice of callings.

Transhumant sheep-owners[1] have now almost disappeared from the village, partly because of the many laws for the protection of agricultural land passed since the eighteenth century, but also because of migration to and settlement in the south and the rising importance of forest land. Yet there is still adequate grazing for cattle in the limited numbers kept owing to the periodic failure of seed crops and consequent scarcity of fodder, and the difficulty of providing byres for cattle in winter. Extremely heavy fines for damage to crops by straying cattle, in some cases amounting to almost the cash value of the animal, also tend to keep numbers down. Disputes between farmers and *ganaderos* are very common, though usually settled out of court because of high legal costs; indeed, it is difficult to see how they can ever cease, having regard to the irregular fragmentation of arable land and inadequate methods of enclosure, and also the lack of any sharp distinction between the two occupations—farmers being in addition *ganaderos* and vice versa. Yet in some ways the two callings are complemen-

---

[1] Only about ten per cent of the total flocks in the region of Soria can now be called transhumant and of these most have made the annual journey to the south by train since 1936 when the sheep routes were disrupted by the Civil War.

tary. Cattle manure is an important fertiliser; hence the need for good pasture.

Wealth is to some extent measured by the number of livestock possessed.[1] Goats are looked after either by the children of individual owners or herded together under a shepherd paid jointly by a group. The animals respond to his early morning call, and the jingling of the bells round their necks announces their return home through the streets at night. From time to time the town council will form a committee of *ganaderos* to decide on the wage claims of these shepherds. Pigs are almost always kept within the house and nearly every family has one or two.

An anomalous position is achieved by the Forestry Commission and the local town council through measures adopted by each to harass the owner of livestock. Natural germination of the wild white pine is effected when the seed falls to the ground from the small cones. The Forestry Commission maintains that livestock ruin many pines by treading on the seedlings or young roots. It is the town council's responsibility to apply this national body's restrictions on the movement of livestock through the forest land. But this council is itself composed of owners of livestock and part-owners of forest land. Draught animals, especially oxen, are needed to haul away cut timber, and it is humanly impossible to prevent some animals from straying, however conscientiously forest land is patrolled by municipal guards. Furthermore, the village is split by strong differences of opinion; many of the shepherds and livestock-owners hold that, though seedlings are indeed trodden in by their animals, so too is seed which the birds would otherwise carry off before it had a chance to germinate, and the soil is thereby rendered more productive. The livestock actually help along the natural process, they imply. A summer visitor from Madrid, a staunch member of one of the religious brotherhoods with kin in the village, was sufficiently convinced by this theory to use his weighty influence with the Forestry Commission to obtain some relaxation of the restrictions on livestock.

Scarcity of foodstuffs limits the rearing of pigs. The few reared in the village are sometimes put out on a fifty-fifty basis with a

[1] Ramosierra boasts 850 head of cattle, 'the best in the province', 50 horses, 82 asses, 475 goats and 2,800 sheep.

local swineherd who takes half the litter. Others are bought from itinerant salesmen who may come from villages up to twenty miles away, driving small herds before them, perhaps to be converted by local traders into spiced sausage meat or ham for the August fiestas. Some are fattened in the home or put out with a swineherd, and are then killed in December at a family feast known as *La Cata* or *La Prueba* (The Tasting); the hams and the yard-long spiced sausages hang from the ceiling, and some may be sold to pay for next year's pig. A few families still observe the pig-killing ceremony on the traditional St. Martin's Day (November 11th): 'a cada puerco le llega su San Martín', runs the proverb ('every pig is overtaken by his St. Martin's Day'). A local wit impudently expressed the pig's importance in the economy: 'No offence to those present,' he said with a quick glance round at a passing herd, 'but there go the riches of Spain!' And as a local proverb says: 'God sends a litter of piglets to the bitch of the man He loves well.'

A hilly terrain, an inclement climate and periodic failure of seed crops do not encourage ambitious farming. The Roman-type plough is still in use. Cereal crops are grown on a very small scale and mostly for fodder. Fifty years ago sugar beet, flax and hemp were commonly grown, and they still are in more low-lying parts of the province. There are no vineyards in this climate, naturally; and there is no orchard produce. Some aromatic herbs such as thyme are grown for household use, as well as manzanilla or camomile for infusion as a medicinal *tisane*. Occasionally, to augment the continuously short supply of fodder, land is left without fertilisers for a time and a specially tough type of grass is grown. An esparto-type grass grows wild; smeared with resin, it used to be made locally into baskets and panniers for mules.

The smallholdings (*parcelas*) are in general the size of allotments —not more than two acres. Disputes over irrigation, though rare, are bitter and may split friends or neighbours who have traditionally shared a small irrigation canal for generations. One party will inevitably oppose another's application to the municipal council for permission to open a new canal, and discord will spread to their families. In most cases leased land is worked by former owners who have had a mortgage foreclosed; some say that one or two of the wealthier landowners (who may own as much as 400 acres in forest and pasture) have been over-ready to lend money and as quick to foreclose, and there is certainly a tendency for the wealthy to acquire more land over the years. After foreclosing the rent is fixed in terms of cash instead of as a proportion of the harvest, which would leave the tenant at the mercy of a bad crop had he not the Pine Luck to fall back on.

Thus the villager's livelihood, like the village economy, is not wholly dependent on one source. Although the forest is the mainstay, arable farming and livestock contribute to a now comfortable standard of living, not to mention occasional shooting of partridge, hare and roedeer and fishing for trout and barbel. It would be misleading to attempt to calculate wealth strictly in terms of one factor alone such as land owned without taking into account the capital and labour invested in it individually and by the community.

There are representatives of most crafts in the village, though the travelling tailor, like the itinerant quack and teacher, has disappeared, as well as the candlemaker who knew everybody's business. The shoemaker who used to make all types of footwear now limits himself to rough mountain boots made from uncured leather, importing other kinds from Soria and devoting the rest of his time to repairs and saddlery. Of the seven carpenters engaged on housing and on private orders for small articles of furniture, one specializes in coffins and is a part-time gravedigger. The blacksmith repairs bicycles as a sideline, but sends all other major repairs necessitating welding to Soria. Few calls interrupt the telephonist, who takes in stockings to mend.

Two bars, where coffee is served unhurriedly from ancient Espresso-type machines, divide the town between them and provide full employment for their managers; the wife of one of them takes in sewing, and both keep poultry at the back. Four of the five general stores also serve drinks over the counter, which thus becomes a bar and is attended by a regular and ageing clientele; what used to be the local inn is now only a bar, when the owner can be persuaded out of his carpentry workshop at the back; many more temporary bars spring up during fiesta time at the butcher's, at the baker's and elsewhere.

No one now has a suit made in the village, and the owner of the one clothing store is the agent for the two important banks in

Soria, as well as being an informal pawnbroker. The one ram-shackle taxi is used, except during fiestas, almost exclusively by the priest for his visits to outlying homesteads; it is owned by a part-time barber. There is besides a full-time barber, who knows all the gossip and is helped by his farmer son at rush hours. The postman, a cheery, rock-like figure as rugged as the very weather he must endure, reads with difficulty and has been delivering the few letters that arrive for twenty-four years; before the Civil War he depended on a tip of five or ten centimos per letter, but now he receives a small salary which he supplements by 'helping out' friends.

Occasionally, a visiting market will be set up in the central square or at the local inn; it provides articles such as crockery and brooms not to be found in Ramosierra. Shopping outside the pueblo is usually done through Leandro, the bus driver, who goes to Soria daily and acts as a general buyer, stating his own commis-sion. One realizes that the scale of preferences in the village has undergone only a slight adjustment since 1936, and the essential economy remains based on the social value of the land, a precious family right.

It is obvious that there is no 'war of prices' here as in Madrid, no cut-throat competition. Plurality of occupation is a necessary rule rather than a leisurely exception, and it is accompanied by an interchange of goods and services between kin, friends and acquaintances in which money in the form of hard cash plays only a secondary role. This is not to say that the people of Ramosierra are unrealistic about money, but that their system is based on values rather than prices. Provincial statistics, which show a startling increase in the cost of living since the Civil War, have less application here. Though the effects of this increase have filtered down through the few imports from the outside world, highlighted particularly in the cost of clothing and cooking oil, they are, of course, also reflected in the rise of the value of the pine, which is advantageous to the pueblo as a whole.

Whilst economic values give significance to people's social be-haviour, they are also related to social distinctions recognized in the community. One of the characteristics of isolated communities noted by Redfield[1] is the predominantly personal relationship be-

[1] *The Folk Culture of Yucatan*, 1941.

tween villagers. In every sale or purchase, in every exchange of goods and services, however small, there is a conscious, mutual recognition of identities between the two parties involved. Each villager knows everyone else by name, by nickname or by sight. Anyone attempting to enter this net of interconnected relations for the first time or after a long absence—a stranger, for example, or a returned emigrant—must take great pains to relate himself as quickly as possible to the interests of the village and its inhabitants. Until he becomes known, it is difficult for an 'outsider' to command any attention or consideration beyond a guarded courtesy; even the split-second relationship between the counter-girl in a big city department store and the most insignificant member of the shopping crowd ranks higher in the scale of social values.

It is not surprising that the continual juxtaposition of relations enforced by proximity and kinship ties greatly colours economic values. It exerts an equalizing tendency which prevents the mere possession of wealth from becoming a social virtue, unless it is used in a beneficial manner. Contrariwise, avariciousness is censurable, for it plays no useful social role; it is, in fact, anti-social. The words *roñoso* and *tacaño* are generally used to mean 'niggardly' or 'stingy'; but their alternative meanings of 'nasty', 'sly', 'malicious' and 'sordid' are revealing. Democratic equality, considered as the worthiest 'aim-action' for money, has already been achieved. And as poverty is not intrinsically despised, the so-called 'rat-race' or 'fast-buck' American mentality is unknown here. Progress is not looked upon as a desirable thing in itself; nor is it linked in the village with material gain.

This ideal behaviour is expressed in the aims of the *Caja de Ahorros* or savings bank. A beneficent institution with provincial autonomy, it has a branch office in Ramosierra run by the proprietor of the clothing-store. It has all the facilities of an ordinary bank but loans at low rates of interest are more readily made. Larger loans are commonly used for buying teams of oxen for hauling timber from the mountain—a yoke of oxen may cost as much as half a year's benefits from the Pine Luck. Profits from this savings bank are utilized for charitable projects such as a summer camp in a neighbouring village for poor children from the towns.

Yet this is 'ideal' behaviour, and even so reflects the comparative prosperity of the times. Fortune has been, is, and always will be fickle; the struggle in a bitter climate, with rudimentary equipment and a general lack of the entrepreneur's spirit, for a bare living, previously afforded mainly by the Pine Luck, has led to mass migration in the past. There remains a desire to appear poor, even if one is not, and a traditional objection to any outlay of money except to save face or with the certainty of a direct, short-term return.

Wealth is not as equally distributed in the pueblo as all this might suggest. Although there is now no real poverty[1] any sharp and continued fall in the value of the pines might in the future affect traditional norms of behaviour. But there is little need for a nagging social conscience on the part of the community in general, or of the rich in particular. Both extremes, the really rich and the least fortunate, are in fact disgruntled; the former feel that everyone takes advantage of them just because they are fortunate, and the latter that they are being exploited for the opposite reason. These attitudes are reflected in the system of bargaining which permeates society at all levels throughout Spain. Both parties to a bargain have a precise preconceived notion of the value of the article in question; both consider the other's price scandalous robbery; both give ground reluctantly under pressure and for fear of being considered grasping. The alternative, to accept the price first named, is to label oneself a *primo* ('sucker' or 'mug'). Pitt-Rivers suggests[2] that deadlock is reached and broken only by the intervention of a professional broker (*corredor*) who saves face for the bargainers by clinching the deal. This is probably truer of Andalusia than of Old Castile, where the professional broker is a rarer bird. His place is often taken by a supposedly neutral party, who is immediately suspect to both sides.

The richer derive their wealth from sources outside the community: the richest man of all is reputed to have a fortune of over sixty million pesetas, from property in the south of Spain acquired by his transhumant shepherd ancestors. Others have increased inherited capital by widespread banking and commercial activities,

[1] This is by no means true of the province as a whole. In 1949, out of the fifty provinces in Spain only Alava contributed less than Soria to the national income.

[2] Op. cit., p. 64.

which have greatly encouraged the general movement away from the land. The returned emigrants on the other hand are without exception self-made men who spent many years in the Argentine or Mexico. They are conspicuous at first for their ready generosity, and the richer among them consider it more 'elegant' to buy their food in Soria.

Money consciousness is more apparent among the young men, largely owing to the influence of provincial capitals, magnified during military service. Films and such media as radio and advertising have, however, had little effect so far; thus there is a comparative lack of subjective wants. Fiestas are occasions for a certain display of wealth and for honorific expenditure; then, indeed, carefree spending and 'treating' are essential for individual prestige, whilst the bigger the bulls and the louder the fireworks, the greater the prestige felt in the pueblo as a whole. Other occasions such as christenings and weddings reveal that spending (of late) is not a question of just 'keeping up with the Pérez' but of outdoing them.

# 4

## THE POWERS AND THE WORLD OUTSIDE

OFFICIALLY Ramosierra preserves the title of *villa* (a municipality enjoying peculiar privileges by charter) conferred on it by Carlos III in 1774. Its semi-isolation among almost impassable mountains and in the harshest climate in Spain largely accounts for the special sense of compactness still felt by the villagers. Partly because snowbound tracks cut them off from Soria for most of the winter, they were granted their own civil and criminal jurisdiction in the eighteenth century, with the right to erect a scaffold and pillory;[1] and they were given a doctor, a surgeon and an apothecary to deal with the frequent accidents caused by falling pines and the careless use of tools in the forest. The appointment of a mayor (*alcalde*), an assistant-mayor (*teniente alcalde*), two aldermen (*regidores*) and a type of attorney-general (*procurador síndice*) laid down the lines of future provincial government by vesting power officially in the hands of an influential few.[2]

In fact, it merely perpetuated the system of *caciquismo* (political squirearchy) which, it has been suggested, is 'so natural a form of Spanish public life, so consonant with the national character, that its extirpation might prove to be a loss rather than a gain.'[3] The parallel between the relations of provincial and local government in the peninsula, and those of the *encomenderos* (military commanders with special rights over a group of Indian villages) and the native *caciques* in the sixteenth-century Spanish Empire is too

[1] The *rollo*, or stone cross, in the central square still stands as a mute memorial to the earlier more extensive local jurisdiction.

[2] The privileges were not a free gift. Each of the then 110 *vecinos* had to pay the King 7,500 *maravedis* (the smallest Spanish coin then, worth about one-third of a farthing) plus half annates amounting to 26,625 *maravedis* every fifteen years.

[3] See Salvador de Madariaga's *Englishmen, Frenchmen, Spaniards*, O.U.P., 1949, p. 165.

close to be ignored. There, it would appear, the crying evil was not so much the system itself as *cacique* oppression.[1] Even today in Ramosierra *caciquismo* is often used as an umbrella term to cover criticism of the rich or of restrictions on individual freedom and progress in general.

This does not mean that mayors themselves have always been *caciques*, though it is largely true to say that they have always been controlled by them. The mayor is, under the present regime, appointed by the provincial governor for an indefinite period and, although unwritten law suggests that this should not be more than four or five years, in practice it is usually much longer. His appointment must be ratified by the central government in Madrid, and thus the person so appointed must be, superficially at least, sympathetic to the cause of the National Movement and the Falange Party. A local chief of the Falange Party is also appointed in the village. Both these men are *hijos del pueblo* (sons of the pueblo).

The governor of the province, however, is invariably not of the locality. His appointment is generally a political favour and his eventual dismissal, therefore, a political necessity. Tension and resentment is generally the reaction to a new governor, particularly when he tries to change traditional practices. A recent governor who attempted to curb boisterousness in the five-day fiestas of San Juan in Soria (dating from the eleventh century) was frustrated by an ugly popular demonstration. He succeeded, however, in reforming into contiguous smallholdings under the same owners agricultural land previously cultivated in separate, isolated strips: no mean feat this, even with the promise of State aid. A vigorous demolition and rebuilding campaign in the slum areas of the provincial capital also stands to his credit. All these matters are vehemently discussed in Ramosierra, where interest and ties in the provincial capital are strong. 'He can make or break you,' they say, and they relate with awesome respect and a certain glee the dismissal of the mayor of a neighbouring pueblo. It was for the official visit of the same governor that this ambitious mayor provided a

---

[1] See J. H. Parry's *The Spanish Theory of Empire in the Sixteenth Century*, Cambridge, 1940, for an excellent outline of this. The word *cacique* came from Cuba and is now used pejoratively to describe the local prototype of a defective parliamentary system in Spain.

lunch the like of which has never been seen since, complete with champagne and the best brandy, reputed to have cost the village 20,000 pesetas. It is significant that after almost every national election in the past governors have *had* to be removed.

In larger matters affecting the province, pueblo unity is liable to be disrupted by the system of *partidos*—the administrative districts into which a province is divided. In the eighteenth century, Ramosierra had its own civil and criminal jurisdiction; it preserves the former and even administers two small hamlets through nominees of its own mayor. But for purposes of criminal jurisdiction it is part of a provincial *partido*. Each *partido* is represented in the provincial council by one of its mayors, elected by all the others.

Medical, pharmaceutical and veterinary services are usually organized on a cooperative basis, the cost being shared by a number of municipalities. On a larger scale the governor of the province may demand cooperation from the *mancomunidad* (commonwealth), and thus enforce a union of all the municipalities in a *partido* for some public works project decreed by the central government. In such cases national pride may override local patriotism, but where no direct short-term benefit can be discerned these projects are regarded as annoying interference on the part of a dictatorial government.

Yet the governor may act on his own initiative. One example was the project of a road to the shores of a large lake 5,000 feet up under the mountain peaks, a popular spot for tourists because of its scenic beauty, a paradise for fishermen, and the place where provincial swimming contests are held. The scheme included the construction of a *parador* (rest-house and inn) for visitors, to have twelve bedrooms and a bathroom. A number of *partidos* were to share the expense, though the lake itself lies on the north-western boundaries of Ramosierra's municipal limits and its contribution was to be approximately 50,000 pesetas. Stubborn opposition was offered by the *ayuntamiento* (municipal council), first because of the cost, and, secondly, on the grounds that the scheme would attract unwelcome visitors. Discussion on this second point even included puzzled annoyance about the inclusion of a bathroom in the *parador*; it was suggested that the appliances usually to be found in a modest modern toilet might attract couples of easy virtue.

Such opinions are given here only in an attempt to point to an attitude of mind which automatically suspects and rejects any change from without. When this individual state of mind develops into a body of opinion it must be studied as a social phenomenon, for it has a bearing on the community's attitude to the outside world. Coolness towards the outside visitor, never apparent on a person to person basis, is manifested by the community as a whole. Opposition to entrepreneurs from outside setting up new industries, to new provincial projects, to applications for residence by summer visitors, is justified on various grounds: that these things will prejudice the local economy, that the cost will be unbearable, that the pueblo will not benefit, that the village will become popular as a health resort and attract people with contagious diseases. On an individual level this attitude may be described as *ensimismadismo* (being wrapped up in oneself), a variant of Hume's 'introspective individuality' and the concern of Spanish writers such as Unamuno. On a community level it becomes a 'sociocentricity'—a community self-centredness which decreases in intensity as the unit widens from the 'quarter', 'village' or 'town' to 'district' and 'region', until it ends in a mere hostile national patriotism.

In any public function where the community as a whole is represented, such as the inauguration of a new school building, the visit of the provincial governor, or the traditional ceremonies connected with the patron saint fiestas, three figures who mark the official triad of local authority are always seen together in the positions of honour. The civil authority is represented by the mayor, carrying the *vara*, a short, tasselled stick, the insignia of his office; the ecclesiastical, by the parish priest, always in his habit; and the judicial, by the sergeant of the Civil Guard in dress uniform. Each of these is the symbol of a nationally imposed system of authority, and therefore no one of them is the freely elected representative of the pueblo. They nevertheless embody at a local level a traditional set of national values which is accepted without question, though the people themselves may be apt, more often than not, to confuse the personality with the institution. Of the three, only the mayor is a local man, for it is national policy to post priests and policemen to localities other than their own.

The mayor, then, is the political head and chief spokesman of the village. He is president of the council, which is composed of six members elected in pairs by the family heads, the *vecinos*, and the *gremios industriales* (syndicates); continuity is ensured by election for a term of six years, so staggered that two new councillors are elected every two years. One of this number is appointed by the president to be assistant-mayor. Serving on the *ayuntamiento* is a responsibility that men are not over anxious to undertake; apathy and fear of criticism play a great part in their reluctance, so that elections are by no means hard fought. During the Second Republic (1931–6), it is said, a Republican *ayuntamiento* discovered a misuse of public funds by a previous mayor and published its findings; two members of this town council were shot later during the Civil War. Such happenings, together with a traditional moderate anarchism which finds expression in a marked mistrust of all forms of authority, have produced a kind of studied indifference to local and national politics.

The day-to-day business of governing a small village is carried out by its civil servants, chief of whom is the *secretario*, who has the only sinecure in the village. His duties are roughly those of an English town clerk and his appointment is made by the central government for life; but as he is the right-hand man of the mayor the rhythm of his activity is largely governed by that of his superior. Asked if he had no other form of employment as a sideline, since he seemed to have plenty of spare time, he replied that it was not necessary. By village standards he is comfortably off; apartments are provided for him on the warm south side of the town hall, with efficient central heating, and he earns 3,000 pesetas (approximately £27) a month paid to him by the *ayuntamiento*.

He and an office staff of two deal with the daily routine of applications for building and trade, family allowances and the collection of taxes, correspondence with the provincial capital and the like. It is the town crier who, by means of throaty announcements preceded by a thin blast on a small horn, keeps the people informed of the mayor's *bandos* (proclamations) on hygiene, common pasture land, the straying of cattle, morals in general, market prices or any special event such as a visit of the Governor, a visiting theatre or cinema show or market, and activities connected with the fiestas. The *secretario* is not distinguishable from the rest of the community by any particular uniform but favours a dark suit with a tie for special occasions, and carries a walking-stick on his rounds of the village. Neither he nor his wife was born in Ramosierra; nor indeed were any of the State employees such as the telegraphist and postmaster, the doctor, the chemist and the schoolmasters.

The position of these functionaries in the pueblo is rather delicate. They lack the feeling of solidarity enjoyed by the ordinary *vecino*, and the rich and influential are loath to accept them socially. We saw when discussing the Pine Luck how the pueblo may resent those born outside it, and 'outsiders' in their turn may react against pueblo hostility. One night during the August fiestas, when the village youth tend to band together for nocturnal activities such as 'singing the rounds' and for a good deal of daring horseplay, the doctor's backyard was broken into and two of his chickens were stolen. The local authorities were prepared to punish the culprits with a fine, but the doctor insisted not only on a retribution of three times the market price of the fowls but also on prosecution in the provincial court.

If the authority of the *ayuntamiento* is accepted as an essential nuisance, the mayor's powers are held in healthy respect. Since he is the personal delegate of the central government, and responsible to it through the provincial governor, his council acts in an advisory capacity only. When things go well, individual and office are rarely confused. Far from being embarrassed by dramatic gestures and rhetoric, people frequently applaud them, but attribute their use to the role an individual is playing. Thus a compliment to the mayor on a fine speech is recognized as flattering not so much the man as the institution he represents. But when the man seemingly arrogates to himself the virtues of public office his role becomes a sort of mask which people jeer at. Furthermore, criticism of an individual official comes more often from a single *vecino* than from the pueblo collectively. Thus the *ayuntamiento* as a whole may be generally censured for laziness in not providing adequate piping for the water supply, or equally blamed as a whole for extravagance in laying down new cobbled paving in a main or side street. But when its decrees particularly affect an individual, his criticism tends to be levelled at one of their number, more often than not the mayor.

A case in point is that of an innkeeper in the main square who was forbidden to unload stores in the square. The inn had been struck off the official list for overcharging tourists (fine, 1,000 pesetas) and because of the owner's refusal to pay his taxes in full, on the ground that he was only really busy for two months of the summer. He insisted that he was the victim of a premeditated persecution campaign on the part of the mayor to get him out. 'What more does he want?' he complained. 'He's got all the power and he still loves ordering people about; he's got more money than he can ever use, but he has to borrow a car to settle the boundaries of his private estate because he's too tight to buy one. I'm richer with my bicycle,' the innkeeper concluded scornfully. He refused to call his 'enemy' (incidentally a distant relative) by anything but his Christian name, omitting the respectful title *Don*, and loudly aired his opinions in the village. The pueblo was well aware of the innkeeper's grievance, but not all its sympathy was with him, for he was considered very independent, a little 'touched', and more than a little 'tight' himself. During the fiestas, however, the sanctions of the law were tacitly ignored by both the executive and the individual victim. The imported band, about seventeen strong, had to be lodged somewhere; and their accommodation was at once good business for the innkeeper and a problem solved for the fiesta organizing committee, the *ayuntamiento* in another guise. No one in the pueblo sees anything odd in such behaviour, indeed it is regarded as the only sensible thing to do. But then the fiestas are an offering to the patron saint of the village, and an aura of sanctity surrounds them, as we shall see later. During the fiestas, too, the pueblo demonstrates its solidarity to the outside world; hence the eagerness of summer visitors and returned emigrants to take an integral part in them.

Although it is not within this book's scope to discuss the merits and demerits of regional characters, it should be pointed out that these are sharp enough to be distinguishable, and that an even greater distinction can be drawn between town and country life and behaviour. Unamuno sees a continuous tension between town and country, and draws a comparison unfavourable to the peasant, whom he accuses of being covetous and small-minded, indifferent to government, believing neither in the law nor in its efficacy, and convinced that everything is achieved through the good graces of the *cacique*.

We have already noted a link between Ramosierra and Madrid

through summer visitors with roots in the village, and a wider network of relationships through emigrants to other countries or other parts of Spain. Without doubt such links are sometimes instrumental in maintaining the *cacique* system, at other times in modifying its effects: in supporting and encouraging traditional customs on the one hand, and in the introduction of new and beneficial practices on the other. It is the summer visitor or homing emigrant who is most enthusiastic and meticulous about details of ritual in fiesta observance; and he, too, who, as a mover in the modern world of great cities in Europe or the sister South American republics, sometimes prevails on local authorities to relax the harsher restrictions on both youthful behaviour and on the introduction of more modern industrial and agricultural techniques.

Close contact is maintained between kin and friends separated physically by emigration. It was an emigrant's boast that anything which happened in Ramosierra, however insignificant, was known within three days in Vera Cruz, though the converse was not necessarily true—nor even desirable, added some. Emigrants can be divided into two main groups: those who went to Mexico and South America at the turn of the century, and those who sought their fortunes in Madrid.[1] The former, almost without exception, became prosperous, and either sent for other members of their families or returned to marry and live in Ramosierra; the latter were mostly young men prevented by tighter immigration quotas from emigrating, but no longer content to endure the hard winters in their native village. The philanthropy of the emigrants from Ramosierra is held up as an example to the whole region, and the pueblo often seems to bask in their reflected glory. The villager will proudly volunteer the information that even the provincial capital did not possess an adequate drainage system before Ramosierra, but only later questioning will elicit the fact that this was instituted in 1919 from emigrants' money. He will agree that Arboleda also has produced a number of philanthropic emigrants,

[1] There has been a sharp rise in migration to provincial capitals since the end of the Civil War. There was an urban rate of 10.47% in Soria in 1950 (only 4.75% fifty years earlier); compare 84.02% for Madrid in 1950 (69.65% in 1900). Accompanying this is a striking increase in emigration since World War II: 15,246 in 1947 but 61,334 in 1951. All but a few of these went to South America. See *Guiá de la Iglesia en España*, Madrid, 1954.

but will declare that the emigrant from 'that' village emigrates *con vicio*, meaning that he is easily given over to vice because he is used to 'an easy life'. Then he caps the argument by declaring that all the big fortunes from abroad were made by men from Ramosierra.

There is a certain romantic allusion here to the clean-limbed, poor but honest emigrant who 'hits the town with five cents', starts with some lowly task like selling newspapers, and builds himself up by sheer hard industry into a leading business tycoon. No doubt this picture contains an element of truth; the early emigrant's lot was almost certainly a hard struggle; but it is equally true that, once he was established abroad, ties of kinship and friendship prompted him and his kind to help those who followed in their footsteps. This 'self-made man' technique is highly applauded in the village, but it does not automatically carry with it any notable prestige. All returned emigrants are rather scornfully referred to as *Indianos*, and it is evident that they are by no means welcomed back to the village fold with open arms. Though their money and their donations may be accepted as a matter of course, the emigrant has to work hard to win his own acceptance; hence his enthusiastic plunging into village affairs and fiesta ritual, and his ingratiating ways and generosity in the bars. Mistrust of 'foreign ways' and the 'city slicker' mentality acquired in the towns and abroad account in part for this feeling, but one of the less publicized, though by no means weaker, characteristics of the Castilian—envy—is its real basis. It is revealed in engaging bursts of candour in the village itself, and by ex-villagers living in Madrid who have no particular axe to grind and have achieved an impartial position.

Every person living in Ramosierra's one parish is a registered Roman Catholic; from this point of view the words *pueblo* and 'parish' are synonymous. It is not the task of the social anthropologist to 'explain' religion, but rather, as Professor Evans-Pritchard has carefully pointed out,[1] to show its relation to social life in general. That it is a social phenomenon and not merely an individual matter is shown by its intrusion into the significant periods

[1] *The Institutions of Primitive Society* (broadcast talks), Oxford, 1954, pp. 5–7.

and events of people's lives. As *rites de passage*, baptism, confirmation, first communion, marriage and death are all naturally the subject of religious ceremonial. But so also, by means of blessings and directed prayers for success, are other activities brought into the religious picture—agriculture or animal husbandry, journeys, the inauguration of new buildings or societies, as well as such implements of these activities as tools, means of transport and the very foundation stone. Thus the Church acts as patron and protector not only during the vital events of the life cycle but in the ordinary daily activities of life.

In this context then, the man of the Church (who in the personality of the parish priest is at pueblo level the representative of the Pope) becomes a figure in the social structure. Here is a society in Western Europe which has not yet made between the popular mind and religion the separation so noticeable in more complex and industrialized societies. There are no mutually exclusive sects based on class or occupation, and thus no 'sub-cultures' brought about by such divisions as are found in the free Protestantism of Great Britain. So, at all strata of society, and in practically all forms of collective activity, the priest is not only an essential figure but one who is naturally accepted. By his Sunday sermons and by admonitions to the individual in the confessional box, the parish priest exerts considerable influence, albeit mainly restrictive, on the behaviour of his flock. Indeed, he would exert more if only more people listened to him and if the bulk of the men did not stay away from his services. I am not concerned here with the rights and wrongs of the methods he employs, but rather with the effect of them on the social life of the pueblo. For the past thirty years in this parish the movements of the faithful have been controlled mainly from the church, the priest having not had much belief in the efficacy of visiting the villagers at home except in the case of serious illness or death. For this reason he maintains close professional contact with the doctor, so that his appearance outside the church often presages ill in the minds of the pueblo.

The practice of holding *novenas* in different houses[1] every night

[1] A nine days' prayer made in preparation for a feast or for a special intention after the example of the Apostles before Pentecost. This is often the excuse for a social occasion with refreshment provided after prayer, as it still is in parts of Central and South America.

with the priest leading a group of relatives, friends and neighbours is falling into disuse. The priest continues to hold *novenas* in the church, sparsely attended by a pious few, mostly *las beatas*, a word once used of women who wore religious habits and engaged in works of charity, but now loosely applied to those who base their lives on churchgoing and surround the priest on every possible occasion. Unfortunately it has a secondary meaning of 'female hypocrite',[1] and it is from these women (as well as from his housekeeper and the local authorities) that the priest learns of goings-on in the parish.

Going to church, and to be seen going to church, still have a social force, because by churchgoing the pueblo reasserts its sense of compactness (as parishioners); so that even the men *en masse* will make at least a token appearance at the services on the more important feast days. Although the authority of the Holy See in Rome may be recognized merely by such formalities, this does not mean that a wholly Catholic nation will not merge religion into the totality of its general culture. Even the most cynical of men will insist that his religion (although he may not practise it) is an integral part of his existence, so that an attack on his religion is also an attack on his way of life and vice versa. Confusion arises from identifying the two at a level where we should make some distinction. Hence, anti-clericalism should be distinguished from anti-Catholicism.

The priest, then, in the role of supreme defender of the faith (and therefore an integral part of a traditional way of life) is also the unique performer of expiatory rites which nullify the effects of sin[2]—effects which may be some form of misfortune in this life or retribution in an after life. To this end, he is empowered to withhold the sacraments which, in the case of baptism, matrimony, and

---

[1] In fairness it should not be forgotten that 'hypocrisy' originally meant acting a part. Sincerity may equally be coupled with dramatization of religious worship, which is common in Spain; but Unamuno, quoting from *Lex Credenti* by Fr. George Tyrrell, S.J., in *Obras Completas*, Tomo 3, Madrid, 1950, pp. 1089–96, implies that women have feminized the cult of Christ, with the Church's tacit consent, to such an extent that men of action are no longer attracted to it. This is a comparatively recent phenomenon and is a far cry from the militant saint ideal of Loyola.

[2] I follow here Radcliffe-Brown's interpretation in *Social Sanctions*, Encyclopedia of the Social Sciences, New York, 1933.

extreme unction before death, may have serious social repercussions; certificates of baptism are demanded for entry to many schools, complete civil rights are given automatically on marriage by the Church under the Concordat of 1953, and the Church may forbid Catholic burial to Marxists, dissidents and 'the unworthy' (i.e. notable sinners). In the very publication of banns the priest is exercising a parochial right, whereas we know that the pueblo itself has its own methods of expressing disapproval of the choice of a marriage partner.[1]

The parish priest's duties tend to merge with those of the executive, as in his chairmanship of committees for administering foundations and trust funds, consisting of money left by rich emigrants, mostly for educational purposes. He is the channel with his parish whereby Catholic Action censors films and plays and provides gift parcels for the indigent through *Caritas*, the social help service first organized at Valladolid in October, 1936, through the women's section of the Falange Party. He is also *ex officio* president of all the *cofradías* (religious sodalities), with one exception, that take a prominent part in feast day celebrations. His leading role in village affairs makes his help desirable—not to say essential—in matters where recommendation and influence carry weight.

The last figure in the official triad of the authoritarian structure in the village is the sergeant of the Civil Guard section. He belongs to a force whose members are the aristocrats of the many police bodies in Spain. Under rigid discipline, their activities are largely confined to the country, where they patrol roads and paths, always armed and in pairs. Originally a holy brotherhood founded by Ferdinand and Isabella in the fifteenth century to put down outlaws in the Castilian forests, the Civil Guard was reformed as a national force after the Carlist War of 1844, when it performed much the same function. It was also the bane of the many roaming republican elements after the Civil War of 1936.

Organized on military lines, the corps has similar ranks to the Army's, and all but the high-ranking officers live in barracks. They are, in effect, soldiers and are noted for their apparent incorruptibility and their traditional support of the established

[1] See Pitt-Rivers, op. cit., for discussion of the *cencerrada*—the Spanish charivari—pp. 169–75.

government, except during the last Civil War. Their provincial organization is based on territorial *partidos*, like the municipalities and the dioceses. Over 50,000 strong, their duties are to protect the civil population and its property from local crime and national rebellion. They are easily distinguished by their glossy three-cornered hats with the flattened brim at the back, a symbol of their 'back-to-the-wall' stand in the Carlist Wars.

The small detachment of six takes little part in village affairs, for they are mostly out on patrol and have no ties of birth or kin with the community. However, they do unobtrusively supervise gatherings of villagers at markets, auctions, dances and fiestas, and casually enforce local hygiene or irrigation regulations. The sergeant, though directly under the orders of the mayor as the executive, also manages to resolve trivial conflicts between families which might otherwise be taken to the local justice; but he does this through the force of his personality and not by virtue of his rank.

Prohibited from intermarrying or even fraternizing with the local inhabitants, the Civil Guard through their dispassionate and ruthless efficiency in times of trouble have become the traditional enemy of the peasants. There is thus a healthy respect for this force, which is typified by an almost total lack of crime in the locality—the occasional prisoner is a dedicated vagabond or a persistent gypsy. Its presence must be considered as a regulatory, balancing factor in social order, though not a naturally integrated one, since its loyalties always belong to the world outside.

Religion, by sanctifying the events of family life, automatically complements and strengthens the force of law. By acting as judge in matters of morality, approving or condemning custom and *mores*, the Church assumes authority over and directs public opinion. This accent on morality rather than on dogma and faith would seem to be a characteristic of the Spanish Catholic Church during the present epoch; a basic conception of man as a being burdened from birth with the vitiating effects of original sin, and beset on all sides by temptation, may in some measure account for this. Faith and good works are reduced to second place, in contrast, perhaps, with more northern Catholic thought and theologians such as Martin D'Arcy and Jacques Maritain who are more concerned with man as a reasoning being and with the explanation of much dogma by the laws of reason. The remarks of a Spanish monk are apposite here. 'For centuries we have been preaching morality to the eventual detriment of our dogma,' he said, 'and now we realize that we lag behind other Catholic-minded countries in our ideas of theology. We are only now beginning to send our priests abroad to study and revivify our faith.' In this connection, too, the comment of a cultured villager may be noted after hearing during the August fiestas a fiery sermon on the virginity of the Virgin: 'For the Spanish Church there seems to be no other Commandment than the sixth . . . you can do what you like, as long as you keep this one.'

Although questions of faith are taken for granted in this traditionally Catholic country, it is doubtful if an explanation of some religious mysteries would be within the ken of simple country folk. The priest's role is therefore largely a monitory one aimed primarily at women and children, for it is through them that the stability of the family is preserved. Thus the content of a sermon or address depends much less on exposition than on a rhetorical, admonitory style—although this is not always in itself sufficient to hold the attention.[1] Nevertheless, the pulpit in Ramosierra is still the best place for reaching the community on matters of traditional importance to the pueblo. Hence, on the day of St. Roch in 1956, the energetic sermon consisted almost entirely of a warning against the gradual loss of pueblo customs and an appeal to young bachelors to join and support their religious sodality. The parish priest, too, in his Sunday sermons in the summer may often be heard declaiming against the insidious influence of the habits of 'strangers from outside'. Though this may not be looked on too kindly by the summer visitors (in most cases relatives of the villagers) the underlying concern to preserve local and traditional values is none the less clear.

The people of Arboleda are sometimes derided for being so ignorant as to maintain a *curandero*, or folk practitioner, in their midst, the implication being that Ramosierra is far above this sort

[1] A visitor-priest observed: 'There are only two types of preachers: those who make the heart move and those who make the "arse" move.' Mass in Madrid is now conducted almost as a background to a continuous sermon which lasts the length of the ceremony.

of thing. But conversation in the village reveals at least a respect for, if not a belief in, this man's powers. Some shepherds apparently still send him tufts of wool from an ailing sheep 'para deshacer el mal de ojo' ('to take away the evil eye') supposedly cast on it. Belief in the evil eye is common enough throughout Spain, and one personal prophylactic is to extend the index and little fingers while repeating the word *lagarto* (lizard); but both reputed effects and treatment vary considerably from region to region. It is thought in Ramosierra that the evil eye may affect livestock through pasture, water or the air. Making the 'circle of King Solomon' with the left hand on the forehead of an affected animal is held to be specially efficacious. Gypsies are commonly believed to possess the power of imposing spells, and in the municipal ordinances of Ramosierra they are forbidden to stay within village limits for more than one night.

When misfortune continually dogs a man he may attribute it not to mere bad luck but to another's evil influence. Those about him, indeed, may darkly suggest that his misfortune is no more than poetic justice for his own misdeeds, or they may go further and imply that he is a kind of jinx or Jonah. In this context they say of a man that *tiene mala sombra* (he has an evil shade or spirit); hence the opposite, *tiene buena sombra*, means to be pleasing or popular, though a commoner expression is *tiene gracia*[1] (he has grace). There is a sharp distinction to be drawn here; having a *mala sombra* is not the same as being possessed. The Church regards the former kind of talk as mere superstition, but recognizes the latter state and has a ceremony for exorcizing evil spirits. Valle-Inclán in one of his novels[2] refers to *La Misa de las Endemoniadas* (the Mass for those possessed by the Devil) held at the shrine of Santa Baya de Cristamilde at midnight. But the popular mind preserves an ambivalence in these matters, and in the same tale, after the Mass the people of the pueblo take their charges naked into the neighbouring sea to be washed clean by seven successive waves.

*Curanderos* and *saludadores* (the popular *cognoscenti* of special

---

[1] To have *gracia* is to be specially gifted by God spiritually, or in speech, movement or wit, inspiring admiration (and envy) in others. The plural *gracias* is used as we use 'thank you'. Consequently to be *desgraciado* (degraced) is to be unfortunate, wretched—to be out of favour.

[2] Ramón del Valle-Inclán, *Flor de Santidad*, Madrid, 1920, pp. 209-15.

charms) also sell love potions and give advice on combating the curses of *brujas* (witches).[1] One way for a shepherd to find out who had cast a curse over his sheep was to throw an ailing animal into a blazing fire, and whoever was first drawn to the scene by the sheep's bleating would be the guilty man; a traditional measure (*carga*) of corn sufficed to buy off the curse. The two worlds of superstition and faith often merge; just as the *curandero* will be resorted to for his use of special powers which the doctor or veterinary surgeon does not possess, so will the saints and the Virgin (also possessors of miraculous powers) be invoked to act as mediators with God or protectors from the devil. Many parts of the body indeed have their own patron saints: namely San Blas for the throat, Santa Lucia for the eyes, and Santa Agueda for the breasts; and these are readily called upon in cases of illness. If a cure is effected waxen votive offerings (*ex-votos*) will be made in the shape of the cured organs. It is well known that when churches were sacked in the Civil War many favourite images, especially those of the Virgin, were left unprofaned even by rabid anti-clericalists. The Republican Government itself gave tacit recognition to these popular cults by setting up a Commissariat-General of Worship in December 1938.[2]

Sometimes a misguided conception of the Church's functions and powers is revealed, as by the man in the story who came to the priest and asked him to say a mass of excommunication against his sworn enemy. There seems to exist in the popular mind an idea of the supernatural which is dissociated from the religious idea— of a kind of no-man's-land between this world and the next in which spirits annoying rather than malignant have free run. The saints and the Virgin, having been completely human beings, must themselves have suffered from the influence and tricks of such spirits, and so they are appealed to as real people who can understand. If as part of this range of remedies and safeguards through invocation the sign of the Cross is frequently made—on leaving the house in the morning, before getting into any form of public transport, by fighters before a match, with saliva on a spot

---

[1] Aitken claims that these have disappeared since apothecaries were forbidden to sell the ingredients for their charms. See B. Aitken in *Folklore*, 1926.

[2] Cf. E. Allison Peers, *Spain in Eclipse*, London, 1943, p. 67.

where pain is felt—this is no more than a conspicuous expression of belief in divine authority and protection. There may be points of resemblance here between this attitude towards mischievous spirits and that of the Irish towards 'the good people.'[1]

Hand in hand with superstitious beliefs goes a strong respect for modern medicine; but, unfortunately, I cannot discuss in detail here the villagers' attitudes towards health and their doctor. The latter necessarily ranks high in any view of village institutions. His work makes him a leading member of pueblo life, with the special privilege of entry into every home. Yet despite his evident skill, despite his education which gives him high status, in some respects he is found wanting in the eyes of the community. His marginal position was to some extent revealed when his chickens were stolen, and he has tended openly to ally himself with the 'outsiders' by his expressions of discontent.

The feeling that everything of one's own is best, and everything about one of the neighbouring communities in particular is worst, is evident in the pueblo's attitude towards Arboleda. By no means the nearest village, it is in fact some nineteen miles away. Only in the last fifty years or so has Arboleda grown to be larger than Ramosierra; but in material wealth it appears to have been always richer.

The phrase 'newly rich' as used by Ramosierra of Arboleda, while not strictly justified, carries all the scorn and disdain (with perhaps a shade of envy) which a seedy nobility might impart to it, for Ramosierra never forgets its days of past glory when its fine palaces housed the king's nobles, nor the comparatively high status of its visiting summer folk today. The villagers deride the fiestas of Arboleda, which they say are a direct copy of their own, but on a larger and vulgar scale. In fact, the fiestas in Arboleda have all the aspects of the Madrid *verbena* or fair. Although the traditional *mayo* (a form of maypole erected in Ramosierra) is not found there, the bullfight is of a much better quality, with professionals in the proper dress, and a presidential stand graced by women in high combs and mantillas. Much of this air of gaiety and tawdry splendour is secretly envied, especially by the young; and it is a favourite practice of young men from Ramosierra to try to 'gate-crash' the bullring in Arboleda.

[1] Cf. C. Arensberg, *The Irish Countryman*, New York, 1950, p. 186.

Many expressions reflect a form of joking relationship between the two villages. Choice curses, though not peculiar to this area, seem nevertheless to be reserved for use particularly between these two pueblos:

¡*seco te veas*! literally 'may you see yourself dry!' (the American 'drop dead!')

¡*centella te aplane*!⎫
¡*mal rayo te parta*!⎭'may you be struck by lightning!'

are among the most common. But it is amongst the women in Ramosierra that the particular scorn felt for Arboleda is most apparent:

> *Quien en Arboleda casa*
> *Mula y mujer lleva a casa.*[1]

This may be taken as evidence of the Arboleda women's industriousness, for which indeed they are famed; but in Ramosierra it is offered as evidence of their brutish habits. Further comment on their supposed coarseness and slovenliness comes out in conversation: 'They comb their hair in the open outside their houses, and pick off each other's fleas.' Even an official of the Ministry of Information and Tourism, himself a native of Ramosierra, quite seriously maintained that forty per cent of the girls who reach the altar in Arboleda are already pregnant.

There is a lower standard of living in Arboleda than in Ramosierra—so they will tell you in Ramosierra; by which they imply that Arboleda tastes are less refined and that its people live badly for all their money. It is true that prices are generally a little lower in Arboleda in spite of the more valuable Pine Luck shares enjoyed by its inhabitants. Ramosierra (particularly through its women) derides the fact that any outsider who marries 'into' Arboleda receives only a half share in the Pine Luck, whereas in Ramosierra he would be entitled to a full share. The point that a half share in Arboleda is now worth more than a full share in Ramosierra is ignored. This feeling of superiority is seen at its highest in the cult of the Virgin of the Pine, the patron saint of the village who gives her name to the parish, *Nuestra Señora del Pino*.

---

[1] 'He who marries in Arboleda takes both woman and mule back home.'

An educated observer of his own village maintains that the cult of Our Lady of the Pine goes back to the fourteenth century and that she commands the worship of men who neglect all other religious practices. In support of this he adds that some members of the *cofradías* or religious sodalities only go to church on one day in the year, August 15th, the feast day of the Assumption of the Blessed Virgin Mary.[1] The cult of the Virgin under different names in Spain is closely associated with locality ties. She takes on the role of both champion and protector, as may be seen in verses such as:

> De las aguas de Ramosierra
> La mas fuerte la del Duero
> Nuestra Señora del Pino
> La mejor Virgen del Cielo.[2]

Myth though this may be, it serves as a form of sociological charter, a justification for social behaviour and ritual which, whilst it both strengthens and illumines belief, also acts as a sanction. When the women with their pine branches tap the men on the head on August 15th they say, 'De hoy en un año' ('From today until a year hence'), thus perpetuating a time-old rite whose significance is long forgotten, but which serves yet as a public reminder of the woman's role in the village and her high status compared to women of other villages. Similarity of role is seen in the yearly offering of three maidens (once demanded as tribute by the Moors) in the fiestas of San Juan at the village of San Pedro Manrique in the same province.

[1] The belief in the Assumption, the ascent of the Virgin's body and soul into Heaven, firmly held in the early church, was defined as a dogma in 1950.

[2] Of the waters of Ramosierra the strongest is the Duero (whilst) Our Lady of the Pine (is) the best Virgin in Heaven.

# 5

## THE PUEBLO FAMILY

DAILY street scenes in Ramosierra reflect the pattern of home life in the community. The men are busy about their work or chatting and arguing in the bars. When and if the women appear, they are usually accompanied by their children and carry a shopping bag or a bundle of washing; or they hurry discreetly, in pairs, on their way to or from church.

In the ideal pattern of husband and wife relationship the husband's distinctive role is that of the authoritarian head of the family who makes all the decisions; the wife's role is to be submissive, retiring, frugal, and uncritical of her husband. Though there may be a certain discrepancy in practice between the ideal pattern and real behaviour, it is precisely the unquestioning acceptance of the ideal relationship that makes for tight-knit family stability and the sanctity of the home. Foreigners are often puzzled, and sometimes hurt, by what appears to them to be a lack of hospitality on the part of Spanish people, which seems to conflict with their evident generosity and humanity. But if the home and the family are two complementary units held in sacred regard, it is not to be wondered at that only kin (or prospective kin) are admitted to this circle and that strangers are entertained outside. From the ideal pattern one might well suppose that the husband is the key personality of the family circle. As a figurehead he is, but the woman is the real power behind the scenes. The Church fully realizes this and depends on its dominion over the women for eventual control of the family. It is true that the majority of women are seemingly submissive and dominated by their husbands—'lo que tu quieras' ('whatever you wish')—is the national cry of outward submission—but in some cases it is a question of keeping small rules so that the breaking of big ones will not be noticed. Wives are nevertheless careful to perpetuate the myth of

55

the all-powerful father figure in their children's eyes, because it tends to stability and, of course, to discipline in the home.

For her part, the woman accepts her secondary role complacently since, being unaware of the so-called advantages of the emancipated woman, she can hardly be expected to envy her. It is she who holds the home together, who is the focal point, or hearth, round which the children huddle to catch the warmth of traditional practice in ritual and religion. From the moment the child is suckled it is projected into a welter of ritual from which it rarely escapes in its lifetime. Baptism, confirmation, first communion, religious teaching in general and the cult of the Virgin and patron saints in particular, fuse the Church and the child's everyday life into an indivisible whole which no amount of liberal or anarchical thought acquired in later life will fully destroy.

As we shall see when discussing the annual August fiestas in honour of the patron of the village, it is the women who play the leading roles and are figuratively saviours of the village and its prestige. In terms of role conflict the man's is continually played down (in subtle ways so as not to offend his manly pride) before the need to recognize the woman's outstanding and more enduring role. But in Segovia, the adjoining province to Soria in Old Castile, on February 5th, the feast of Santa Agueda (Saint Agatha), certain villages still elect a mayoress for the day with special privileges,[1] following an age-old custom given royal recognition by Philip IV. There exists a kind of Santa Agueda association, a form of religious sodality with an entrance fee and officers designated for the year. Even in Ramosierra pregnant women donate votive offerings to Santa Agueda 'so that the breasts will not run dry', since she was the saint who before being martyred was debreasted. In the past, in some areas around Soria male and female roles were definitely substituted for one day: the men did the housework and the women, called *Aguedas*, had the right to choose their partners at the village dance.

The many superstitions and prohibitions affecting women during menstruation or pregnancy would, in a primitive society, be interpreted in the terminology of taboo. In Castile they tend to sur-

---

[1] See Gabriel Maria Vergara y Martín, *Provincia de Segovia*, Madrid, 1900. Saint Agatha was martyred in Sicily in Roman times after refusing the Praetor's suit on the grounds of being a Christian.

round a woman with a profane aura, for she is considered to spread an area of danger about her and must therefore take care of herself and be humoured. At one time only virgins were allowed in vineyards and even now, in some vineyards and cellars, all women are barred at the time of grape crushing, for it is said that a vintage would turn to vinegar should a pregnant woman approach the wine vats. Flowers and plants dry up if touched by a menstruating woman, hair will not curl, mayonnaise will not mix—these are common superstitions among Ramosierra women and among most poorly educated women in Spain. Another very generally diffused superstition is that of *antojos*, based on the need to satisfy a pregnant woman's whims and appetite. If her desire for any type of food is not immediately gratified, then, wherever her hand touches her body just after, on the selfsame part of the child's body will appear a mark in the form of the object denied. Since the woman's major duty in life is childbearing these attitudes are not perhaps surprising.

It follows that the ideal woman's simple, home-loving but dignified role cannot fit her for an active life outside the home she creates and the small community circle of which it forms a part. The importance of her role automatically limits the range of its social distance, a fact implicitly recognized by a decree of the State of October 7th, 1937, which made obligatory six months social service for all single women between the ages of 17 and 35. This is organized by the Women's Section of the Falange Movement,[1] at present under the leadership of the sister of the founder of the Movement itself, Pilar Primo de Rivera. We shall see when discussing life in a Madrid parish that the certificate issued after this six months' service is a necessary prerequisite for application for a majority of posts, situations, degrees or diplomas, and, of course, passports. Far from creating conflict in the future roles of husband and wife, this social service is aimed at perpetuating the myth of the ideal woman, concentrating as it does on the values of

[1] Under the official auspices of the Franco regime, *La Sección Femenina de la Falange* largely confined itself to nursing and general care of the soldier in the Nationalist zone during the Civil War years. It has since shown more pedagogic tendencies, and organizes regional and national contests of music and dancing, the winners of which have, in later years, been taken on world tours. Affiliated to *La Sección Femenina* is the social help organization, *Auxilio Social*, which is a women's voluntary association.

the home and of Spanish Catholicism, with a dash of the correct political views to flavour. The semi-military discipline, the wearing of dark blue shirts and the injection of Party political conscious-ness are never aimed at making a woman more independent, which would be even more futile than undesirable. The introduc-tion of the female vote in 1933 left women embarrassed and be-wildered and, according to Peers,[1] since they were largely illiterate and in the main influenced by the priests, it had precisely the opposite effect to that desired by the Republicans. However, the appearance of the State as a kind of 'mother figure' at a national level is something new for Spain, and must be taken into considera-tion in any further study of the emancipation of women, especially in urban areas.

In the home the woman exerts her influence mainly through the children and the frying-pan. Meals still retain a certain social utility, occasioning a rigid grouping of the family unit at least twice a day (breakfast and 'tea' are not considered formal meals). Lunch and dinner are never taken in the form of snacks—the hurried sandwich of the American makes the Spaniard raise his hands in horror; they are leisurely and usually heavy meals (three or four courses at least) taken at the kitchen table, where family affairs and problems are discussed. No one would dream of having these meals elsewhere than at home and, when in Soria for shop-ping, markets or business, the family seeks the warm, informal cosiness of the family type restaurant rather than the cold imper-sonal atmosphere of a hotel dining-room.

At about two or half-past two in Ramosierra, there is a general exodus from the fields and bars; and the streets and countryside give no apparent signs of life save for the wisps of smoke curling lazily from conical chimneys, until the reappearance of the men for their coffee and cognac at half-past three or four o'clock. Dinner is rarely eaten before ten o'clock at night, and on ordinary days there is little or no activity after this final meal. During the extraordinary celebrations of fiesta time the men tend to ignore this rigidity, much to the annoyance of the women.

---

[1] E. Allison Peers, op. cit. There was always a higher rate of illiteracy among women. In 1900 over half the entire population was illiterate; by 1950 this had been reduced to one-fifth, but of those over 40 one in three was still illiterate.

Potatoes, kidney-beans, garlic soups, with occasional variations on eggs and meat, form the staples of the villager's diet. *Chorizo*, a highly-spiced pork sausage cut into strips, is an additional treat, much in evidence after the pig killing in November or December. After the men have killed and skinned the pig, the women make the sausages and hang those not immediately eaten with the hams from the kitchen roof to smoke. Some specialize in *carne mechada* made from slices of pork with stuffing in the centre, roasted with garlic and salt to taste; but this is not peculiar to the locality. Unlike some other regions, Castile has no typical dishes worthy of note, for in general its hard subsistence economy does not lend itself to imaginative sauces and the like. 'Aquel es buen día cuando la sartén chilla' ('That is a good day when the frying pan spits') is an old proverb indicative of a low standard of living. Some housewives still bake their own daily bread—the women in the outlying hamlets have no choice—and produce from the family fields makes most households practically self-sufficient in the kitchen.

The woman's scale of preferences is limited and is unaffected by advertising, for though the few families which have radios[1] (and use them) may learn to choose between manufactured products they rarely if ever see them at village level. Where choice is necessary it is the shopkeeper who exerts influence. Hence the Ramosierra woman has none of the worries of a modern urban housewife who, racked with indecision as to both price and choice, may be lured from one shop or product to another by the promises and enticements of manufacturers.

The daily tasks of running the house, feeding the chickens and milking the cow or goat fall to the women whilst the annual ones, especially in the agricultural round, are carried out by the men. At crucial points in the year which call for special effort the whole family works as a team, for there is no hard and fast rule for the division of work between the sexes except that of decency and common sense.

Let us examine the daily life of the village woman in some detail, for it will serve as a comparison later with that of the urban housewife in Madrid. The winters are long and hard so that the family spends most of its time indoors in the warmest part of the house,

---

[1] The number of radios in the village is, however, increasing rapidly. Only 15 licences were issued in 1941, but 74 in 1954, and over 100 in 1957.

namely the kitchen. 'What do you do all day in the two or three
months when all outside work is paralysed?' I asked. 'We keep
warm,' was the answer. On a normal day the woman will rise at
about 8 a.m., and prepare a relatively heavy breakfast of garlic
soup, ham, *chorizo*, bread and chocolate, for 9 a.m. After tidying
the house for an hour or so, she will, if weather permits, take the
cattle or goats to the common pastureland and return to busy herself over the large pots at the open fire.

Shopping is not an essential daily task in the pueblo as most of
the housewife's supplies are already stored in the house. Cooking
the thick soups and *cocido* stews which are preferred in the cold
weather is a slow business, and she will probably attend to some
sewing as she casts an occasional glance at the fire.[1] Tending the
fire, hungry for wood, in fact takes up much of her time, because the
right heat must be maintained if the food is not to be spoilt. After
lunch, there are the rough wooden or earthenware dishes to be
washed without any modern aids such as soap powders or the like.
Invariably the afternoon is taken up by sewing and mending,
especially if the family is a large one. But by five o'clock, before it
becomes dark, the woman will hurry to the mountain slopes to
collect the cattle, install them in the byre or in the stable next to the
kitchen, and rake out the *berzas* (a kind of savoy cabbage) which
serve as their fodder. The pig and chickens must similarly be
attended to, and the goats or cow milked. Cow's milk, however, is
somewhat of a luxury in Ramosierra. Twilight is the time for a
little relaxation and gossip with a neighbour or close relative, with
whom she probably goes to the Rosary service at the parish church.
By 9 p.m., however, she is always back at home to put the final
touches to the dinner in readiness for her husband who returns
shortly afterwards from his favourite bar. She may then nod over a
little more sewing after dinner until midnight, when the whole
family retires to well-blanketed beds.

As in Madrid, the week is broken up by specific tasks which
must be fitted into the daily routine. Of these, the most important
is *la colada* or weekly wash, which takes up the whole of Monday

[1] It is worthy of note that, in the relatively few cases where a joint
family is found living in the same household, each nuclear family has its
own kitchen (or at least its own fire and hearth) though the joint family
as a group eats together.

and Tuesday. When the weather is not totally inclement, the house-wife invariably prefers to go to the washing point at the river below the church where the complicated procedure is easier and where, too, she can exchange the latest news and gossip with the other basket-laden women. The clothes are first washed lightly and left soaped and stretched on the grass verge to catch the midday sun while the women go home to prepare and eat lunch. Later they are again washed, and thoroughly, and again stretched in the sun until it sinks low in the sky. A third time the clothes are washed and soaped, then left in the basket for the night. In the morning they are rinsed and laid out to dry on the river bank. The three opera-tions in washing, known as *ojos* (literally, 'eyes'), are calculated to clean and whiten the clothes through the additional use of *lejía* or lye—a solution made from pouring boiling water over ashes. Except for Sunday, which apart from the care of animals is wholly a day of rest, the remainder of the week is given over to the pains-taking repair and care of linen.

In spring and summer, however, the days are longer and the woman's work harder. She is expected to help in the sowing and weeding of the small corn fields and vegetable patches, but in practice usually limits herself to spreading the manure fertilizer. During the short harvest (*la siega*) in summer, she will rise as early as 5 a.m., and help the men reap the grain, but she takes no part in the gathering of herbage or grass for fodder. Sometimes she must take both breakfast and lunch to the fields for the whole family, in which case meals are earlier than on a normal day. In the minor threshing operations (*la trilla*), which begin at about 8 a.m. when the sun is warm in July, the woman will help her man prepare the *parvas* or circular heaps of unthreshed corn. She also joins in the winnowing, either by tossing the corn into the wind or by driving a horse-drawn threshing board over it. This toboggan-like harrow has three or four rows of metal teeth set at an angle; the metal teeth, however, wear out within a year or two, and so these are supplemented by many more rows of sharply pointed flints, which hardly ever need to be replaced. Whoever is in charge of the horse (or ox) sits on a small box or cane chair on the board holding the reins, with a wary eye and a bucket at hand to catch the droppings of the animal. Threshing only stops when the sun fades, for the night humidity, like the early morning dew, causes the grain and chaff to stick together. The later the threshing and other joint family tasks occur in the summer, the less the women participate. From the beginning of August they busy themselves in preparing their costumes and whitewashing the house in readiness for the patron-saint fiestas.

The real education of the child begins and ends in the home, and is the largely unconscious result of example and imitation. The child grows up in a society where the roles of each sex and age are clearly defined, and this society in its own mind makes a plain distinction between *enseñanza* ('book-learning') and *educación* (the basic education in manners and morals). Part of his training is directed to accepting the father's word as law and to viewing the mother as the source of all virtue. Respect for authority and virtue, embodied in the parents, is therefore instinctively acquired by the child and extended to all parents and adults, particularly close kin. In every gesture, moreover, the boy will portray the manliness of his father and the girl will typify the submissiveness, virtue and tenderness of her mother. This duplication of character and personality is further enhanced by the adoption of the same Christian names for the children as those of their parents or grandparents; but as the pueblo always refers to them as 'the son (or daughter) of so-and-so', this also helps to define their social identity in relation to their parents and fuses their own personality into the greater one of the family.

Love binds the members of these families together as tightly as a tree is attached to its roots. Love for children is not the tight-lipped, restrained emotion of the northern European parent but an overwhelming, uninhibited gush of love and affection which makes the air at times positively resound with great, smacking kisses like pistol shots in the dry mountain atmosphere as family and friends, unable to resist the chubby infant cheeks any longer, swoop on them with shrill cries of love. Children are continually under the parental eye and the smaller ones are never left to roam alone. Parents accompany them to school, and their older brothers or sisters accompany them on errands or in play. Grandmothers or aunts and, in Madrid, family maids take over the extra-familial care. Children's gangs are almost unheard of in Spain.

An average couple in Ramosierra has four or five children now. Thirty years ago, one out of every eight children died; but this high rate of infant mortality has since been cut by half. In the past nine or ten children to a family were not uncommon, but as one elderly villager explained wryly: 'I had ten children originally but four died . . . of what? . . . of being too small.'

Religion enters the child's life from the moment he is slapped as a newly-born babe and his mother thanks God for a safe delivery. Baptism follows as soon as is humanly possible, for until then, in familiar parlance, the babe is considered to be *un judio* (a Jew) or *un moro* ( a Moor), i.e. one not of the true faith. The christening ceremony is always followed by a celebration in the home to which close kin, intimate friends and the priest are invited. With due reverence, comparisons are drawn between the male baby and the Child Jesus as represented in 'cribs' at Christmas; and the child is constantly urged to emulate this figure and those of the saints. For a girl-child, the model is of course the Virgin Mary. Since Catholic custom demands the aid of a sponsor when a new member is brought into the Church, the child's range of patron-protectors is extended through the special spiritual relationship with his godparent or *padrino*. In most parts of Spain it is common for the sponsors of the marriage to act as godparents of the first child of the union. When possible they are usually the brother of the bride and the sister of the groom. Religion also permeates the many lullabies, stories and games (particularly those of the girls) that surround the child in its early years. Unlike those of the Irish, Spanish stories are unconcerned with the antics of 'the little people' or fairies, although they recognize their existence. Instead, they weave into nature, legends and songs feelings connected with the saintly life and death.

Present-giving highlights the successful achievement of certain stages in the life-cycle of the child and, conversely, of its parents. Sometimes these presents are traditional ones, but tradition may be broken to meet the needs of the moment and the desires of the recipient. The new mother is almost always given a cake soaked in sherry by the senior maternal aunt; and godfathers, when they can afford to do so, often open a savings account for their godchild. The godfather also distributes coins and caramels to the children who attend the baptism. The State in its turn presents the parents with a reward in the form of a family subsidy which, beginning with the second, increases considerably with the advent of every successive child. When the boy reaches the age of thirteen or fourteen, depending on his size, he will be given his first really 'grown-up' suit with long trousers and, to mark the event, his parents may present him with a watch. Similar presents are given to the girl when she has her first party dress, and some parents feel that a social injustice is done to the boys by the generally greater fuss made of the girl once the age of puberty has been reached. This is especially the case in Madrid, where 'coming out' parties are given by quite humble families.

Special suits and dresses of fine material, which often cost the parents more than a month's income, are provided for the Church ceremonies of Confirmation and First Communion. It is not uncommon to see diminutive boys of seven or nine resplendent with shining face and hair peeping out from the full-dress uniform of an admiral, or indeed to see their angelic seven-year-old sisters struggling with the wings and haloes of their cherubim costumes. Present-exchange is customary at the more important religious festivals such as Easter and, particularly, the Epiphany, when the children are led to believe that those who supply the gifts are the Three Wise Kings; the children show their credence in this myth by placing a few strands of hay under their beds for the camels.

Age is relatively unimportant. Birthdays as such are not celebrated unless they happen to coincide with the child's name-saint's day. Present-giving on the saint's day is an annual recognition of the child's religious personality expressed in his Christian name, rather than a yearly celebration of the mere date on which he was born. Many of the older people are very vague about their real age in years (though not to the extent found in most primitive societies) for the critical dates in life are not so much the days of birth as those on which some change takes place in their religious or family status. Thus, a man will fix a date in the past not by reference to the year but perhaps by his marriage; a woman, by the birth of her children; and a child by his inception into a religious sodality or into a new state of grace through a church sacrament. Of course, dates may be fixed by reference to 'Acts of God', which may be either natural phenomena like floods or typhoons affecting the whole village, or personal accidents. In all cases, the event takes precedence over the date.

Desegregation of the sexes is achieved domestically through gatherings of the extended kin-group in the home and publicly through fiestas and weekly dances, which are all channels of courtship. The engagement period (*noviazgo*) begins from the moment the couple are said 'to have relations' or 'to be talking', and ends in marriage. Courting is always begun with a view to a permanent union and the founding of a family. It is not only a sociological truism that full adulthood is reached only by marriage; in Ramosierra the establishment of a permanent household is a necessary condition for full participation in the common patrimony of the Pine Luck. For this reason frivolity in courting is rare and is censured as showing a lack of 'formality'. As the engagement period is rather long interest is maintained by a feigned battle of the sexes in which the whole gamut of tricks of coquetry and petty jealousies is run.

A dying form of manhood rite is that called *hacerse mozo* (literally 'to make oneself a young man') when the boy of 15 or 16 enters upon the age of courting. It consists of paying for a round of drinks at some selected moment during the village dance. *Hacerse moza* for the girls seems to occur when they stop dancing among themselves in pairs and accept boys' invitations to dance. At one time in the past the favoured youth would be presented with a special pastry (*rosquilla*) baked by the girl on the occasion of the next village feast day. The old custom of electing a 'mayor' from among the youths (*alcalde de mozos*) for the August fiestas now persists only vaguely in the somewhat diffident acceptance of a natural leader for erecting pine trees, organising the bullfighters and 'singing the rounds' (*La Ronda*) on the last day. This leader is nevertheless given tacit recognition by the local authorities and the fiesta organising committee.

Serenading, which takes place only on feast days, is a group activity, and special verses, made up for the occasion, may be sung outside the houses of respective girl friends. 'El Yanguanito'— the innkeeper—is one of the few to be fined in his younger days for singing particularly bawdy verses. A *novio*, or suitor, who is not of the village must first satisfy local opposition by 'paying his entrance' in the tavern before he can continue serious courting. A young man's life is ideally epitomized in a verse popular in the village:

*La vida del mozo es saltar tapias y corrales,*
*Dormir en camas agenas y morir en los hospitales.*[1]

But this role of the reckless devil-may-care young gallant is one that the village youth can seldom hope to play.

Much of what used to be hidebound custom has now been lost to the pueblo, for both Church and State have waged ceaseless campaigns in the past against pagan excesses associated with religious feast days wherein courting customs were much in evidence. Where such customs are remembered, they are apparently rather ridiculed. Ramosierra regards with disfavour, or so it would seem, the intemperate festivities connected with San Juan in Soria. Needless to say, this somewhat prim attitude galls the youths of the village, who talk with glee and envy of the good times to be had in the provincial capital. 'El que San Juanea, Marzea', they say with mischievous grins, meaning that he who enjoys himself in the fiestas of San Juan (in June) has sown wild oats which will bear fruit in March. Certainly, village girls still pray and offer candles to San Antonio in the hope that he will provide them with a husband; and the boys in a group brew up chocolate in the open at sunrise on San Pedro's day, to which alfresco feast the girls, suitably chaperoned, are invited. But, lacking the public opportunities provided by the less inhibited fiestas, courting tends to go underground and seek the romance of the illicit. The thick woods surrounding the village are always at hand: 'entran en el bosque dos y salen tres' ('two go into the forest and out come three'), commented a cynic when questioned on the changing habits of youth.

Throughout the engagement period the girl spends much of her time preparing her trousseau (*equipo*), a truly impressive stock of linen and clothes, some of it handed down by her mother, but all involving fine needlework and intricate hand embroidery. Ready-made articles are heartily disdained and could never compare in quality and workmanship. Other than this there is no recognized dowry.

Couples rarely decide to get married before the man has finished his military service, and since they will not qualify for

[1] A young man's life is to leap over walls and fences,
Sleep in the beds of others and die in the poorhouse.

the Pine Luck until one or other is 25, this is the commonest marrying age. In this Ramosierra conforms to the national pattern, for only twenty-five per cent of the population marry between the ages of 20 and 24, while more than half marry between 25 and 29. Except for a sharp drop during the Civil War years, the annual number of marriages has remained fairly constant over the last half century, the slight increase being proportionate to the rise in population. Once the decision to marry has been taken the *novio* (prospective bridegroom) and his parents come to the house of the *novia* (prospective bride) to ask her parents formally for her hand. The traditional gift to the girl at this stage is a bracelet, but this varies if there is a prized family heirloom to be passed on and may take the form of a ring or even a diadem. There is no formal ceremony; the visit usually takes place at about 7 p.m., the hour of *merienda*, of which the visitors partake. From this moment onward, the boy and girl are mutually committed to marriage, which takes place very soon afterwards. Only death, or something very drastic and 'ugly', will prevent it.

'The most brutal crimes . . . have been those committed in country districts by peasants . . . Experience shows that repugnant, bestial criminality is in inverse proportion to the density of the population.'[1] Unanumo's generalization is not borne out by available statistics, although national *suicide* rates do reveal that the highest proportion by far (40 per cent) is among the agricultural class. In Ramosierra the only homicide within living memory took place when a marriage had been arranged, the girl's hand asked for, and a house for the young couple already bought. It was the girl herself who decided to break off relations with her *novio*; and in a heated discussion with her near her house in the higher, less-frequented part of the village, he split her skull with the forest axe that he was carrying. He then turned the axe upon himself. Though he survived and was sent to prison for eight years, he served little of this sentence and is now in a mental hospital in Soria. Some say that the girl was brutal and tactless in trying to end relations so brusquely. Her family at the trial accused the boy of trying to abuse her; but ready tongues point out that the parents had in the past allowed them to go alone to nearby fiestas and return as late as four in the morning, so that the young man had already

[1] Unamuno, *La Civilización es Civismo*, 1907.

had every opportunity. The murder almost ruined his family; the mother sold all that she had to save her son at the trial. The subject, needless to say, is tactfully concealed in the pueblo and never discussed. Nor is it discussed here from any wish to be sensational, but rather to show that any departure from the accepted code of social behaviour always brings its retribution, whether it be the censure and wrath of the pueblo or the act of an individual agent.

Marriage considered as an institution in this society is a free agreement between individuals, a contract, unlike the enforced rights and obligations existing between parents and children. It brings with it added prestige which cannot fail to place the two partners in a higher status group: spiritually, because marriage is regarded as a vocation; materially, because of the money acquired through automatic entitlement in this community to the Pine Luck; and socially, because the couple can now, as part-owners of the patrimony and as heads of an integral family unit, pass this right on to future generations. Breaking a marriage contract is therefore a threat to the social structure of the community and so, in the case I have cited above, pueblo opinion was against the girl.[1] Marriage is a focal point round which human relationships revolve, and its social function is to defend the social order against attack by individual nonconformists. Hence the pueblo's hostility to remarriage of widows and widowers, and the censure implied in saying that a spinster over marriageable age has 'failed'.

Marriage, though enabling the parties to play a full part in the affairs of the pueblo, does not command, as it once did, the interest of the whole village. No one in particular used to be invited to the ceremony since it was assumed that all who could would attend. Now the custom of issuing invitations, in numbers agreed by both sets of parents, is creeping in from the towns. In practice, of course, anyone may enter the church, and there are always more than the number invited present; but the tendency to print wedding invitations is a dividing factor, and, although only indulged in by 'pretentious' folk (they would be called *cursi*), creates ill-feeling in the pueblo.

Marriage institutes a new web of social relations and also implies an adjustment in existing ties of kin, and sometimes of

[1] They were highly amused in the pueblo to hear that breach of promise is often the subject of a legal action in England.

locality. Loyalties are widened or narrowed to accommodate the new member into the two family groups; new responsibilities and obligations are created. A brief explanation of names and their use will help us in our further consideration of the extended family.

Both boy and girl have one or more Christian names, plus two or more surnames which are the patronyms of the paternal and maternal grandparents. Two surnames only are required for official purposes, but pretentious folk tend to use as many as four or five; for easy reference in the pueblo one is sufficient. So, although Serafina Varona Cano was known simply as Serafina Varona before she married Hilario Vasquez Maldonado, on her marriage she acquired her husband's patronym without losing her own names. Officially, therefore, she became Serafina Varona Cano de Vasquez, but a shorter mode of address would be Señora de Vasquez. She is probably still known in the pueblo as Serafina Varona, or simply as 'Serafina, the wife of Hilario Vasquez'. Sons and daughters will adopt the first surnames of their parents. Thus the woman's patronym is preserved by her children, though not by her grandchildren.

On a summer's day in 1774 the parish bell summoned the 110 *vecinos* of Ramosierra to discuss their new municipal status. Most of the surnames of those present can be found in any list of *vecinos* today. Many of the names are recognizably Castilian, and to any native of the province of Soria are also indicative of the locality. Of the 315 *vecinos* listed for the Pine Luck in 1956, at least forty-four bore one or both surnames in common. Earlier, we noted that cross-cousin marriages were not unusual. Two brothers may put off dividing an inherited family field in the hope that it will be retained intact in the family by a marriage among their progeny; and such marriages are facilitated by the naturally closer contact between cousins, which (especially among timid folk living in isolated hamlets) makes courting easier.

First cousins are close enough relatives to be considered members of the family at any special gathering; as such, they are known as *primo carnal* (i.e. cousin of the flesh) or *primo hermano* (brother-cousin), and the intimate form of address is used with them. All other degrees are classed under the term *primo político* (cousin-in-law), or simply *pariente* (relative) which, within the village, implies no ties of loyalty on grounds of kin but only the normal ties set up by friendship. Indeed, there may be cause for regret when the relative is not *simpático* or friendly; as may be seen from the innkeeper's outburst against his distant relative and close enemy, the mayor: ' . . . and what's more, to crown it all, he's a relative of mine'.

*Primos* was a term used by earlier kings of Spain when referring to grandees; but just as relations at court were often uneasy and favourites ephemeral, so among distant cousins too much emphasis should not be placed on mere kinship ties. The more colloquial use of the word *primo* is for one who is easily beguiled—a simpleton, a 'sucker'. It has, too, the meaning of first (in ordinal numbers) and thus is aptly used to denote the primary consanguineous relationship.[1] Nevertheless, it must be stressed that even first cousins usually belong to completely independent households, even if their relationship and their awareness of stemming from the same set of grandparents often pave the way to a genuine friendship.

One case was met where a comparatively young man addressed both his first cousin *and* his uncle by the same term *tío* (uncle), but this could not be substantiated elsewhere and is not offered here as a general rule. The word *tío* may also be used colloquially in a genial way to mean 'bloke' or 'character', as in 'es un tío muy gracioso' ('He's a very amusing character'); in a pitying way as in 'pobre tío!' ('poor chap!'); or in a rather disparaging manner, as in 'Entonces viene este tío y me dice . . . ' ('Then this "guy" comes up to me and says . . . '). The feminine *tía*, strictly used to mean 'aunt', also has a very common colloquial use to refer to old women of mean class, instead of the title Doña, as in 'Da esto a la tía Isabel' ('Give this to old Lizzy'); it can be employed to refer to someone who is easily deceived as in 'Cuéntaselo a tu tía!' ('Tell it to your grandmother!'); and, finally, in a far more disparaging way than its masculine counterpart, it may be used to describe an old crone or a whore.

Relations between uncles and nephews, aunts and nieces are based on friendly contact; and these kinship ties seem to be particularly strong among the women, where rights and obligations

[1] It has been suggested that the system of reckoning by first, second and third cousins originated in Spain and Portugal as a result of Teutonic invasions; see A. R. Radcliffe-Brown and Daryll Forde, editors of *African Systems of Kinship and Marriage*, O.U.P., London, 1950, p. 16.

include care of the children in time of need. Kin-terms are much more in evidence in daily conversation than they are in our own society; 'son', 'daughter', 'brother', 'sister', 'cousin', even 'wife' are modes of address heard frequently between relatives, and all of which tend to sharpen the relationship. Both obligation and sentiment govern the degree of mutual help and attendance at family gatherings, weddings, and funerals, but these follow no fixed pattern and their very fluidity makes them extremely difficult to plot.[1] Family ties which might be distant and weak in the village often seem to strengthen in proportion to the physical distance from the pueblo, granted that contact is still possible. Summer visitors who are quite remote cousins will be given the hospitality of the home in Ramosierra, for one never knows when their help or influence may be needed. This is particularly noticeable in the case of emigrants, for it is outside the pueblo that the real sense of community exerts itself as a bulwark against the unknown dangers of a strange world. So, in Madrid, even a fellow-villager might be greeted warmly as a country 'cousin', though no real relationship exists other than a comforting sense of 'togetherness' in a big city.

Another artificial extension of family ties is the spiritual relationship set up by godparenthood (*compadrazgo*) between the real parents and the godparents, and between these and their godchildren. First, we must distinguish between the terms *compadre* and *padrino*. Compaternity springs from the custom of the early Church (later recognized by Canon Law) requiring a sponsor at baptism to prevent the entry of bogus, 'spy' Catholics during periods of persecution. The special quality of the spiritual affinity created between the sponsor and the parents of the baptized person was recognized by the mutual use of the terms *compater* and *commater*, which are the Spanish *compadre* and *comadre*. From the sixth century onwards this affinity was considered a bar to marriage, as it still is in the popular mind. This prohibition naturally extends to the child sponsored at baptism, who talks of his sponsors

---

[1] In general I agree with Pitt-Rivers, op. cit., p. 106, speaking of Andalusian kinship, that 'it is a facultative rather than a firm bond'. In other words, the family relationship is there if you want it. Further indication of the weakness of these ties is that in discussion cognisant range of kin rarely extends beyond second cousins.

as *padrino* (godfather) and *madrina* (godmother). Until the Council of Trent in 1545 evergrowing exogamic groups made up of these spiritual relatives came into being, for by then as many as thirty baptismal sponsors were permitted. Gradually the system had become closely associated with the use of influence through the good graces of a wealthy and distinguished sponsor.

We see this idea persisting in the secondary meanings of the terms, for *compadre* may also be used in the sense of protector or benefactor, whilst another use of *padrino* can be that of patron, or one's second in a duel. In mediaeval times, the system increased class solidarity in a given locality and so, in Andalusia particularly, the word *compadre* can mean friend or neighbour, as indeed it does generally in South America. In the province of Soria however, a common greeting is the word *paisano* (countryman), which expresses a solidarity based much more on common territorial origin. On the feminine side it is not difficult to see why *comadre* has also come to mean midwife or *accoucheuse*, and *madrina*, patroness or bridesmaid; nor is it difficult to imagine why the additional meaning of 'a gossip' was adopted in both cases. The old Scottish word 'cummer' is, after all, not a far remove from *commater*—and 'god-sib' easily becomes 'gossip'.

Two further distinctions must be drawn between *padrinos*, for there are *padrinos de boda* (marriage godparents, i.e. the equivalent of best man and bridesmaid in Britain) and *padrinos de bautizo* (baptismal godparents). The more aristocratic families and some of the rich families which ape them now tend to pick the father of the bride and the mother of the groom as wedding sponsors, while a further choice, where feasible, may be made from the baptismal godparents of either bride or groom.

In Castile their obligations are few and extend only to the payment of church ceremonial fees, the provision of the *arras* (thirteen symbolic pieces of gold or silver given by the groom to the bride), and the arrangement of the wedding feast afterwards. Since they are usually close relatives, the question of spiritual kinship and consequent impediments to marriage hardly arises. The obligations of the baptismal godparents are, in the same way, to bear church costs, to provide the white baptismal smock, and to cater for the post-baptismal gathering at the parents' home. Moreover, in theory, the godparents are responsible for the spiritual and physical welfare (should the parents die) of their god-child.

This relationship keeps them in close contact and is often forma-lized by frequent gifts during adolescence, perhaps a boy's first suit or a girl's first long dress, as well as a special gift on Passion Sunday during the last week of Lent, which the godchild recipro-cates with a palm on the following Palm Sunday. Appeals to god-parents by their protégés in time of need or for favours are normal, and are accepted in the general pattern of the patronage network. This is frequently the reason for not choosing a close relative as godparent but, rather, a rich or influential friend, perhaps from outside the village, since it is an artificial way of widening the range of patronage. In Castile the important relationship is that established between godparent and godchild, not the curiously formalized relationship found in Galicia, Andalusia and South America between *compadres*, which is akin to a blood brotherhood. Thus another link in the functional chain is established. Apart from this, and beyond the elementary family unit, few structural bonds exist; there are otherwise only *ad hoc* groupings arising from a given situation.

In passing I may profitably mention two weaker types of *padrino* relationship which are nominal only. The division of baptism and confirmation into two separate rites dates back to the eighth cen-tury; now, although a sponsor is necessary at confirmation when the child is supposed to reach the age of reason, his obligations cease with the ceremony and no lasting spiritual kinship is implied. The sponsor, chosen by the child, may be a friend or parent, but is more often selected from among his or her religious or lay teachers. Finally, the Church through such religious bodies and organiza-tions as Catholic Action and *Auxilio Social* (Social Help) offers the services of more disinterested *padrinos* (bearing only the cost of the ceremonies necessary) to poor families who, from indif-ference or lack of funds, have failed to undergo the rites of the Church; and particularly to those who went through only the civil form of marriage during the government of the Second Republic (1931-39). This type of sponsorship has a businesslike function; it rarely creates that spiritual and thus honorary mem-bership of the family unit found in the other forms.

Although the pueblo itself shows no marked censure of a

family which has not undergone these basic religious rites (providing the decencies of respectable family life are maintained), it is difficult indeed for such a household to resist the fulminations of the priest from the pulpit, the insinuations and gossip of *las beatas* at the washing-point or in the shops and, above all, the dreadful, shameful lack of conformity, which is probably the greatest strain and pressure of all. For even if a couple could tranquilly live together without having been married in church they would not wish their own shame (in the eyes of the pueblo) on to their children. In the same way, the main anxiety of every mother is to have her child 'named' as soon as possible after birth, for although the pueblo will no doubt dub the child with a nickname anyway, no mother in her right mind would run the risk of having her offspring called a Moor or a Jew. Nor would she wish to prejudice the child's chances of immediate salvation in the event of an untimely death and have it languishing in Limbo.

Death and its inevitability permeate many of the nature legends and songs of the pueblo, so that the child quickly accepts the fact with little fear except that of accounting to his Maker:

> *Yo no temo la muerte,*
> *Que morir es natural;*
> *Solo le temo a la cuenta*
> *Que a Dios le tengo que dar.*[1]

But the crisis of death causes a realignment in kinship ties and, incidentally, heightens the sense of community. No one in the pueblo recalled the custom of hiring professional mourners which foreign novelists so enthusiastically refer to when writing on Spain. The reason is simple here; all six sodalities in the village are in fact mutual-aid-in-burial societies and their members are pledged to assist at every funeral.

For most relatives and friends the feeling of obligation to take part in the wake is still strong. The Church has just officially revived the Easter Vigil on the night after Good Friday. The corpse is left in the bedroom flanked by candles, all mirrors in the house are blacked over with cloth, and window-shutters are opened. The Rosary is recited around the body by visiting women whilst the

---

[1] I do not fear death, For to die is a natural thing;
I fear only the account that I must render to God.

men, having grunted their condolences, sit in the living-room or kitchen drinking coffee and anisette until early morning. There is a solemn but not sepulchral air about the proceeding.

Once the funeral (attended only by the men) is over, a *novena* or nine-day prayer meeting is held either at the house or in the church. There on the floor of the church, if the family can afford it, an engraved flagstone will mark the resting-place of some relic of the deceased. Relations will surround these stones with a small mat, a stool, and a burning candle to make, as it were, an extension of the household in the church, where the survivors can feel that the deceased is still a member of the family.

# 6

## STATUS AND MORALITY

IN A SMALL relatively isolated community such as Ramosierra
an arbitrary imposition of our own concept of class would be misleading. Social distinctions are not immediately observable. The
very principle of equal shares in the Pine Luck has a levelling effect,
and conformity to the pattern of the ideal family only emphasizes
an egalitarianism among Spaniards in general which has always
been noted with surprise by foreigners. The distinction which
villagers and townsmen alike make between personality and social
position overrides the concept of class, and has been expressed as
'a respect for human personality rather than for human rights.'[1]
Such a distinction has as its basis a system of social values linked
to the ideal behaviour by which a man is judged. Here manners
are not separated from morality; custom is not a mere ephemeral
fashion.

The esteem of one's neighbour is far more significant in the
pueblo, where anonymity is impossible, than in a city, and the
individual's status is more closely associated with that of his
family. Moreover, although village life calls for a greater self-
sufficiency and leads to a manifested self-centredness, this does
not result in such a conscious pursuit of personal or group interests,
to the detriment of the social order, as it does in the city. In fact,
there is a marked reluctance to withdraw into any kind of exclusive
group such as a club or party. In the absence of class-consciousness, therefore, we must re-examine the significant roles played
by various members of the pueblo in the light of the social distinctions recognized among them.

As a working guide, we will divide the community into leaders,
controllers, and servers. In the first group, I include the mayor,
the priest, the doctor, and certain members of the richer families.

[1] Pitt-Rivers, op. cit., p. 66.

They constitute the *élite*, they have the power and, in a sense, are the 'gatekeepers' who play a leading role by guiding the pueblo in its dealings with the outside world. In the second group I would place the police sergeant, the town council staff, the industrial exploiters of the pine, the teachers, the women, and some of the older men—those, in fact, whose main role is to preserve the *status quo* and guard tradition. It is true that the teachers are also at times innovators, in that they may bring new facts and problems into the ken of the villagers; but in Ramosierra at least they cannot be included among the leaders, for they have neither the power nor the personality to warrant it. Finally, among the servers, I would incorporate the young and those who minister functionally to the needs of the community—such diverse folk as craftsmen, swineherds, the town crier and Leandro, the bus-driver. Arbitrary though this division may be, it gives a clearer pattern than any stratification in terms of class. To substantiate it, I intend to review social distinctions made on criteria of age, sex and birth, wealth and occupation, names, speech and appearance; by relating these to social values and behaviour, we shall then conceive some idea of status in the pueblo, which is no more than differentiated social position.[1]

Clearest of these social divisions is that between youths and elders. The social distance that separates them is based on experience and age and is expressed in their mutual disdain. The elders consider the youths to be soft, spendthrift, disrespectful, unchivalrous and addicted to vice. The youths think the elders decrepit, mean, dictatorial, hypocritical and old-fashioned; some they also consider to be addicted to 'vice' of a more private nature. Though neither group is compact in its sense of awareness, each is consolidated on occasions when their interdependence is enforced. For there are multiple daily tasks on which the brawn of youth and the experience of age must combine; a simple example from leisure activities concerning the pueblo as a whole will suffice as an illustration.

Two special pine trees (mayos) are erected in the two squares for the August fiestas. The elders of the fiesta organizing committee, the senior members of the religious sodalities and the generous

---

[1] See R. M. MacIver and C. H. Page, *Society*, London, 1949, p. 353; and Pitt-Rivers, op. cit., p. 65 note.

returned emigrant who supplies the refreshments cannot put up the pines without the aid of the youths. The youths cannot put up the pines without the experience and technique of the elders; moreover, they are disinclined to work hard for no pay in their spare time. Appeals to conscience and sense of community, plus the bribe of refreshments, were not enough three or four years ago; authority, in the form of a special edict from the mayor through the town crier had to exert itself; the youths were commanded to present themselves as a labour force on a boiling hot afternoon.

Transition from the one to the other group begins when the youth starts courting. Marriage and maturity at the age of 25, besides qualifying a man for the Pine Luck, form also the point at which he will automatically transfer into the married men's sodality from the unmarried men's brotherhood. It is the older men who most carefully preserve the ritual of the fiestas, and it is experience combined with age that fits a man for the Pine Luck selection junta, as well as for election to the town council and the syndicates. The respected elder, who often merits the title of *Señor* from the young, relaxes in the sun on the stone benches around the church or squares secure in his authority, which springs from his practical knowledge and familiarity with village lore.

Women are not dismayed by the fact that divorce (except in very rare cases) is unobtainable in Spain; nor do they fret because they do not vote, or because when they are married they suffer many legal disadvantages compared with their husbands. Their seeming lack of independence does not affect their independent spirit; they conform to their role and make of submissiveness a virtue. The essence of ideal womanhood lies in a cult of virtue, the model for which is the Virgin Mary. With virtue go the concomitant qualities of grace, tenderness and beauty. The language is redolent of such expressions and, indeed, makes sharp distinctions on all things aesthetic; so that *feo* (ugly) is an operative word extended from aesthetics to ethics. As the embodiment of the ideal of virginity a woman is pledged to virtuous behaviour, wherein shame plays an important role. The loss of virginity involves loss of shame only when it is not consecrated by marriage.

Pitt-Rivers[1] considers *vergüenza* (shame) to be the feminine counterpart of manliness, and defines it as 'the regard for the

[1] Op. cit., pp. 112–13.

moral values of society, for the rules whereby social intercourse takes place, for the opinion which others have of one. But this, not purely out of calculation. True *vergüenza* is a mode of feeling which makes one sensitive to one's reputation and thereby causes one to accept the sanctions of public opinion.' Such an interpretation has much to recommend it. Although the definition itself seems to dwell on the idea of personal reputation, its author brings out in his text that *vergüenza* has an innate and hereditary moral quality. I liken it to a precious inner dignity maintained by strict observance of established codes of behaviour by which not only the individual but also his family are judged. It is truly a cultural value and a measure of status.

This concept, which applies also to men, therefore has a positive value and cannot be wholly interpreted in the negative sense implied by the inadequate English translation. But its force is particularly active in Andalusia, and its overtones are not comprehensive for Castile. Here, we must emphasize the spirituality of moral values in a society which regards the 'mother' as the secular model of the greater Virgin Mother. The cult of the Virgin Mother, so fervent throughout Spain, has its greatest supporters among the men and should not be confused with mere religious practice, at which the women excel. It is, moreover, a cult of an '*Immaculate* Virgin' who, according to the dogma of the Church, was conceived without the least guilt or stain of original sin. The clue then to the picture of the ideal woman lies in the dual ideas of immaculateness and virginity. I think of it as the 'Immaculate Mother' complex.

It follows then that sex is a field in which not only should *vergüenza* be particularly displayed but honourable intention be inherent as well. *Formalidad* (formality) implies an established mode of behaviour of which earnestness and reliability are the important bases. 'Un poco de formalidad, ¡por favor!' ('A little more formality, if you please!') is the oft-heard cry whenever the bounds of decency have been overreached.[1] In ideal sexual relations there is little room for the erotic or for the institution of the mistress. Where sexual relations fall from the ideal they are regarded as the passing satisfaction of appetite and relegated to

[1] I have heard it used even when a man took off his coat at an informal gathering and when foreigners lazily stretch themselves.

the province of 'shameless' men. Hence a prostitute does not constitute a threat to the social order, for she has lost her shame, if she ever had it. Otherwise the sexual act must occur only within the blessed sanctity of the home. The spirituality of his guiding values tempers the sensual in the Castilian. Out of passion is wrought not carnality but purity, for sex and romantic ideas of love are dissolved in the greater union of the family and parenthood. Tirso de Molina makes one of his characters say:

' . . . bien o mal nacido, el más indigno marido excede al mejor galán.'[1]

Hence the myth of Don Juan Tenorio, the greatest gallant and seducer of all, properly belongs to the cradle of Andalusia, while that of Don Quixote remains an heroic and essentially Castilian illusion.

Bearing all this in mind, we can now re-examine the concept of shame. It may be related to timidity, which means having too much of it, or to *educación* (good manners) which shows the right amount. *Cara-dura* (brazen-faced, cheeky one) is evidence of too little, and *sin vergüenza* (shameless one) means a complete lack of it, displayed, in the eyes of the pueblo, by gypsies, certain types of beggar, and other rebels of society. In this latter sense the term is used as a powerful insult, reflecting indirectly on the parents, and particularly the mother, who should have inculcated a sense of shame in the child.

'You shameless one!' may also be used affectionately to a baby or to one loved implicitly whose actions can involve no sense of shame. The feelings of the suitor in the verse:

'*Anda y rézale a la Virgen y dila que no entro a verla,*
*Que me da vergüenza 'icile' que te quiero más que a ella.*'[2]

reveal how closely love and shame are related.

Summer visitors incurred reproach by bathing (albeit in swimsuits) in a natural pool in the forest at least 300 yards

[1] 'Whether of high or low birth, the most unworthy husband surpasses the best gallant.'
[2] 'Go and pray to the Virgin and tell her I do not enter to see her,
That I am ashamed to tell her that I love you more than her.'

from a public footpath—at any rate until after the participation of a personal and influential friend of the mayor. If a sense of guilt is a matter for the individual conscience, a sense of shame is the social expression of this in the 'public' conscience. For the pueblo shows little patience or forbearance with any straying from accepted codes of behaviour, and an individual is quick to censure publicly acts to which he might well be inclined, or might even commit, in the privacy of his own home.

A nagging concern for honour, authority and economic independence helps to shape the external role of the man who is the guardian of the household. Its internal harmony is ensured by the woman, who is not expected to do man's work or spend time unnecessarily outside the home, and therefore confines her activities as far as possible to that home, visiting other women only occasionally, and going to church, which is beyond reproach, but never of course indulging in masculine practices such as smoking and drinking in bars. The wife of the café-bar manager is regarded as unfortunate because she has to help behind the bar, but as this is really part of the home the work is accepted as 'decent'. Everyday news is gleaned from gossip in the shops and at the washing-point by the stream below the church. Conversely, it is unmanly for the husband to help with housework, essentially a woman's task.[1]

For a man is a creature of action and passion; he demonstrates courage and strength and has 'spunk'. To be accused of 'not having testicles' carries the slight of cowardice, and a man who does not take up the challenge will be dishonoured. There is little homosexuality in Spain, and the word *marica* has a contemptuous and ugly ring. In its most offensive form this studied manliness (*hombría*) is exaggerated into the hooliganism found in Madrid, while the new, popular, but vulgar term *macho* has reduced it to the level of a male animal. Hooliganism has even penetrated to Ramosierra; as one of the elders sorrowfully put it: 'Ever since the *caballero* [cavalier, gentleman] descended from his horse he has been descending more and more.'

In its less harmful form *hombría* perpetuates the myth of Don Juan, of a hungry male virility causing women to be ever wary of

---

[1] On the other hand I found that some wives dealt with the town council's paper work, either because the men 'would not be bothered' or because they were working in the forest all day.

their virtue. The language reflects this in its use of the word 'to love,' not the abstract *amar* but the forceful *querer*, implying complete possession, not only in the physical sense. It implies a certain shamelessness which allows a much greater wandering in sexual relations to a man than to women, who expect him to be 'naughty'. This is an attitude which condones adultery, but only when the sanctity of the home is not affected by it and the wife's honour is respected. Nevertheless it makes the man in his contemplative pride extremely sensitive to ridicule. Hence, the extreme conformity in behaviour and dress everywhere. And in the professional bullring also it is revealed in the apparent obliviousness of danger by bullfighters, aped during the August fiestas by the village youths; the spectators are equally ready to deride signs of cowardice in bulls which do not turn out to be *bravos*.

Such attitudes, moreover, promote the segregation of the sexes and a mutual, only partially veiled hostility, well expressed in the proverb, 'Al marido, ámalo como a amigo y témelo como a enemigo' ('Love a husband as a friend and fear him as an enemy'), and many others which point out the pitfalls of marriage. In church and in religious processions, in school, in play and in the evening promenade, the sexes are always divided. The *cofradías* or religious sodalities are all-male associations since, in theory, it is their task to guard the patron saints of the village, which is a man's job. This extreme segregation makes an ordinary friendship between the sexes very difficult for, in the case of the unmarried, it would be assumed that they are courting; and in the case of married people, their friendship would immediately be suspect. A man never shakes the hand of a woman. Even I was kindly warned that my well-meant chivalrous action in pulling up a chair for a married lady might be misinterpreted if indulged in too often.

Where it does not affect the unity of the household, a husband's infidelity is accepted with resignation by the wife; but the infidelity of a wife is the grossest possible degradation for a man. This is not only because it sullies his manliness, with the added implication that he is unable to satisfy his wife, but also because it threatens the very base of the household structure, which it is his responsibility to guard and preserve. More important still, it is a testimony of lack of shame in his wife, whom he should view as the ideal type of unsullied motherhood. For every man sees in the girl he courts a future mother, and the worst insults in the language are directed against the individual's parentage.

In popular terminology a wife's looseness is reduced to the level of mating among goats. I was assured by a shepherd that when two male goats fight over a female the winner covers her first and then allows the loser to do so. To call a man a 'buck' or 'he-goat' (*cabrón*) is the worst possible insult, the important implication being that he consents to the adultery of his wife. When referring to a cuckolded husband, it is said that he has been given 'horns'; 'el mal del cornudo, él no lo sabe y sábelo todo el mundo' ('The trouble with the deceived husband is that he does not know and everyone else does'). The wearing of horns, figuratively, seems to be as general throughout the Mediterranean area as it was in Elizabethan England;[1] folk tales say that Eve obtained from the Devil his chieftain's horns as the price of her complaisance and presented them to her husband.[2] In sociological terms, I suggest that the infidelity of the woman constitutes a danger to the essential structure of the elementary household, and that the symbol of the horns (representing the power of evil operating through the woman) is derisively attached to the man for his short-comings in preserving the established social order.

The families, therefore, whose members most faithfully live up to the required social values are granted a status which is not based on class, like birth into an aristocracy, but rather on honour. Not only has the honour of their men remained unstained but that of their women has been defended, for they have never lost their 'shame'. Certain families who have played a leading role in pueblo affairs are held in high regard—a street is named after one of them —and some of their branches usually have connections with the outside world. Vera Cruz in Mexico, I am assured, is full of 'good names' from Ramosierra. These families are usually prosperous and are looked upon as being influential and original, so that even their occasionally eccentric behaviour is tolerated. It is said of Baldonero Varona (a middle-aged man) that on his patron saint's day 'the street is not wide enough for him', but in fact he provides

[1] There are several references by Ford and Mistress Quickly in Shakespeare's *The Merry Wives of Windsor*, and the term 'horn' is used concurrently with 'cuckold' throughout the play.
[2] See F. T. Elworthy, *Horns of Honour*, London, 1900.

fun in which everyone eventually participates, as distinct from mere hooliganism.

Class is not so important as being a 'son of the pueblo', a fact clearly seen in the scorn levelled at the neighbouring village, Arboleda. Being a Castilian is of secondary consequence, useful for distinguishing oneself from gypsies or foreigners. There are only two or three families that could be said to move in high society outside the pueblo, and the aristocratic summer visitor, although his noble birth is recognized, is quickly assimilated into the corporate pride of the locality. The villagers' lack of self-consciousness and the fluid mixing of groups are evidence of this. The foreigner, too, is classless and blameless (like a baby) until he proves otherwise.

Occupation and wealth are two other criteria which have more significance in the town. Here in the country, when a man is a forester, an agriculturist, a herdsman, and perhaps a carpenter to boot, any distinction made on grounds of occupation alone is apt to be misleading. Personality counts more than profession, and even a swineherd could become mayor or take holy orders, if he were capable. There are, in fact, as many or as few social classes as we choose to make. Friendship and mutual interest based on *simpatía* (congeniality, not compassion) are the motive forces for groupings which are not easily plotted. Temporary *ad hoc* groupings are also apparent in the traditional refreshments taken after religious ceremonies during the fiestas. Only one of these refreshments is open to the pueblo as a whole. The others are attended either by the mayor's special clique (a group of potentially influential friends) or by members of the respective religious sodalities in their captains' houses—prestige groups formed on membership lines, though not exclusive.

A few years ago, however, Leandro (the bus driver) and Donato (the poor son of a respected landowner who died bankrupt) organized a private dance in the streets surrounding their houses, in the centre of the pueblo. Bunting was stretched between the windows, a small orchestra was engaged from Soria, drinks were provided, and a small group of intimate friends with their families was invited. Everyone had a gay time and they intended to repeat it the following year, but enthusiasm waned. They were not celebrating any special event; but it is significant that both the organ-

izers frequently complain of *caciquismo* and lack of opportunity
in the pueblo, and also have money troubles. As we noted earlier,
no real prestige is gained or lost by living in any particular part
of the village, nor is poverty considered in any way shameful, nor
mere possession of wealth a social virtue in itself. Many of those
not invited to the dance criticized the organizers for their extravagance and restless discontent—'trying to set themselves up as
somebody'—while Leandro and Donato in their turn condemned
their critics for being envious.

For envy can have a levelling down effect in that it reduces its
victim to the level of his critic; and a less successful villager will
often blame it as the reason for his failure. It is not just a passive
sentiment or even a greedy coveting of another's possessions and
good fortune. It is far more an active desire to see everyone
'in the same boat' and with the same troubles. Jealousy is directed
against the affection desired for oneself; envy, perhaps, against the
affection manifested by God in a man's success. Although the
Church's teaching is based on the brotherhood of man, this does
not preclude inequality. In every Castilian there is a potential
anarchist, a state of mind helped by his excessive concern with
personal honour. More endowed with individuality than with
personality, he faces up to the world with such vigour that he
obeys only himself and a supernatural Being.[1] Each therefore sees
himself as apart, as specially chosen by God, which may partially
account for the profusion of 'Great Captains' and *conquistadores*
in Castilian history. But envy, the legacy of Cain, is largely responsible for this sense of individuality. Plutarch even thought
that envy was the driving force behind the 'evil eye'.[2]

Mistrust and envy of one's neighbour, plus a regard approaching veneration for the elementary family unit in the home, account
largely for the *ensimismadismo* or sensation of being wrapped up in
oneself felt by the villager. Although the emigrant constitutes
an extension of the village household abroad, on his return he
encounters opposition because of envy and because of his connection with the alien, hostile, outside world. He must reinstate himself by acts of generosity and the establishment of a separate household based on the original ideal model. The villager's conservatism

[1] See Unamuno, op. cit., pp. 338–400 and 850–56.
[2] See A. C. Haddon, *Magic and Fetishism*, London, 1906, p. 34.

therefore lies not in his mental poverty, but in the strength of his social organization whose foundation is the elementary family unit. A Castilian's home is his castle.

'Loving thy neighbour as thyself' is interpreted in the context of friendship rather than of neighbourhood. Indeed, one of the first signs of a really charitable twentieth-century social conscience (from a welfare State point of view) owed little to the Church and less to the State. The impetus was that of the young widow of a former Falangist leader, Onesimo Redondo, who in October, 1936, at Valladolid founded the 'Auxilio Social' (Social Help) movement, which even now forms the basis of charitable works in most parishes throughout Spain. The energetic 'do-gooder', however, is by no means a common figure in either urban or rural communities. The nearest approximation is the man respected for devotion to his family and a selfless interest in the pueblo, whose advice is frequently sought.

Yet such a man does not necessarily wield any real power unless he belongs to the leading group. If he is a leader, he will act as patron to many of the controllers and servers who seek his favours. All leaders at some time or another play important roles (as do the saints and the Virgin) in the patronage system which, again, has as its aim the levelling out of inequalities. The leaders themselves have still more powerful patrons in the national and provincial capitals, and these may sometimes visit the village in the summer. It is through these greater external patrons that a controller or server who has run foul of his village patron may bypass the influential local leader. In this way, Donato's brother, whose application was previously blocked, won his present appointment as forest guard. For it is the power to do good (or evil) for the pueblo or for individual clients that gives leaders their status, not just the posts they hold or the occupations they follow. By the same token, it is not the quantity of wealth that is important so much as its beneficial employment; for there should be an ideal fraternity in riches too.

Do names, speech or appearance help us to delineate status? Apart from his dual surname a child may have any number of Christian names, but the pueblo swiftly recognizes the clumsiness of formality by immediately applying the diminutive or a nick-name, as indeed do most of the parents. The very compactness of the village encourages the use of single Christian names, sometimes in the affectionate form: for instance, Jaimito (for Jaime) or Perico (for Pedro). So the popular manager of the syndicate bar is always known as 'El Quico' (for Francisco), and the bar is never given its formal title, 'Educación y Descanso', but becomes 'Quico's Bar'.

The nickname can act as a force in social behaviour. It is not simply a natural reluctance to grapple with cumbrous dual surnames that moves people to relate a child to his household by referring to him as 'the son of so-and-so'. In fact, outside the household, it is doubtful if the full surnames even of close kin are known. Only the priest, the secretary and the townhall staff, the Civil Guard sergeant, and the leaders of the religious associations are likely to have any comprehensive knowledge of them through their dealings with records and registers. Even they will resort to a more familiar nickname at times to make themselves clearly understood.

Let us consider some of the better-known nicknames. (The choicer ones are not readily disclosed to an outsider; this would be *feo*, or incorrect behaviour.) There are those that help to define the individual in relation to his present household or to that of his ancestors; some fix his place of origin or that of his family; others define his profession, interests, or peculiarly personal characteristics. Still more describe groups within the village or whole communities without.

The innkeeper is invariably known as 'El Yanguanito' and has this name painted on a signboard above the entrance to the inn. He inherited it, like his father before him, from his great-grandfather who once lived in a house called 'La Yanguana' because he originally came from the neighbouring village of Yanguas. At one time, the pueblo dubbed him with another—'El Corcho' ('The Cork')—because he enthusiastically samples his own wines; but this never caught on with the same strength as his traditional name. 'Pedro el de las Truchas' is a barber who has little interest in trout fishing; it was the nickname of his father, a gamekeeper.

Yet the nickname need not be passed down in the male line only. The daughter of 'El Vitillo' became 'La Vitilla' when her father died from the effects of the chorea—the St. Vitus's dance—from which the name seems to be culled. 'La Vitilla' inherited a good deal of money but few good looks. Nevertheless, she had no difficulty in marrying a farmer now known as 'El Manténme' ('The keep-me one'). Previously, he was called 'El Pelo Blanco' because of his father's white hair, despite the fact that his own hair is black.

Terse nicknames define certain professions as they do in Wales. 'Santiago el Tumbas' ('James the Death') is a cheery grave-digger; 'Pedro el Botas' ('Peter the Boots') is the shoemaker. Both the male nurse and the doctor are grimly referred to as 'El Matasanos' ('The Killer of the Healthy').

Personally descriptive nicknames are the commonest and cruellest of all. 'La Loca' ('The Mad One') is a thick-set woman whose sexual prowess, they say, has lost her two husbands. 'Leandro el toca'o' ('Leandro the Light-Witted') is the punch-drunk bus driver. 'El Aguado' ('The Watery One') was applied to a rich but thrifty man who was teetotal, but this has not passed on to his son for obvious reasons. The cheeky, cheery grocer is 'El Quitapenas' ('The Remover of Care'). Spanish kings in the past were similarly named—Sancho the Strong, Peter the Cruel, Henry the Impotent. The use of these names is not always malicious. Although they are generally uncomplimentary, there may exist kinder alternatives sometimes used by the man's friends. Everyone is aware of his own nickname, yet the force of it lies in never using it in his presence. Communal satire is permitted; individual incorrect behaviour is not.

For this type of nickname can act as social satire ridiculing a man's nonconformity. Where village moral standards are affected, it acts as a sanction of the entire pueblo and not just of the person using it. Its function is clear, for it is given only to a person who in the fullest sense 'belongs' to the community. No summer visitor would be given such a nickname, however deep his roots in the village. Even if one had been associated with him originally, it would die when he left the village and ceased to take an active part in its affairs; for he would then belong to the wider outside world.[1] This distinction can be noted in the case of the emigrant who may receive once more the nickname he had before he left the village, provided he takes up permanent residence again. The nickname is,

[1] Strange visitors such as foreigners who simply do not fall into any recognizable category may be given a purely temporary nickname. I was known as 'El Mister' and, later, 'El Irlandés' (because of Irish ancestry).

therefore, the sign of entry and acceptance in the community's social structure. It is a definition of status.

Those cursed or blessed with a specific nickname do not fall into any definable social grouping within the pueblo except 'las beatas' ('The primly-pious ladies') and 'Los Roques' (the members of the bachelors' sodality), both of which cut across the pueblo structurally because of their semi-religious activities. In contrast to the inter-personal relationship covered by nicknames within the pueblo, there do exist group nicknames for the inhabitants of certain other villages or towns, notable among which is 'Los Bretos', of obscure meaning but derogatively applied to the people of Arboleda. Other regions, and foreign countries too, also come under collective nicknames, but these are less common and, when used, almost always manifest a latent hostility. A young French visitor, who enthusiastically tried to join in the village dance, had all kinds of practical jokes played on him. When at long last he took offence, mouths were drawn down in disgust at his behaviour, and shrugging shoulders accompanied the comment: 'i Esos malditos Franchutes!' ('These damn Frogs!')

In short, nicknames help to personalize relationships, but there are no fixed rules for applying or transmitting them. If they help to place a man quickly, or if they are descriptively apt and successfully carry the sanction they imply, they will stick. They can be used as a form of social satire behind which lurks scorn and sometimes envy, but the nickname is never taken as an insult except when it is used in the recipient's presence, for it belongs to the pueblo as a whole. Though it may seem grossly unfair, even damning, it cannot be escaped except by leaving the pueblo. It is, in fact, the judgement of the community.[1]

Villagers cannot be socially graded by their way of speaking, since this is not linked with individual intelligence. Ignorance of matters not directly concerning the pueblo, such as are found in newspapers and books, is not despised. Even illiteracy, highest among the 40-year-olds and over, is no bar to active entry into the affairs of the pueblo, and in no way embarrasses the forester

---

[1] Unamuno's theory that country people choose the stranger sounding saints' names to avoid others calling their children by an ugly nickname cannot be substantiated for, amongst other things, it does not explain the transmission of the nickname.

working on the mountain slopes. The important thing is to speak 'Christian', which is their synonym for Castilian, and the conversation of many unlettered villagers who have been no farther from their pueblo than the main road is quite surprisingly articulate and wealthy in metaphor.

As the spirit of conformity lacks a stimulus in itself, this is provided by dramatic expansiveness, exaggerated gesture and an evident sententiousness. For the language used in the pueblo is full of proverbs which reflect its history, adages and short pithy sayings which are sometimes devastatingly scurrilous in their application. With such a range as Castilian supplies the illiterate scarcely needs to think grammatically when he can reach out to an apt maxim to serve any occasion. Where logic fails in an argument the confident use of a proverb may succeed.

In such propitious soil gossip is bound to flourish, and as a form of social sanction lies largely in the hands of such women as 'las beatas'. It is often the quickest and most direct punishment of the moral code. It does not ostracize or outlaw the culprit; it 'in-laws' him by relating his behaviour to a particular household.

The formality of the language is used to maintain social distance. Though the intimate *tu* is generally used throughout the pueblo, the respectful third person *Usted* is used by youths addressing elders and sometimes by children to authority-conscious parents, or whenever the formality of the occasion and lack of acquaintance-ship demands it—for instance, with strangers and foreigners. When used in excess the heavy courtesy and endearing phrases may cloak indifference, envy, or even hate. When the youths serenaded an attractive French visitor to the pueblo two or three years ago the words became elaborately, even insultingly, fulsome after she had rewarded them with only a trifling gift. Professional serenading, that is, expectation of actual money, is something quite new.

The people who give themselves airs are usually those who would like to merit the title *Don*. This is an important term of social dis-tinction and, like *Señor*, deserves consideration in our discussion of status. The use of *Señor* implies respect for age or possessions, and is sometimes used cautiously where the status of a person is not immediately recognizable. It can mean lord, master, or the owner of property. So God is 'El Señor', the mayor is sometimes jokingly called 'El Señor (or El Amo) del pueblo', and the word would be used when asking for the man of the house. It is used as a title to a superior, like 'Sir' or 'Sire', or to an equal like 'Mr'. So boys will use it to their schoolmasters, and women particularly will use it when speaking to the priest, who is known as 'El Señor Cura'. Employees do not use it to their employer's face, though they might do so behind his back in reference to him and in the presence of a visitor. Thus 'Es un señor mayor' ('He is an old gentleman') was used for my benefit to describe an old man who takes the sun in the square, but amongst themselves he would be 'Old Manuel'. Again, a man might introduce his wife to me (an outsider) as 'mi Señora', but this would be considered high falutin' compared with the usual 'mi mujer'. The difference is something like that between references to 'the wife' and 'my wife' in England. Occasionally 'Señor' may be used contemptuously of somebody one dislikes and without the usual implication of respect. 'El Yanguanito' referred to the mayor in this way; or perhaps the literally translated example, 'The Señor Picasso is a painter who ought to be shot' makes the use clearer.

Its diminutive, *señorito*, is the form sometimes applied to the young son of a rich and influential household, who does not 'belong' to the pueblo. A humble but rich forester has four sons who qualify for the title as they spend most of their time in the capital cities. It is often used with sarcasm to describe fashionable idlers, and so is occasionally employed to refer to a particularly lazy youth.

*Don*, the supposed Spanish title for 'gentleman', has subtler uses and connotations. It also implies respect and may be employed in deference to age, occupation and the influence implied by material possessions. As with *Señor*, the presence of others may demand its use; or it may go with an official title as in 'El Señor Alcalde, Don Ramón Varona' ('His Worship the Mayor, Mr Ramón Varona'), though only the town hall staff and humbler people seeking favours would actually address him as 'Don Ramón'. It is the equivalent of 'Mr', but must always be used with the Christian name; so Rodrigo de Huesca, a rich emigrant returned from Mexico, is known as 'Don Rodrigo' to most of the younger men outside his own clique, but his son is known merely by his Christian name, Manolo. Like 'Esquire' it is found on envelopes in personal and formal correspondence; so 'Thomas

Atkins, Esq.' would become 'Don Tomás Pérez', but 'Muy Señor mío' ('Dear Sir') would be the usual opening for the actual letter.

Professional men merit the title because their education for a career elevates them above ordinary pueblo status, and in general, it will be given to those with a university degree (like 'Dr' on the Continent). 'Don Agapito' the priest has it not only because of his education but also because he represents the power of the Church. The doctor should have the title by right, but because of his unpopularity few accord it to him. Schoolboys use it of their teachers, and so do parents, but in their case only out of respect to those from outside the pueblo, even if they are younger. It is closely associated with full adulthood so that only middle-aged married men will qualify in the pueblo. Occasionally, it is applied jokingly to the snobbish visitor from Madrid, and there is a special name, 'Don Guindo,' really a nickname, for one who boasts of learning he does not possess.

What must be stressed is the deep sense of fraternity felt among the villagers, so that the ridicule occasioned by the misuse of these terms implicitly controls their use. As we have shown, very few men in Ramosierra merit the titles. Apart from showing courtesy before strangers, they are used only of those few who in fact constitute the power élite which wields authority in the village. Almost without exception, 'dons' and 'señors' do not fully 'belong' to the pueblo, for by virtue of their wealth, power or education they have interests linking them to the world outside. These terms, therefore, which to some extent measure social distance, single out those individuals whose failure to conform exactly to the pueblo's egalitarian values sets them apart as a force to be admired and cultivated—or to be reckoned with. Outwardly expressions of respect, such terms are sometimes based on fear: a fear manifested by those who use these terms even of the police sergeant.

No social distinction is made on grounds of dress or appearance. Sobriety is the rule; the villagers wear no 'outlandish' cuts or colour schemes of the type which make tourists so laughable in their eyes. Women mostly wear black or grey, which are serviceable and also suitable for the long periods of mourning; they do not consciously follow national or foreign fashions, but vie with each other at fiestas and on Sundays in a purely personal rivalry. The men favour corduroy for their working clothes, shave infrequently (but never wear beards or exaggerated moustaches) and sometimes sport a tie with their neat dark lounge suits for Sunday mass. The black beret is the popular headgear, and only the mayor regularly wears a trilby and a waistcoat, for reasons of health. Men began to put off their distinctive provincial dress in the 1890s, but women wear theirs for at least one day during the August fiestas, while some of the older ones still favour a less formal version of the same costume for everyday wear, topped by a heavy black shawl.

Do the people themselves make any such social divisions in their minds? A final glance at the language will give us some indication.

1. *la gente gorda*: literally, 'fat' people: a grouping based on sociopolitical power and influence—those who 'run' the pueblo; it includes the mayor (and by extension the Governor), the priest and the Civil Guard sergeant, not because of their personalities but because of the power behind them. It may be associated with wealth, and would thus include some of the richer ex-emigrants, but wealth alone is not enough to secure inclusion in *la gente gorda*. Most *Dons* and leaders fall into this grouping.

2. *la gente rica*: a division made on grounds of wealth alone. It would include the present mayor and most of the ex-emigrants (but not all of their sons, some of whom are hard-working farmers) as well as the mistrustful forester who keeps his money under the mattress. Their generosity in the pueblo and donations to its funds might win them the title of *Don* eventually. The possession of money by *la gente rica* is not important, but what they do with it, *is*.

3. *la gente de carrera*: i.e., those who have studied for a particular career. The professional and university group is included here; the mayor, the priest, the apothecary, and some of the summer visitors from Madrid, but (for personal reasons only) not the doctor.

4. *la gente inteligente*: a sub-grouping based on a secondary education of some kind and the intelligent application of it to everyday affairs. The Varona brothers are placed under this heading for their business-like exploitation of the pines; the doctor too, for his technical ability, and of course the teachers, except for one who is considered knowledgeable but 'stupid'.

5. *la gente lista*: a similar sub-grouping based more on astuteness and 'animal' cunning. It is closely associated with success in one's particular field. The sergeant of police is deemed to be *listo*, and so is 'El Quitapenas', who is a keen business man.

6. *la gente educada*: applied to all those who have been properly brought up, who show persistent good manners, who are chivalrous and graceful in their behaviour. Inclusion in this class is a tribute to the parents.

7. *la gente simpática*: only those whose charm of manner and genuine friendliness overcome all other considerations are included here. As these qualities form the basis of most friendships, this grouping is the most likely to cut across all others.

8. *la gente decente*: judged on questions of morality; 'decent folk'; generally applies to the honest hard-working type with no pretentions who maintains the traditions of the pueblo. Most people would like to think themselves among *la gente decente*.

9. *la gente vulgar*: the 'plebs' of the village; those of humble origin. The expression would be used only by those who consider themselves superior, in other words those who do not fully 'belong' to the pueblo. The ex-villager who has made good in Madrid and is a 'social climber' might use the phrase to describe his own people. So might the much-travelled emigrant who has seen the world and mixed widely. They themselves would undoubtedly be thought of as snobs by *la gente vulgar*.

10. *la gente ordinaria*: applied to those whose behaviour is the opposite of those under heading 6. They are generally rude, and thus the phrase is a censure on their parents. It may be applied to people like the innkeeper who, although he clearly knows full well how to behave, often ridicules the excesses of traditional etiquette. 'El Quitapenas' who was fined for rude jokes on the bus, and Leandro the driver for allowing him, would be placed under this heading by some of the more easily-shocked women.

# 7

## THE PATRONAL FIESTAS

BETWEEN August 14th and 18th every year special fiestas are held in honour of the two patron saints of Ramosierra: Our Lady of the Pine (Nuestra Señora del Pino) and St. Roch (San Roque). Each patron is represented by a male confraternity[1] led by a captain, a lieutenant (*alférez*) and a sergeant, who are in charge of the ritual around which the fiestas take shape. All members of the confraternities are obliged to take part in the ceremonies; no villager can ignore them. For two of these fiestas are holy days of obligation, and these I shall describe in some detail; all five are communal holidays in which everyone joins.

Throughout the morning of the 14th, sweating bands of youths directed by the elders erect two of the tallest pine trunks, called *mayos*,[2] at least sixty feet long, and freshly felled from the surrounding forest. One is placed at the entrance to the village and the other in the main square. Ribbons of the national colours flutter from the tops of these pines, and the red and yellow flags are hung out over the balconies of houses. The church bells have been ringing all morning and fireworks drown the throaty announcement of the town crier, which marks the official inauguration of the fiestas at midday.

Little of importance occurs until twilight when a tour is made of the village by the confraternity sergeants carrying their chased steel halberds and accompanied by pipe (*gaita*, in reality a chanter,

---

[1] There are other sodalities in Ramosierra whose importance lies only in their activities on their own patron saint feast days and at members' funerals. They are, in fact, mutual-aid-in-burial societies.

[2] Really a summer form of maypole—*mayo* (May). In some other villages of the province they are erected in mid-summer; very few are put up as late as August.

the pipe part of the Galician bagpipe) and kettle drum (*tambor*). These are soon joined by an imported band, smart in uniform and marching step, whose blaring brass brings the people streaming out of their homes to attend *La Vela*—the first ceremony of the fiestas.

*Vela* has the double meaning of both candle and wake, and the idea (if not the practice) of the wake is significant on this eve of the feast day of the village patron. The principal role in the ritual is played by the mayor's wife or other female representative in her capacity as *Mayor Dama* (First Lady) acting on behalf of the whole pueblo. Dressed entirely in black with a high comb in her hair and a delicately embroidered mantilla over her head and shoulders, she walks in solemn state to the church, guarding the flame of an intricately fashioned candle. Normally donated as an act of penance, the candle is fully two feet long. There in the three-naved, eighteenth-century parish church, now beautifully transformed by a mass of colour, and ablaze with light from hundreds of altar candles, the priest in his heavy ceremonial robes is awaiting her. Kneeling, she gravely offers up the candle, together with a nominal sum in cash, to the primary village patron, the Holy Virgin of the Pine.

A short service follows during which the civil authorities and the visiting ecclesiastics occupy their privileged position at the side of the altar. As the priest turns to the altar and begins to intone the Latin prayers, the music strikes up. It comes tentatively from a wheezy eighteenth-century organ, a violin and a flute. Small orchestras in Spanish churches are as common now as they were in England a hundred years ago, though there is a tendency to reserve them for very important feast days, weddings, and special high masses. Much favoured are pieces like 'The Indian Love Call' during Mass, or the triumphal march from *Aida* as the priest makes his exit. For these holidays a choir has been formed consisting largely of summer visitors (who have relatives in the village), backed by two determined professionals imported from the provincial capital. Now, as they sing a spirited Salve Regina, with the seventeenth-century retable brilliantly illuminated to reveal that rarely-painted scene of Christ's Circumcision, with the side altars beautifully draped and flanked with clusters of burning candles, with the music flowing out to the small waxen-faced image of the Virgin above the central altar, this large but simple village church takes on a new grandeur.

It is obvious that a great deal of work, money and pride have been expended for the villagers' own satisfaction and not merely to impress the visitors. There is much fidgeting during the service; veils are adjusted, covert glances are taken to see if one's neighbour is there and what he or she is wearing, and an unaffected interest prevails rather in the decoration of the church than in the actual ceremony. This dedicatory service ends abruptly when the priest wheels round to announce the masses for the morning, which is the signal for the 'Mayor Dama' to leave again in procession.

As she comes out of the church, one senses a gayer note in keeping with the march struck up by the waiting band. Now the procession is led by two sidesmen who rush ahead waving spluttering fireworks which throw dancing shadows in the dark lanes. With the children leaping about in anticipation and everyone chatting animatedly, it is not at all the solemn affair that started out for the church. Through the twisting cobbled lanes the procession makes its way to the main school building where it mounts the stairs, followed by a milling, noisy crowd of villagers, who seat themselves like pupils at the long benches. The municipal authorities and the parish priest with his adjutants seat themselves on the raised dais at the far end, whilst members of the religious sodalities, acting as waiters, scurry about with *el refresco*.

This refreshment of specially-baked light biscuits washed down with cinnamon-flavoured diluted red wine is served first to the authorities—with the exception of the mayor who (as he is still acting in his capacity of formal leader of the pueblo) is given only a glass of water. Then, as it was next doled out on the basis of 'two for the brothers [i.e. members of the confraternities] and one for the others', I suddenly realized that this was one of the oldest customs of the village. For the strength and quantity of these refreshments have been strictly governed throughout the history of religious sodalities and, reading between the lines of ancient statutes, one gathers that abuses made such rationing necessary. Hence the mayor now makes only in water his special toast to all present, saying: 'I toast you for the favour which I have received from you all,' which ends the ceremony; there are no speeches and no other ritual. The significance of the final toast seems to be a recognition of the implicit trust (theoretically) placed in the mayor as the steward[1] of common wealth, for this is a ceremony at which all are entitled to attend and partake. They no longer understand why they do these things; dimly they realize there is a value in them which is being chipped away by the lack of interest among the young and the apathy of many of the older people.

Here, at this point, the last link with public ceremony is broken for the day. The mayor returns to his house where he entertains a group of men invited either because they are of his own clique or kin, or because they are potentially influential friends. Elsewhere, whole families drift off to the bars or to walk in the square until dinner. Greetings are warmer and longer than usual tonight; a festive spirit pervades the narrow streets and excites the children. After dinner, from about 11 p.m. to 2 a.m., there is a village dance around the *mayo* in the main square. To the hired band's spirited but inaccurate renderings of popular Spanish and Latin-American rhythms, the young shuffle about rather self-consciously under the benign gaze of their elders, and split up immediately the music ends. Many of the younger girls dance together and some others, more mature, lead their clumsier male partners. Summer visitors show off their sophisticated dance steps and their town clothes.

Soon, the older men, having put in an appearance, stroll once or twice around the square and then deliberately retire to a round of the many temporary bars. Cheap brandy and *anis* stimulate the flow of conversation up to 3 a.m. in groups which change constantly and rarely harden into cliques. Here, a shepherd talks freely and easily with a visitor who is a Professor of Law; over there, the town crier is arguing a point with the doctor. Their conversation almost always concerns the affairs of the pueblo, and critical comparisons are made between the organization of the present fiestas and that of previous years. There is much animation but no evident drunkenness.

Eventually the band goes to bed and the bars slowly close. Yet boisterous groups of young men continue to roam the streets

---

[1] *Mayordomía* (stewardship) is, in Mexico, an institution involving ceremonial sponsorship by a group of people of an image in a church. Candles are burned and meals are given in its honour. See Geo. M. Foster, *Empire's Children*, Smithsonian Institute, 1948.

aimlessly seeking a diversion which only they themselves can provide. Tomorrow the elders will good-naturedly complain of noise and nostalgically recall their own lost youth. At dawn, the young revellers are still in the main square tiredly brewing up mugs of chocolate over an open fire.

On August 15th, the day celebrating the Assumption of the Virgin, High Mass is scheduled for 11 a.m., but the square outside the church is quiet except for the play of a few uncommonly well-brushed children in their best clothes. The church bells have been ringing continuously for over an hour and soon they are joined by the sound of the pipe and drum accompanying the confraternity sergeants who are off to collect the captains and members. In full procession, the captains bearing the sodality flags, the lieutenants with their staffs of office, the standard-bearers holding aloft the insignia of their respective patrons followed by the sergeants shouldering halberds, both sodalities march to the church to receive a blessing.

Outside, an expectant crowd awaits them for the ceremony of the *Revolteo*[1] or twirling of the banners. When the robed priest emerges, he takes up a central position with the mayor, flanked by the Civil Guard. Each captain in turn then faces them and, taking off his beret, he salutes first the authorities and then the public with a sweeping gesture, which they acknowledge by a bow of the head or by raising their own headgear. He then grasps the large flag and, unfurling the heavily embroidered cloth bearing the name of his sodality, he waves it slowly in a fluttering motion, first three times to the left and then three times to the right. This calls for a certain skill and not a little energy, and shouts of approbation or derision from the crowd spur on the competitive efforts of the two captains. Each then gravely retrieves his beret from the ground and again salutes the company.

By this time, the images of the patrons have been brought out

[1] The *Revolteo* may well be a ceremonial relic acquired from the reviews of the old Spanish *tercios* or infantry regiments in Flanders. The pipe and drum, the weapons, the flags and insignia, all lead one to suggest that these sodalities are merely the religious successors of the old sixteenth-century local militia. These were raised by local councils for defence purposes in areas newly reconquered from the Moors, and even then were known as 'brotherhoods' (*hermandades*).

from the church and are carried in procession through the village, mounted on small wooden platforms borne on the shoulders of the brother-members. Today the Virgin takes precedence for it is her feast day; tomorrow it will be Saint Roch's turn to lead. Chanting a hymn, the procession makes the regulation tour of the village but, though it does not lack a simple dignity, it is hardly a solemn affair, with children dancing in and out of the column. By means of a swaying step, the bearers of the images make even them 'dance', and there are shouts of 'Viva la Virgen!' answered by 'Viva San Roque!' from enthusiastic spectators—hushed by the more pious. But there is nothing studiously pious in the chatter of the participants and the remarks of the spectators from the balconies.

Once back at the church, High Mass begins. Each *cofradía* stations itself within the altar rails in the church, which again is packed. Apart from the ordinary village folk are the school children, marched to the service by the schoolmasters, with cuffs for the laggards in the rear. At the Offertory of the Mass, the parish priest, assisted by two visiting priests for the occasion, turns to face the congregation, and the mayor and the captains of the *cofradías* come forward to kiss his hand and present him with an offering (now in money) on behalf of their respective bodies. Once again, the mayor is acting in the name of the whole pueblo.

High Mass during these two special feast days is marked by fiery sermons given by a visiting priest who, since he has gained a reputation for his delivery, demands a special fee. Many tongues are only too eager to begin wagging against the cupidity of the clergy, yet they are equally ready to point out that a good professional merits his pay. The preacher I heard on two separate occasions was a rubicund figure in his early thirties already showing the signs of good living. He was in fact the nephew of the 'Secretario', a 'magistral' (prebend-preacher) in the provincial cathedral. Majestic in his scarlet robes, he well befitted the title in the arts both of oratory and preaching. His rich and mellow voice filled and reverberated through the high-ceilinged church; now trembling with emotion, the next moment thundering in anger, it was emphasized by pleading, all-embracing gestures or by pounding of fists on the pulpit rail, to such effect that the congregation seemed fascinated and spellbound. The theme of his sermon was the virginity of the Virgin and, throughout, the necessity of keeping the sixth commandment, 'Thou shalt not commit adultery', was reiterated.

From the choir, however, where the band, the singers and some thirty or forty villagers had gathered, there was a distinct migration. As soon as the sermon began, small groups quite casually left their seats and climbed into the belfry, there to enjoy the landscape for twenty minutes or so. Those remaining in the choir showed little interest in the affairs below; the singers compared notes, the organist berated the children who had operated the bellows, and one member of the band went to sleep in the corner.

It would be rash to conclude that the main congregation below would have behaved in the same way, had not their sense of delicacy prevented them. No two people have exactly the same religious fervour, and most choirs, where they cannot be seen, are renowned for their isolationism except when in song. Some of the congregation had previously expressed the view that even the visit of a priest famed for his rhetoric was not enough to hold their attention, since the words would be the same even though his delivery might be more 'showy'. Nevertheless, later discussion among the villagers who had attended in the naves quite clearly brought out the pleasure they felt that their special festivities were graced by such men of high rank and talent; that, in fact, they were getting good value for their money. All who had listened praised the preacher rather than the sermon itself, and thus the praise, by inference, was extended to the institution that he represented; once again the distinction was drawn between the role and the individual.

After High Mass, the *Revolteo* of the flags takes place once more, and then the members of the religious brotherhoods stroll off informally to their respective captains' houses for the regulation refreshment. The *cofradía* of the Virgin is accompanied by the parish priest on this day, and he and the captain are given water whilst the other members drink the diluted wine and eat the thin biscuits. After a discussion of the past ceremonies with the priest (who is their honorary head, since this is the married men's sodality), the captain ends the meeting by drinking in water a toast to those present. The formula 'I toast you all for the favour which I have received' is the same as that used by the mayor to the pueblo as a whole on the previous day. The time is now near two o'clock and the streets are deserted, for the women have gone off to prepare lunch whilst the men are having a final aperitif in the bars. Lunch will be late today and no one will mind, for the fiestas have really begun.

As the men are finishing their after-lunch game of cards in the main bar at about 5 p.m., the sound is heard once more of the pipes and drums. Without insignia this time, the sodalities are proceeding to collect the parish priest and the town council; later, led by the brass band in triumphant march time, the group makes its way to the fields of San Antón. The 'Campo Verde' of San Antón is a stretch of open pastureland in the valley to the north where the now derelict shrine to the saint stands. A large crowd of villagers and summer visitors has gathered to watch the ceremonial dance which follows.

A statutory *Revolteo* of the flags accompanied by pipe and drum opens the function. Then, at a signal from the parish priest, the same musicians break into the rhythm of a *jota*, which, in this form, is of Aragonese origin, rather like a Scottish reel. The order of the dance is ritually complex, for each official of each sodality plus the mayor must dance a chorus with his female representative —his wife, mother or sister—and then further choruses with the female representatives of the other sodality. It is obviously a stimulating but exhausting experience for the older people.

The task of organizing the dance is jealously controlled by the captains, who take their duties very seriously. Indeed, throughout the fiestas great care is taken that traditional detail of the ritual is preserved. There is always an ancient member whose advice is sought when in doubt. They do not know the origin of the dance, and only do it now because 'they have always done it'. Its origin may be the same as that of the English Morris dance, taken from the word *Morisco*, i.e. 'Moorish', which became fashionable at the time of the Reconquest in masques and court dances. If so, it may be interpreted as a mock battle in dance form between Moors and Christians, which from Aragon in the twelfth century spread all over Europe.[1] This interpretation is supported by the *Revolteo* of flags which accompanies the ceremony and gives it a military flavour. There is no procession as such back to the village, but members of the brotherhoods tend to keep together, for they

[1] See V. Alford and R. Gallop, *The Traditional Dance*, London, 1935.

return to the captains' houses to take yet another regulation refreshment.

At twilight the church bells announce the beginning of the Rosary procession in which the images of the patrons are again carried through the streets in the same order as in the morning, but this time without the guard of halberdiers. It should be mentioned in passing that only a facsimile of the real Virgin of the Pine statue is carried; the original legendary image, reputed to be eleventh-century work, is never removed from its niche above the altar, where it is fixed to a pine trunk. During the procession the sexes are segregated; the men lead with the statues whilst the women follow in a disorganized crowd, wending their way through darkness relieved only by the light of naked torches flanking the statues. Prayers are in Spanish and the singing is a chant in the Gregorian style, accompanied only by the doleful pipe. The atmosphere is suffused with that mixture of deep piety and frivolity which one associates with a people whose religion is merged into the totality of their general culture.

When the images are returned to the church, a ceremony similar to that of the previous night in which the mayor's lady offered up a candle takes place, with the captains' female representatives now playing the leading role. Precedence in these two offertories falls to the *cofradía* of the Virgin, and by chance neither the captain nor his wife were of the pueblo, although they had kin there. Both women, the one a wife, the other a mother, acting on behalf of the two brotherhoods, revived an old custom of wearing the colourful provincial dress for the occasion, instead of the normal black. There was much favourable comment on this, including a slightly regretful feeling that it took 'strangers' to revive the old tradition. Again a short service follows, and afterwards the brotherhoods go back to the captains' houses to take yet another refreshment.

The number of regulation refreshments during these days suggest that the ceremonies of the past were a good deal longer and more strenuous than they are today. For the *cofradía* of the Virgin, however, this one is rather more significant, since this is the day when the insignia are handed over to the new officers, automatically elected by seniority of service. The other brotherhood will do the same tomorrow on the feast day of San Roque.

A.    Alcázar, the old fort.
B.    Mozárabe quarter of San Ginés.
      and the 'vicus' of San Martín.
C.    Moorish settlement.
D.    Jewish settlement.
      Inclosures in the XV and XVIII
                          centuries.
I - 12  Modern urban districts.

The Growth of Madrid.

After dinner, another village dance is held around the pine *mayo* in the square. The swarm of villagers is swelled by an increasing number of town visitors (who have come specially for the well known ceremony on the morrow) as well as a number from the lonely hamlets dependent on Ramosierra. Whole families arrive in groups, for during fiestas kin ties are strengthened by house-to-house visits formalized by refreshment with the familiar diluted sweetened wine and biscuits. It is a fine though chilly night, and the well-wrapped spectators sit on the stone benches surrounding the square, or on the church steps. The scene is much the same as on the previous night; the young people dancing, the older women watching, and their menfolk drinking in the bars. Only a firework display at midnight brings them all together. The highlight of this expensive display of rockets and sympathetically detonating lines of multi-coloured fireworks comes when a picture of the Virgin bursts out in a frame of colour. It is greeted with hand-clapping and the playing of the national anthem by the band. As this is a special occasion the dance goes on until three in the morning.

On August 16th the pueblo celebrates its second saint's feast day, that of San Roque, patron of the bachelors. As early as 7 a.m. the sound of the now familiar march from the hired brass band rends the air and one feels (remembering their earlier stint) that they too must be feeling the strain of these protracted holidays. The march is shortly replaced by the sound of pipe and drum calling together the brotherhoods. With flags and insignia, they make their way from the captains' houses to the church, where they collect the priest and the civil authorities. Though today is 'San Roque', this call on authority is actually the privilege of the *cofradía* of the Virgin since the ceremony of the *Pinochada* later in the day revolves around a legend in which the Virgin plays the central part.

From the church a now warlike procession makes its way to the lower part of the village, for the officers have suddenly acquired swords and brass-studded shields instead of the usual halberds. Outside the shrine of the Virgin of Loneliness (*La Soledad*) near the second pine *mayo*, a number of women in traditional costume carrying short branches of pine await them. Here, a special Mass is said during which the mayor, and the captain, lieutenant and sergeant of the brotherhood of the Virgin each offer up a candle to their patron. After the Mass they return to the church for the blessing of these pine branches which are to play such an active part in the proceedings to follow. But meanwhile, there is a short interval for their breakfast of coffee or chocolate and buns.

It is not long before the main square begins to fill not only with villagers but also with bus-loads of visitors from the provincial capital and nearby villages, with the notable exception of Arboleda. They are joined at about ten o'clock by the married women in costume and carrying their pine branches. Their beautiful dress merits a short description.

The long vermilion skirt has three bands of black velvet just showing beneath a black embroidered lace-edged apron; a heavy white petticoat worn beneath the skirt sometimes peeps from below it, and white stockings complete the lower half of the costume. A silk, satin, or brocade bodice with red ruffs at the sleeve is covered by a mantilla which varies in colour and style; at one time it was evidently black satin bordered with black velvet, but now the *manila* type—a richly embroidered, highly coloured shawl with a long fringe—is favoured by those not fortunate enough to have inherited the traditional type as a family heirloom. The motif of these shawls or *mantones* is usually floral, and the word *manila* recalls the time when these were commonly imported from the city of that name. Very few now own or wear the old merino shawls bordered in black velvet, which also covered the head and are relics of the days when the pueblo economy was bound up with transhumant sheepherding. Instead, they wear a large white square which, more often than not, they carry in their hands. To complete the costume, a black velvet neckband is held together at the front by a jewelled brooch; some of these are obviously valuable heirlooms. Two vertical strips (rather like lawyer's neckwear) dangle at the back of this neckband; this eye-catching adornment is familiarly known in the village as the *i sígueme, pollo!* ('follow me, young man!'). The whole outfit is known as the *pinorra*; the pine branches they carry are called *pinochos*, and the ceremonial fight with them that follows is the *pinochada*. All these terms are derived from the basic word for the pine—*pino*—the tree which nourishes the village economy.

On the whole, the married women are very young or middle-aged and are very few in number; in 1954 there were only ten, but three years later there were sixteen. The older generation are quick to deplore this poor turn-out of the married women and complain of the modern girl's indifference to village customs. Others admit that the costume is extremely expensive to replace once it is worn out through having been passed down, mother to daughter, over several generations; it rarely seems to be replaced in fact, so that the number of women participants in future years should decrease, unless the costume changes. Another simple explanation is that many of the married women are undergoing one of the long periods of mourning which prohibits them from taking part in any public functions; this is pueblo custom and not imposed by the Church, although it may encourage it.

The fact remains, however, that at least twenty per cent of the married women are summer visitors, and that they, like their men, are the most enthusiastic in maintaining tradition in the village. Nor does their enthusiasm entirely make up for a noticeable apathy among the villagers themselves towards the dying away of tradition once so jealously guarded. Several times the remark was heard that the lack of animation in fiestas these days was due to lack of money, or at least a reluctance to spend it; whereas in the past the very attitude that money was necessary would have been deplored.

After a pause, the unmarried women are played into the square by the brass band, and I noticed that the women *capitanas* of both brotherhoods had affixed to their pine branches a small replica of the brotherhood flag. Ages of the new arrivals varied from toddling infancy to the late twenties. The spinster who, in the eyes of the pueblo, has lost her chance of marriage does not make an appearance at this ceremony, although it may be viewed in the light of a courting relationship from the sociological standpoint. (That this is not entirely true will be borne out in the narrative.) In 1954, their number was seventy-five, and in 1957, eighty-six, if one counted the children. Though the type of shawl varied in colour and style, the rest of their costume adhered strictly to tradition. This seemed to belie the older people's previous criticism of the married women, but was explained away by saying that the young girls were always glad of the opportunity to show off their finery. Also carrying pine branches held vertically in front of them, they formed up in line on two sides of the square. Thus three sides of the square were lined by women in costume, leaving the centre empty. Spectators crowded at the back and at every window and balcony that overlooked the square.

An historical explanation for the *pinochada* ceremony can be found in a simple territorial dispute of forest-land between the two villages of Arboleda and Ramosierra. In Ramosierra this has been romanticized by a religious legend which is firmly believed. They say that 'many' centuries ago an image of the Virgin materialized between two pine trees in the hills, on the frontier of the two villages, and was seen by rival groups of shepherds. When their initial awe had passed, they disputed as to whom should fall the honour of carrying off the image. Fighting broke out, reinforcements arrived and the battle swayed back and forth for several hours. Then the men of Ramosierra, in desperation (some cynics say), sent for their women to come and aid them. When they arrived, they tore branches from the pines and, striking these into the eyes of their opponents, they turned the scales of the battle in favour of Ramosierra, afterwards bringing back the Virgin in triumph to their church. If this be a myth, as seems likely, the people of Arboleda perpetuate it by saying: 'Ya tenéis la Virgen, pero nos quedamos con los pinos' ('You have the Virgin, but the pines stay with us') which, incidentally adds weight to the historical version. It is true that the terrain of Arboleda is much richer in pines, and I have earlier commented on the rivalry still existent between the two villages.

Meanwhile, with flags and music, swords and shields, the brotherhoods of the Virgin and San Roque have entered the square and go directly into the church, in that order. There, they have a brief dedicatory service to prepare them for the mock battle which is to ensue and, leaving the church, they place their flags on the balcony of the 'Casa Consistorial' or town hall (that of the Virgin on the right and that of San Roque on the left). There is a great air of excitement and expectation among the villagers, and much explanation is offered to the 'strangers' of what is to occur.

Suddenly the band starts up with a martial air which is the signal for the attack. Two groups, each of six men including the officers of the brotherhoods, form up in opposing ranks, with arms encircling each other's shoulders. The third man from the left in the Virgin's group, the captain, bears the round embossed shield; the third from the right of the San Roque group bears a similar shield. All others carry naked swords. They wear no special dress and some merely take their coats off. Now the pipes and drums take over from the brass band and, in opposite directions, the two parties begin to trot around the square passing each other when they draw abreast. This trotting, which is in reality a form of high-stepping dance, is the prelude to the fight and is meant to signify the original distance marched to do battle. It also serves to raise their spirits in a mutual exchange of insults, shaking their swords as they pass. It is in fact the ancient play of challenge and war.

On circling the square for the third time, however, the two ranks quicken their pace and meet with wild cries. Each shield-bearer dashes his shield against the other's, then, covering his head with it, allows the opposing party to rain sword blows on it to simulate the fight. These tactics are repeated three times until, finally, the San Roque rank disintegrates and the Virgin's throw their hats victoriously into the air. Cheers and handclapping from the crowd. It should be noted here that this hardly tallies with the legend if the San Roque men are supposed to represent Arboleda, for the legendary battle was not resolved until the Ramosierra women arrived. I suggest that this is really a symbolic victory of the married men over the unmarried. So ends the first round of *simulacro*.

The second part of this mock battle begins immediately after-wards when the shield-bearers (who are the captains) regain their breath and go to collect five members each from the ranks of the married and unmarried women. They include the women *capitanas* carrying the replica banners on their pine branches, and all briefly visit the church to bless themselves and their weapons for the fray. Once more in the square, the *capitanas* step in turn to the centre (the Virgin's representative taking precedence) and perform the same ceremony of the *Revolteo* of flags which was executed by their men folk at previous ceremonies. The tiny replica is waved three times to the left, three times to the right, and thrice over the head to the spectators. Then, each group of five women, the married and the unmarried, forms a file behind the male cap-tain of each *cofradía*. The brass band has sounded the attack and the pipes and drums begin the rhythm of the march. As did the men alone, so all now circle the square with the same tactics, but their progress is notably more sedate and there is much less jeering at the opposing party. Three times they meet; the men captains clash together their shields, and then hurriedly protect their heads as the women use their pine branches. There is no lack of enthusiasm for this part of the ceremony, and the women lay to with a vengeance. Again the file of San Roque disintegrates in defeat, and the victory of the married group is greeted with cheers.

As the tempo of ritual has increased, so enthusiasm everywhere has mounted, but when the female *capitanas* terminate the mock battle by a victorious *Revolteo* of their miniature flags, all the men about the square begin to look apprehensive. They have every reason to do so, because the rest of the women can hardly wait for the end before they are off in a flash chasing any man they can find and using their pine branches freely. For twenty minutes or so they are complete mistresses of the pueblo. There seems to be no definite seeking out of sweethearts on whom to deal the first blow; the chase is indiscriminate. Some are even allowed into the church to strike the statue of San Roque with their pine branches on the grounds that he is a man. Strangers and bachelors are particularly besieged, and any man fool enough to come from Arboleda would have no respite. None is supposed to resist, and if he does (as many do, to add fun to the proceedings) he is pursued and given a double dose. Men are chased through the streets, upstairs, into the fields and into cafés, all with obvious good humour, although there is nothing light in a blow from a prickly pine branch; country women are no weaklings. The priest avoids trouble by delicately retiring to his presbytery.

A formula accompanying the touch on the head is always the same: 'De hoy en un año' ('From today until a year's time'), to which the man who has received the *pinochazo* must reply 'Gracias' (Thank you). For me, the important conclusions to be drawn from this *pinochada* ceremony are not only the supposed victories over the neighbouring village of Arboleda but also the true dominance of the woman in her sociological role, and the symbolic triumph of the married state over the unmarried. If it were simply a ceremony in honour of the Virgin, there is every reason for it to be held on the previous day and not on the feast day of the bachelor patron, San Roque.

Now both *cofradías* collect their flags, briefly offer up thanks to their patrons in the church, and go off to their usual refreshment in their captains' houses where officers for the following year are nominated. The programme then is identical to that of the previous day, but with precedence in ritual given to San Roque. The sermon during High Mass is naturally about the saint, and the pueblo likes to indulge in the story of a past preacher who repeated to an extraordinary extent the name of 'Roque' throughout his talk; it is said that the members of the brotherhood had offered him one peseta for each mention. Having formalized the change-over of officers and their insignia by his official blessing, the parish priest divests himself of his robes and joins the large crowd waiting outside the church. The ceremonial dance of 'the lone man' ('Baile de un hombre solo') is about to take place.

Seated with the mayor before the town hall, the priest gives the signal to the new captains to perform the *Revolteo* of the flags. This done, each of the old officers, in descending order of rank, steps out into the space in front of the authorities, doffs his hat and salutes the company; he then executes a solo dance of the *jota* type to the music of pipe and drum. After two or three choruses he stops, picks up his hat and, saluting as before, steps forward to kiss the priest's hand, which is a sign of dismissal. Each of the new officers does the same, and the last, a sergeant, has the right to pick on any one of the male spectators to follow him in the dance. Since the spectators are usually liberal with their criticism he often picks one of the most vociferous; or, as a prearranged joke, his choice may fall on a stranger (such as myself) whose attempt to imitate the dance provides great amusement.[1]

The ceremony is regarded by the pueblo as simply a tribute of respect to authority by the outgoing and incoming officers. That it is held so near the church suggests, however, that it was originally a part of a larger ceremony which took place inside the church with dancing, a practice which was officially forbidden by the Council of Toledo in A.D. 539. Like the 'Campo Verde' dance of San Antón, it might also be interpreted as a funeral dance, which often took place in the main square or outside a shrine.[2] The

[1] From another point of view it is also a method by which the pueblo proves its solidarity by showing up strangers in a ridiculous light.

[2] See A. Capmany, *El Baile y la Danza, Folklor y Costumbres de España*, Vol 2, Barcelona, 1931.

smaller *cofradía* of San Antón is, in fact, a mutual-aid-in-burial society.

The parish priest then honours the new captain of San Roque by going to his house with the others for refreshment. It is a typical peasant's home, owned by the captain's widowed mother who swiftly brings in the refreshment and as swiftly leaves, for to have the priest in her house is both an honour and an embarrassment. Children come to gape by the door and go into shivers of indecision when called upon to accept a biscuit by the old priest. They look ragged but well-fed, active and healthy, and are sternly ordered out when business begins. For the brotherhood has to discuss a crucial moment in its history. A maximum membership of fifty is fixed by statute but, for many years, interest (and consequently, membership), have been decreasing, until in 1954 there were only seventeen members, some of whom were boys of ten and eleven.

In theory, the two important brotherhoods should mutually feed each other with members. Marriage should transfer them to the *cofradía* of the Virgin, and their children should come to swell the ranks of San Roque. They complain that in practice this is not so, and the priest is silent. The older men are almost without exception bachelors who live in Madrid, and they act like an infusion of new blood into a worn-out body. But they alone cannot break the apathy evident in the group, and no one discusses the future.

Membership is now open to outsiders, even foreigners, so that a few more young men joined in 1957. Their only obligation is a yearly fee of ten pesetas and participation in the August fiestas, but those who live away from the village may, and frequently do, nominate substitutes for their own turn of office. Discussion is ended by the usual toast in water from the captain. Apart from the Rosary procession in the evening with their patron's statue, their duties are finished for another year.

The climax of the fiestas has passed. During the dance and firework display after dinner there is a general feeling, fostered by the young, that tradition has been satisfied and now they can get on with the business of enjoying themselves. This is not to say that the ceremonial ritual of the past two days had been performed grudgingly, but it points to a new attitude which is tending to divide, more and more, lay celebrations from the religious. Everyone stoutly affirms that the latter are 'absolutely necessary' or 'essential to Spanish life'. One wonders to what extent they have also become tiresome.

August 17th, the fourth day of the fiestas, is completely taken up by the bullfight, a relatively recent (some 200 years) acquisition for this village and copied from the ancient solstice festival of San Juan in the provincial capital. Every carpenter in the pueblo busily hammers from seven in the morning till noon, transforming the main square into a bullring. At one time only wagons were used as a barricade and as a point of vantage; now trestles and heavy beams supplement these to form modest stands. The wagons of old never collapsed; the stands of 1956 did, killing one and injuring several others.

This is a day notable for the fanfaronade of virile youth—the one day in the year when the young man can epitomise to a swaggering extreme the values of manliness and bravery which the male holds dear. What he lacks in valour he will make up in 'Dutch courage' at the bars before the fight. Flamboyant dress and the professional trappings of the bullring, the sword, the cape, the expectant crowd, the stirring music, but a pitifully small bull, will lend him a daring which he must vindicate at all costs. For the pueblo in general is judging him and, in particular, the elders in authority and his prospective wife are critically looking on. In the bull the youth has a traditional 'enemy'.

Chosen by their age-mates, some twenty-five youths go through an antic-full process of playing and killing three bulls, purchased out of the festival funds to which the whole pueblo contributes. By the meanest aesthetic standards it is still a sorry spectacle, yet its justification lies much in its circus value for all concerned. It is not a sport since the bull, destined to be killed, has no sporting chance; nor is it regarded as such. For all their professional emulation, the young men pursue an amateur blood-lust of sacrifice which must be satisfied. They will bask in the glory of a newly-won prestige for months to come.

At night, during the village dance, surveillance by the older generation is noticeably weaker; four days of serious drinking and disturbed nights are beginning to take their toll. The dark lanes around the square echo the murmurs of young courting couples whilst the band conscientiously plays to the more discreet until 2 a.m.

The last day of the fiestas is a practical affair. Three bulls have been killed and must be eaten. First, their offal is auctioned to an all-male clientele in the slaughterhouse at the back of the butcher's shop. Once a 'typical' custom marked by much merriment and drinking, the morning auction is now bureaucratically and dully controlled by the authorities. It is enlivened only by the local wits who punctuate the proceedings with coarse jokes aimed especially at the embarrassed buyers of the bulls' testicles and horns, both highly esteemed as table delicacies and no doubt ordered by the wives for lunch. All monies from this sale go back into the fiesta fund.

Vagabonds have suddenly appeared this day in the pueblo drawn by the prospect of the public feast—*La Caldereta*. They make the rounds of the better-looking houses and, knocking boldly on the front door, shout 'Ave Maria', a time-old greeting which people in the more isolated country districts still use. If the family from within calls out 'who is it?' the beggar will reply stoutly, 'un pobre' ('a poor man') and, on receiving some food, money or clothing, he will take his leave with a gracious 'Dios se lo pague' ('May God repay you!'). I never saw one refused bread or a few coins even when the number of callers must have been exasperating. This type of beggar is the modern relic of the old begging pilgrim who fulfilled a social role as a visitor of holy places and a bringer of news. They answered questions with an old-world courtesy and polite interest. Some had left Madrid in May, on foot, and were filling in time around these villages, taking advantage of the fiestas, before going north to La Rioja and Logroño for the late grape harvesting. Proud and never cringing, they did this every year, but one ancient thought he was getting a little too old to continue so much walking. Asking to be excused as he had so much to do, he wandered off, stick in hand, to another house. These are never harassed by the Civil Guard during fiestas; only the gypsy or the 'shameless' whining beggar is moved on.

In the evening, a little before dusk, the village is left deserted as family groups congregate in a forest clearing below the church where communal kitchens have been set up to roast the meat of the dead bulls. Again this custom seems to be a copy of the

*Calderas* of Soria, which may be a relic of the private armies of feudal-type families divided into companies each with its own banner and cooking equipment. But the pueblo does not think on these lines. For it, the custom is a picturesque part of the fiestas which break the monotony of the daily round, slacken the severity of the social order, and are marked by special friendliness and ease of manner. This extends to the vagabonds who are there in force, and no one is refused food. But they, the band and, of late, the young men form separate eating groups. The night chill breaks up the circles of dancers, and fires are kicked out as families wend their way back to the village.

The last dance in the square at night is definitely the swan-song of a community rather bored with its own merrymaking. Only the younger element is determinedly gay, whilst the chaperones and older folk lose interest shortly after midnight; and the band, after playing to a few tenacious couples, soon blows the final blast which marks the end of these holidays. By 1 a.m. the square is strangely quiet and the tall elegant *mayo* starkly silhouetted against the moonlit sky is the only mute survival of these festivities, past now until a year hence.

I have chosen to describe these fiestas in some detail because they represent the only occasion in the year when the pueblo as a whole is united in its leisure. Other fiestas linked to the four saints to which shrines have been erected last merely for one day. Notable among these is that of San Pedro when the young people leap through midsummer fires. Yet these, and the national holidays, lack the preparation, the ritual and the wholesale participation which characterize the patron saint fiestas in August.

Life in the pueblo is a constant round of toil, and daily relaxation is derived from simple pleasures such as the evening promenade in the summer months or cards and billiards in the bars for the men. Only on rare occasions is this routine lightened by a visit from strolling players (*titireros*) or the screening of ancient films by the provincial mobile cinema. There are no organized sports or club activities, nor is there any desire for such things. The pueblo is sufficient unto itself.

# Part II

# THE URBAN PARISH

# 1

## SAN MARTÍN: A CAPITAL PARISH

STOP a man in any of the main streets of Madrid and ask him to direct you to the 'Centro' district; his brow will knit and he will wave vaguely towards the centre of the city. If you ask him further for the parish of San Martín, his brow will clear and he will give you precise directions to the church of that name. The district is an official, impersonal creation; the parish is a living entity, not simply a geographical location.

At some 2,000 feet above Mediterranean sea level, Madrid lies almost in the very centre of the peninsula, in the province of New Castile. For a modern European capital it has a surprisingly compact look. There are no sprawling suburban approaches that herald an untidy agglomerate of factory stacks. Outlying villages clustered around are linked to it by modern tarmac roads cutting through the tile-red, dusty soil relieved occasionally by lonely fields of corn. Madrid has no heavy industry and its province is as poor a producer of the staple foods as is the province of Soria. Wheat for the hungry mouths of the growing capital must come from the rich fields of Leon; cement for the new skyscrapers must be imported from the factories at Toledo.

To the west and north the peaks of the Sierras of Gredos and Guadarrama attract streams of perspiring weekend trippers in the summer; in the winter their snow-fed, kidney-searching winds sweep down to lay the city low with influenza. 'Nine months of winter and three months of hell', is the proverbial description of Castilian weather. To the south lie the mountains of Toledo and the arid landscape of Cervantes. Likewise, the southerly extension of the Iberian ranges has always made communication with the eastern approaches of the Mediterranean a problem; only in 1946 was Valencia directly connected to Madrid by rail, and even now it is quicker to go by road. Yet, with no economy to justify it, the web of the national railway system is centred around Madrid.

Small wonder, therefore, that the capital's continued growth is considered parasitical by other regions. Its history shows, however, that it was deliberately chosen as a rival to dominate the other primate cities of Barcelona, Valencia and Seville, and the events of this century prove that its continued policy is to check the ambitions of Catalonia. Geologically, politically, and geographically, Madrid is the heart of Spain.

When Alfonso VI captured it in 1083, 'Magerit', as it was then known, was a comparatively minor Moorish fort overlooking the gorge of the shallow River Manzanares below and guarding the passes of the Guadarrama. Conjecture has it that the Greeks founded a settlement there 417 years before the rise of Rome. Ptolemy refers to it as 'Mantua' and the Romans first called it 'Ursaria', because of the numerous bears to be found in the surrounding forests, and then later, 'Mayorito'.[1] Excavations have proved its antiquity as a populated site, but while in Moorish hands it served simply as a fortified hill nucleus like countless others, from which a small settlement or *almedina* expanded outside the walls. Here, in 1098 on the site of this old Mozárabe community, Benedictines founded the monastery of San Martín—an offshoot of the main religious house, Santo Domingo de Silos (not a hundred miles distant from Ramosierra in Old Castile). They were encouraged and aided by Alfonso VI who granted them large tracts of land over which they held a feudal-type control, a control which persevered in somewhat more attenuated form until the disestablishment of the monasteries in 1835.

Madrid's pure waters, the game in the forests, and its central position attracted Philip II enough for him to transfer his court there from Toledo in 1561. Within ten years the population was doubled, creating a housing problem from which Madrid has not yet recovered. Eighty per cent of the houses were of one storey only, and built in such a way that it was impossible to divide them up for lodgers. These celebrated *casas a la malicia* were the cause of much compulsory lodging of the King's household in the parish district of San Martín. Influential nobles built their mansions there, some of which stand today, and this increased parish prestige in both the city and at court. Side by side with these new

[1] See Federico Carlos Sáinz de Robles, *Historia y Estampas de la Villa de Madrid*, Madrid, 1949.

developments came another feature of the post-conquest social structure; the now Christian settlers from the north tended to separate themselves into *barrios* or quarters according to their points of origin, and representatives of different crafts and industries also gathered together in distinct quarters, a tendency which persisted until the eighteenth century. Closely grouped into three recognizable but separate clusters then were the regional migrants, the craftsmen and the courtiers. Occupational guilds, called *hermandades* and founded on religious lines, developed in powerful association with the parish church so that the religious character of the parish also significantly reflected the increased wealth that the area had acquired as a trading and commercial centre, quite apart from its function as a purely ecclesiastical unit. Street names still indicate this.

Throughout this period, the individual was a parishioner first and a subject of secular authority second, in all aspects of life and death. Then came the change from mediaeval localism to baroque centralism, neatly summed up by Mumford: 'from the absolutism of God and the Roman Catholic Church to absolutism of the temporal sovereign and the national State'.[1] Despite the later prestige building of Carlos III and other Bourbon monarchs the configuration of the parish of San Martín remained comparatively untouched, but its face radically changed. As the power of the capital in general waxed, so the influence of this parish in particular waned. Enforced selling of its lands and the encroachments of surrounding parishes then reduced its limits to a fraction of what they once were. Nevertheless, if space permitted, it could be shown that the territorial core of the parish still remains as the true centre of the city.

Before we consider the distinctive areas within the parish itself, two other factors must be noted which transformed its perspective and had consequent repercussions on its social structure. During the French occupation of the city between 1808 and 1812 the church and monastery of San Martín was partially destroyed and robbed of its treasures.[2] The destruction was completed in 1834. An outbreak of cholera which started in the San Martín area swept

---

[1] Lewis Mumford, *The Culture of Cities*, London, 1938, p. 77.

[2] Many of its ninth- and tenth-century Visigothic manuscripts were sold to the British Museum by Joseph Bonaparte.

the city, and the people (who accused the monks of poisoning the wells) began a wave of church-burning which spread to other large cities. The parish centre, once the favourite of royal families and the territorial hub of a web of influence, moved north under a cloud of disfavour from its traditional eleventh-century site to its present, comparatively humble church in the narrow street of Desengaño, then one of its poorest areas. No longer was it fashionable, or even wise or beneficial, to live near the parish church.

The second, more important, transformation of the parish area and, incidentally, of the whole city, was brought about by the building of the Avenida del Conde de Peñalver in 1911. It was renamed Avenida de José Antonio in 1939 after the founder of the Falange Party, but its far more common and popular name is, and always has been, the 'Gran Vía'. Originally, it would have cut the parish area through the middle, but the plans were altered so that the road would skirt a church (an annexe of San Martín) and the houses of certain men of influence. A popular verse records this decided kink in what is now recognized as the 'Main Street' of Madrid. Broad and sweeping, it runs along the southern boundaries of the parish so that nearly half of its length is within parish limits.[1] This entirely new prestige area, with its high property values, contrasted sharply with traditional divisions in this ancient parish.

Each parish has a focus of unity in the name of the saint (or it may be that of the Virgin Mary or Christ) that it bears. With perhaps the addition of the place-name, this distinguishes it from all others in the diocese. But whereas the municipal limits of the village of Ramosierra were coterminous with those of its one parish, Madrid[2] is divided into ten municipal districts comprising fifty-two parishes at present, and this number will presumably increase correspondingly with the rise in population. Each district is further divided into a number of *barrios* or quarters, parts of which may belong to several parishes. Few people will be able to state

[1] The parish of San Martín has control over thirty-eight complete streets and parts of seventeen others, which it shares with the eight parishes immediately surrounding it.

[2] But the geographical extension of the diocese corresponds almost exactly to that of the civil province.

without hesitation which *barrio* they belong to; most, however, are categorically certain about their parish.

A parishioner will direct others by reference to a well-known building (or to where it used to be), or to the name of a boundary or 'linking' street in the parish (which usually survive in popular usage any official changes), or even to a popular café. Newer streets tend to be named after a public (usually political) figure; needless to say, these are the streets whose frequent change of name cause some confusion. The four main streets which bound the limits of the parish are the Gran Vía, San Bernardo, Pez and Fuencarral, and the street linking all of them is Luna with its continuation in Desengaño where the parish church stands. All the boundary streets are mixtures of shopping, business and residential areas, the general pattern being a shop on the ground floor with offices or private homes above it. The linking streets of Luna and Desengaño, once entirely residential, are now dotted with shops, which increase in number around the parish church and the entrances to the boundary streets. Interconnecting side-streets are mainly residential areas.

Identification of area with community is necessarily vague in San Martín. Whereas in Ramosierra the word *pueblo* was synonymous with the word *parroquia* (parish) and either could be used to describe the village, parish, villagers and parishioners, in Madrid the sense of community as one *pueblo* is of course slight. It comes to the surface only when the city as a whole is competing with other large cities, for example on the occasion of a football match. San Martín's size and mobility within the parish make similar identification of place and community difficult, but such identification does manifest itself particularly when San Martín is competing with other parishes in religious processions and fiestas. Normally the parishioner will centre his sense of community around the neighbourhood in which he lives;[1] yet this cannot be defined in terms of *barrio* since one street alone may belong to two, three or more quarters. Proud consciousness of belonging to a

[1] On these grounds, the word 'community' is unsatisfactory to describe either the city or the urban parish. The sense of neighbourhood, apart from defining an area of common living, seems to have limits which fluctuate according to the situation; in general, these limits are fixed by those neighbours whose opinions one trusts or fears.

definite quarter, which died away in the nineteenth century, was typified in the *majo* of the 'low' quarters—Lavapiés, Embajadores, El Rastro and Las Vistillas—immortalized by Goya.

No distinction can be made within the parish on ethnic or religious grounds, but a brief survey of the main street areas will show that other criteria of prestige, rent, property values, economic and social function help to disclose a recognizable pattern. As a guide, I propose to consider the so-called boundary and linking streets of the parish as spheres of influence which react on other areas both inside and outside parish limits.

1. *Gran Vía*: forms part of four separate municipal quarters— Senado, Alamo, Tudescos and Estrella. It is distinguished by a high fluidity of money, an accent on entertainment and leisure, and the marked social mobility of its population. This is the area of expensive clothing and jewellery shops, department stores, plush cafés and nightclubs, palatial cinemas, skyscrapers, airline offices and tourist hotels, and complicated neon advertisements. Permanent stalls for the sale of lottery tickets, tobacco and newspapers dot the main street and squares, where point-duty policemen and automatic lights control the traffic. Its three Metro underground stations, two five-storey garages, and covered market are always busy. This is the newly-rich prestige area of the parish.

2. *San Bernardo*: forms part of the municipal quarters of Senado, Alamo and Estrella. This area is distinguished by its academic, professional and public life. If the parish has a political centre it is here. The Faculty of Law of the University of Madrid, the Ministry of Justice, the provincial headquarters of the Ministries of Supply and of Labour fill the larger mansions which once belonged to nobles of the Court. A seventeenth-century Benedictine monastery, just beyond parish limits, is partly given over to a residential college; and private academies and institutes abound. Doctors' and lawyers' signs are sandwiched between bookshops and stationers. It has one medium-priced and one cheap cinema, a Metro underground station, and one policeman on permanent point duty outside the Ministry of Justice. The recent removal of the tramlines has only mildly relieved traffic congestion in this main street, which cuts across the Gran Vía.

3. *Pez*: belongs in part to the municipal quarters of Estrella, Muñoz Torrero and San Ildefonso. This is the popular shopping

area of the parish, especially for the poorer families. Small shops supply all the staple foods, and general stores offer a variety of household goods. Cheap clothing and furniture stores advertise goods on the instalment plan, and here also numerous shops devoted to repairs and to the sale of second-hand articles are to be found. This area has some of the oldest and lowest buildings in the parish, and one cheap cinema. Its north-easterly tip abuts on the market of San Ildefonso whose parish was once an annexe of San Martín, and it is full of busy taverns.

4. *Fuencarral*: forms part of the municipal quarters of Muñoz Torrero, San Luis, Jardines and Carmen. A predominant business and commercial activity marks this area of banks, offices, the central Telephone Exchange, and the type of shop which deals in manufactured goods such as radios, typewriters, office-equipment and shoes. Dozens of tailors squat over their sewing in the upper storeys of old buildings and the side streets are studded with craftsmen's workshops and the comfortable family type of restaurant, notable for its kitchen rather than its prices.

5. *Luna—Desengaño*: belongs in parts to the municipal quarters of Estrella, Muñoz Torrero and San Luis. This is the least definable area of all since its limits link up and merge with all others. Most of its buildings are residential, but the four churches[1] it contains also make it the centre of ecclesiastical influence.

The population of Madrid has trebled in the last fifty years and continues to grow in an increasing proportion; in 1958 it was estimated at 1,887,000. This rise owes much to migration from the country districts, especially those of the south because of the fall in real wages. Even in Madrid's own province the gain at the expense of the country areas was nearly 2,000 in 1956. Within the city itself, the birth rate has dropped by almost one-third over the same fifty years and, as in all the primate cities, was below the average of 23.43 per 1000 inhabitants in 1953. Urbanization in Spain generally is distinctly correlated with a fall in reproductive rates. In San Martín the parish church declares that it is in contact

[1] For, besides the parish church, there are three other churches in this area; two are attached to secluded communities of nuns, the Mercedarias and the Benedictinas, and the third, whose popularity competes with that of the parish church, is governed by the friars of the Mercedarian order.

Two views of Madrid. A Mingote cartoon from the Madrid newspaper *ABC*

with some 5,000 homes, but admits that the total population of the parish fluctuates between 25,000 and 30,000. As the average size family is four or five, the overflow is taken up by approximately fifty hotels and 150 *pensiones* (boarding houses). Density figures of 847 (12 square metres per inhabitant) show that the housing problem is acute, and San Martín is, in fact, expanding upwards in the form of higher buildings. In the narrow back streets one commonly finds old houses whose bulging walls have been shored up by heavy timbers, often stretching beyond the pavement on to the road surface. When these finally topple the landlord is only too pleased, for the rents of pre-Civil War tenants have long been controlled and tenancy secured. Although he must find alternative accommodation for his old tenants it need not be in the same area; the loftier the new building, the higher the new rents, so that the previous occupier often has to move out of the parish. Thus, the demographic changes induced by the double decline in births and deaths are linked to an increasingly rapid change in the composition of the parish population. Money is ruthlessly finding its own level in housing, and as the wave of wealth sweeps from the Gran Vía to trickle away into insignificance in the poorer areas of Pez, so those who cannot enter the economic swim are driven farther away from the centre of the city and their traditional parish. Two of the highest buildings in Europe now tower over the parish from the Gran Vía area. These skyscrapers, full of offices, flats and hotels, are also a home from home for Americans who administer their military bases in Spain under the pact of 1952; they supply much employment to the local parishioners. The new pattern evolving, therefore, may roughly be explained in terms of a correlation between the height of the building and the income group and the degree of density of population in the parish. The two opposing poles of this correlation are the Gran Vía and Pez areas, ten minutes' stroll apart.

There are no detached or semi-detached houses in this built-up parish; and no front or back gardens. Buildings form part of blocks whose rear may overlook communal courts. These are either mere wells criss-crossed with washing-lines from window to window, or more spacious ones used for commercial purposes, such as scrap-iron storage yards. A sense of neighbourhood is, therefore, enforced by the number of families crammed together in one building whose ground-floor tenant usually acts as porter and general informant.

A certain privacy is ensured for households who have separate access to common landings or to a staircase, but the entrance is invariably overlooked by a porter's window. Yet this modicum of privacy is being invaded by the increasing clamour for accommodation. More and more 'apartments' are being created out of old reception rooms or spare bedrooms. Humorists publish exaggerated cartoons in which even a large wardrobe or piano have been sub-let to the desperate homeless. Few families are owners of the houses they live in, but many more have a long-term lease of the floor on which they reside. Some of the ancient three-storeyed mansions, now converted into flats, have separate entrances and staircases for the use of owner and tenants.

Four-storeyed buildings of grey stone, with attics jutting out of red-tiled roofs, and railed balconies at the French windows of each floor, are still the most common in the residential areas. Some of the tenement-houses have roof-terraces, access to which is usually a bone of contention.   Only the more modern and higher buildings have central heating and originally-planned bathrooms. On the hot summer nights the side streets are full of the chairs and stools of family groups until the cool breezes of early morning. For the privilege of living in this parish a working-class father in the older houses may pay as little as the equivalent of one United States dollar a month—a controlled rent; but this is probably a sixteenth of his weekly income. Rents which are uncontrolled may be as high as 2,000 pesetas[1] a month or more.

The sanctity of the home throughout Spain has never encouraged the casual Anglo-Saxon habit of 'dropping-in' for unexpected visits. For a family of six, cramped in four rooms in Madrid, the enforced proximity of the neighbours scarcely permits the degree of self-imposed isolation which it would obviously prefer. Even if it could get on the depressingly-long waiting lists of the State, Syndicate or Church housing projects in the suburbs, a typical family would be reluctant to move from the familiar parish area; meanwhile it regards with a resigned surprise the restora-

[1] Approximately £17 10s. ($49); but economists in 1956 considered this as a necessary *minimum* monthly wage for a married labourer with a family.

tion of ancient castles, and derives a mocking pleasure from the splendidly unfinished ministries and monuments begun by a display-minded regime.

The feeling of belonging to the parish as an ecclesiastical unit consists in being a *feligrés*—a parishioner inscribed in the parish register. This entitles him to take advantage of the essential sacraments of baptism, marriage and extreme unction, and of the religious associations, charities and their services. Official status as a *vecino* in the district is acquired by a minimum of six month's residence for all Spaniards of 21 or more, or for those of 18 or above who are legally living apart from their parents and are inscribed in the electoral census as heads of households. The municipal *Padrón* is the civil register of those liable to pay taxes within the Centro district. All those listed therein are required to carry an identity card with photograph and, if qualified for social insurance benefits, to acquire on marrying a Family Book from the so-called Ministry of Grace and Justice.

The difference between membership of the ecclesiastical and civil units cannot be considered wholly in terms of the voluntary and the compulsory. Except for an insignificant percentage of Protestants, there is religious conformity within the parish, and social and religious obligations often dovetail; for religion is not yet merely a personal affair, and the parish still exerts certain controls. These will be discussed in the next chapter, where an examination of the political structure of both Church and State will reveal the authority and influence each wields.

The aim of this chapter has been to paint the background and landscape of the Madrid picture. The subsequent pattern that will emerge will not be the comparatively regular one of the pueblo but, rather, a jigsaw of interlocking social relationships which merge their various forms and colours.

# 2

## THE AUTHORITIES AND THE
## WORLD AROUND

AN AUTHORITARIAN triad composed of mayor, police and priest, similar to that found in the village, exists in the city but in a more impersonal form, which only adds weight to its authority. It helps to create awareness of community among all who share a common mode of living in the district and parish, divisions which are themselves part of a nationally imposed political structure. For not even the rural parish is an autonomous, integrated whole wherein everything that happens is functionally interdependent, and the urban parish is much less so. San Martín is at the heart of the nation's government; and interaction between the superstructure of the capital as a whole and the local parish unit becomes clear only when the institutionalism of authority in general is examined.

It is not my task here to go deeply into the historical causes of the existing system, or to evaluate the political structure. A distinction must, however, be drawn between that which is traditional and enduring and that which is the result of current political necessity.

When, in the sixteenth century, the country quickly fell under a bureaucratic absolutism pride was lost in the provincial *fueros*, in municipal liberties, and in the rights of the Cortes of Castile. Imperialism, Parry says, killed the best political thought in Spain. Later, as an aftermath of the Napoleonic wars, the pendulum of government swung from reaction to counter-reaction. The political instability and internal strife reflected by the ninety-eight changes of Cabinet between 1834 and 1912—a period which saw revolutions, regents, pretenders, new monarchs, the First Republic, military coups, a Restoration, and the humiliating loss of the last of Spain's New World possessions—made the populace apathetic and destroyed its little faith in government. This is very quickly revealed in the parish by the reluctance to discuss the past, except that during which Spain was dominant in world affairs. Past experience has not apparently deterred this people's search for heroic leaders rather than for an abstract political ideal; the comparative success of two dictatorships and the failure of the Second Republic in this century might be adduced in support of this view if one were concerned with political theory.

Government in Spain continues to rest on the three institutions of an hereditary monarchy (rejected by two short-lived republics), the parliament of the old Castilian Cortes, and an extensive Civil Service, with a permanent staff except for its highest officials. Spain is at the moment a kingdom without a king. The Franco regime has committed itself to the maintenance of the monarchy as an institution by the 1947 Law of Succession and the Referendum of the following year. Meanwhile the regime, in its own words, is 'a representative, organic democracy in which the individual participates in government through the natural representative organs of the family, the city council and the syndicate'. Of these three organs one—the family—has continued to participate through the parish in the election of another—the city council of Madrid—since the fourteenth century.

Syndicalism can be considered as a twentieth-century edition of the mediaeval *gremios* or trade guilds, which were themselves linked to both the family and the parish by their religious activities and the practice of spiritual sponsorship. It grew in the cities, not in the country areas, and was closely associated with anarchism in the past before the Falangists and Catholics made it 'respectable' in its current form of national verticalism. It has the effect of combining all elements of the economic process (including the liberal and technical professions) into a single organization. Each service or branch of production is arranged in hierarchical form down to the lowest level, all under the watchful eye of the State and, incidentally, the Falangist party—every syndicate official is supposed to be an active member of the 'party', which has always claimed to be national-syndicalist (after the style of Fascist Italy). Apart from the economic and production policies formulated in its vast modern blocks of offices, syndicalism actively reaches out into affairs of a social character—sports fields, social benefits, education and the like. It has had little to do with the few wage increases since the Civil War, which were ordered directly by Franco; nor is it bothered with strikes or lock-outs, which are illegal, since Franco's ideal is to have neither idle rich nor idle poor. For other than the dedicated party man, the general view expressed by the ordinary worker is that the syndicate organization is unnecessarily top-heavy and provides too many easy jobs for the 'right' people.

The functions of the family, the city council and the syndicate are largely based on the concepts of *caudillaje* (leadership) and its concomitant, submissiveness, the social values for which are found in the ideal types of man and woman in marriage.[1] General Franco, 'El Caudillo', is first an heroic leader of the 'empire' and people, and only secondly an absolute ruler 'responsible only to God and history'. His leadership and the people's submissiveness, therefore, bear a personal character into which a special loyalty enters, whilst both concepts are modified and coloured by the ideal of a 'crusade' based on a mixture of religiosity and anti-Communism. The Falange[2] and the Church, Franco's two most staunch supporters, echo this cult and encourage the virtues of submissiveness. Parishioners who air their opinions are divided on this point, for not all are Franco's men; but the regime's appeal to tradition and Hispanity, plus its continual condemnation of the 'Black Legend', does have a unifying effect, if only to be found in an active xenophobia. This was never more apparent than during the United Nations diplomatic boycott imposed on Spain from 1946 to 1950.

Hispanity evokes the peculiar and precious Spanish way of life but also has political overtones. The Falange's cry 'una libre y grande' ('one, free and great') is related to the idea of a greater Spain embracing the whole of the Iberian peninsula and sister Latin-American countries too. It is a handy slogan for Spanish nationalism. As for the Black Legend, one may describe it as the

[1] I do not intend to explain the whole social system by the use of these concepts, even if that were feasible, but their importance in this society should, nevertheless, be stressed.

[2] The F.E.T. y de las J.O.N.S. (Falange Española Tradicionalista y Juntas de Ofensiva Nacional Sindicalista) was founded by José-Antonio Primo de Rivera in 1932 and is the only permitted political party. It has never been numerically very strong and its influence now is waning, though its founder's name is immortalized in streets in every village and town.

anti-Spanish propaganda (both public and private) which has pervaded foreign literature ever since the colonization of the New World and the Protestant Reformation. With its base in economic, religious and national rivalries, it is malicious calumny, according to the Spaniards; to the world at large, it might be regarded as a 'bad press'.

Madrid rules and influences all other provinces in the peninsula. In this rule San Martín plays a leading part since many of its parishioners have always been directly concerned with the government of the kingdom. The first Cortes, a war council (for the attack on Granada) of the kingdoms of Aragon, Leon, Asturias and Castile, were held in 1329 at the monastery of Santo Domingo in the parish of San Martín. The present Cortes, re-established in 1942, are still largely a council of nobles, clergy and municipal representatives, as they were under the mediaeval and imperial pattern. A revival under an historic name of Primo de Rivera's 'National Assembly', it is a parliament without legislative power. The decrees and laws it passes are initiated by the Chief of State, though there are signs now of a greater independence, such as parliamentary questions to Ministers.

The Mayor of Madrid and province, who is usually a member of the nobility, often a grandee, is nominated by the equivalent of the Home Secretary for an indefinite period. His adjutant, and representative when he is absent, is at present the Mayor of Centro District, a parishioner of San Martín whose nomination, duties and dismissal lie entirely in the discretion of the City Mayor. On taking office, before he is given the *vara* (wand) of authority, he must swear an oath of loyalty (before a crucifix) to Spain and to the Chief of State, promising 'to foment the interests of the Municipality and adjust (his) conduct to the dignity of (his) post'. The Civil Governor then replies: 'If so you do, then God and Spain will reward you, but if not, they will make claim on you.' The District Mayor's favours are earnestly sought by individuals and associations within the parish, for he is by right a member of the permanent commission of the City Council and a man of immense influence.

Parishioners directly participate in the government of their district through the election of councillors by the three groups of family heads, syndicate representatives and delegates of professional, cultural or economic bodies, each of which elects a third of the total number. The last group is itself nominated by councillors elected by the two former groups. Interest in these elections is realistically cynical and lukewarm; they are decreed every six years by the Cabinet and largely organized and controlled by the Falange at the booths and by blaring public-address vans patrolling the streets.[1] Voting is not compulsory, but a family head is under great pressure if his job is in any way dependent on the good will of the syndicates or the party. In some instances, certificates of voting are demanded by employers. But in any case, the parishioner rarely thinks objectively in these matters and often votes to oblige a friend, or a friend of a relative.

The day to day business of government is carried out by bureaucrats whose power lies in their capacity to apply the principle of the law strictly or flexibly, as the mood moves them. They are a paid legion of civil servants, and are accused by the general public of being neither civil nor servants. The sheer impersonality of officialdom places them at a distance from the parishioner, which in a sense gives them still more power. Departmental procedure requires an enormous bulk of documentation at every turn and induces a procrastination (increased by the supineness of poorly-paid[2] officials), which is said to breed corruption in the upper strata and to occasion letters of recommendation by the hundred to the humblest office manager. 'Don't they work in the afternoons?' asks the irritated caller on finding the Ministry offices closed; and the porter sourly replies: 'They don't work in the *mornings*, they don't *come* in the afternoons.'

*Cédulas* (certificates) are necessary for mere vicinage, for social benefits, for all kinds of trading and economic activity, for migration (a man may now be sent back to his pueblo unless he can prove that he will live with relatives or has a house to go to), and even to prove receipt of the sacrament of Communion; they are usually in triplicate and must be countersigned, usually somewhere else. In the San Bernardo area alone there are four agencies which deal with the whole procedure of official applications for a small

[1] In the city elections of 1954 there were 12 candidates and 1,138,111 votes cast. The four replacement councillors nominated by large majorities were all active members of the Falange party.

[2] They, like the military, also fall outside the national social security plan.

fee. Otherwise the man claiming sickness relief or a housing permit must lose many mornings' work waiting in government offices. Sometimes the wives go in their stead, taking their sewing and a sandwich, especially if they have to wait at the window counter marked 'Urgent'. Once made, the application takes months to clear and its success is always in doubt.

This frustrating procedure can be eased only by having a 'friend' in the right place. To have *enchufe* (literally, 'plug')—to be able to make profitable contact—is the modern equivalent of having a friend at Court; it is a short cut through the maze of authority and relieves the tension persisting between State and community. The diversity of urban life, and the existence of specialized agencies for functions which in the pueblo would be discharged informally, produces complicated strata of power and authority which can be dealt with only by cultivated friendship and by patronage. Most bureaucrats themselves owe their positions to more influential friends and relatives. They thus tend to perpetuate a practice to which they are indebted and committed.

When I speak of patronage I refer to a special and durable relationship between patron and client whereby the former acts as a protector, at times as a model to copy and always as an intermediary to deal, in times of need, with persons or situations more powerful than the client—one who avails himself of a patron's services and maintains a reciprocal beneficial relationship with him. Everyone is at some time or another (in one role or another) both patron and client, and the richer and more influential one becomes the more clients one will acquire. God is the ultimate patron, and the Virgin and hundreds of patron saints are thought to intercede with Him on behalf of their clients.

There are several reasons for the specially intensive form of patronage in Spain. A general acceptance of the idea of hierarchy on earth and the inequalities—sometimes crippling—that go with it, is one. But a singular respect for authority arising out of this is accompanied by a fear of power misused. Patronage is one method of levelling out some of these inequalities and avoiding the abuses of powerful superiors. Again, God's ways are mysterious; luck is fickle. It is not surprising that the element of chance is a strong social force in Spain startlingly apparent in all walks of life and expressed in one form at least by a wholesale recourse to decision by lot. Patronage therefore provides at least one down-to-earth insurance policy. Finally, one should not ignore a real sense of the obligations to give, receive and return, and the emotional satisfaction that springs from them.

Whatever form it takes it is effected on a personal basis. The 'arranging' of affairs with officialdom, the lobbying for highly prized and exclusive concessions such as scholarships, sinecures, even import and export licences, the seeking of a cure, or a job, all become the concern of the patronage system. Godparenthood is woven into the system too, and introduces a particularly protective type of patron. Mere caprice does not govern favouritism, and the 'right' man, in terms of patronage, should not be confused with the 'best' man, in terms of efficiency. A battery of recommendations, usually in the form of visiting cards, from a client's various patrons are arms hard to resist.

Yet it would be wrong to assume that patronage always exploits the mass to the advantage of the few. A bad patron, it is true, may feather his own nest at the expense of others but even he has recognized obligations to his protegés or clients. Reciprocity is the first rule of patronage, which is not merely a one-sided affair. The client has a strong sense of loyalty to his patron and voices this abroad. By doing so he constantly stimulates the channels of loyalty, creates good will, adds to the name and fame of his patron and thus ensures him a species of immortality. Moreover, when patrons and clients are in close contact a patron's various clients are an invaluable source of information to him.

All this supposes a much more durable and functional relationship (in which the element of real friendship often enters) than that which we tend to associate with the 'bribe' situation. For the client, there are material advantages to be gained, and at the back of these there lies not only a striving to level out inequalities but also a fight against anonymity (especially in the urban setting) and a seeking out of primary personal relationships. For the patron, there is his 'investment' in supporters—his clients—and, between patrons, a comfortable cementing of relationships. Crises clearly reveal this when protestations of loyalty and support significantly show the alignment of different patronage forces.[1]

[1] See my article in *Anthropological Quarterly*, Washington, January 1960, for a fuller treatment of patterns of patronage.

Conscious use of patronage permeates the whole society. Even the porter's nine-year-old daughter explained away her adverse school report on the grounds of not having enough *enchufe* with her teacher. Friendship has perhaps never been completely disinterested, and in Madrid its obligations are based on a reciprocity of favours which is more important than any mere duty to an employer or to the State. One may be drawn into aiding a friend of a friend of a cousin one has never seen. This sort of extension of patronage annoys many. I liken it to the 'throwing stick' of the primitive hunter, for it is used by the family unit to extend its range and power in dealing with the excesses or defects of authority.

Spain has been called the land of the *patria chica* because of the strength of municipal feeling and the desire to live in compact communities. In the urban parish the social picture is, rather, one of small, mutually competitive groups, each clustering round a figure of influence. Thus bureaucrats and others build up their little worlds about them, and each 'minister' of government, high and low—each individual, in fact, who has power to wield—is a power unto himself. Everyone wants to be a 'chief'. The concept of personal rule (*mando personal*) is not peculiar to the Franco regime. It creates a pyramid of authority and patronage, so that the nearer one is to the 'big chief' the more powerful one is likely to be. This accounts for much of the confusion between government departments and for their lack of coordination. Another result of this system is, of course, the reluctance to take a decision at the lower levels and the exclusiveness of separate patronage groups. The *ensimismadismo*, or sense of being wrapped up in oneself, of the pueblo easily becomes in the town an indifferent attitude of the 'couldn't care less' variety; one minds one's own business and, incidentally, that of one's favoured group.

The business which does affect the parishioner daily is in the hands of city council commissions which operate through the district mayor, secretary and staff.[1] The town crier of the pueblo

---

[1] *Comisión Municipal Permanente*. A permanent committee composed of the mayor, district mayors, secretary and comptroller.

*Comisión de Hacienda: Comisión de Policía Urbana y Rural; Comisión de Gobierno Interior y Personal*. These deal with public finance and administer the legal sanctions of the civil and criminal codes.

*Comisión de Abastos; Comisión de Acopios; Comisión de Fomento*. These

is replaced by poster decrees on walls or occasional radio talks by
the mayor, obedience to whose commands (*bandos*) is ensured
by the urban police. In general, the city council is thought of
as a necessary but often ineffectual nuisance, especially in view of
the unsolved problems of transport, housing, and road repairs,
favourite themes of the cartoonists. Failure to solve the transport
problem means that the San Martín parishioner, too, must wait
impatiently in queues for the smoke-belching buses or be squashed
in the mephitic Metro like others. Only the rich have cars, and
only delivery boys use bicycles, though motor-scooters are seen
in ever-increasing numbers.

Events which occur in the parish and district are always
related in the popular mind to the greater whole of the city.
Multiple loss of life by accidental tragedies such as fire, inundation
or collapse of buildings in San Martín is mourned not only by the
bereaved families themselves but by the capital as a whole.[1] The
Mayor symbolizes this by funeral notices in the press on behalf of
the entire city council and the celebration of public death rites.

Conversely, the weight of municipal authority is felt in every
street and home in the parish; for instance, through the ban
(operative since August 1956) on the sounding of klaxons and on
excessive noise from radios and family gatherings. Offenders are
fined and people are exhorted to inform on neighbours. Officially,
too, police and the neighbours' permission is required for any
gathering of fifteen or more persons. Daily and automatically the
parish is drawn into the larger corporate life of the capital,[2] so

---

control the local economic structure by licensing and inspection and the
supply of fuel and power.

*Comisión de Ensanche; Comisión Especial de Limpiezas; Comisión de
Beneficencia y Sanidad.* These are responsible for public works, public
safety, urbanization, monopoly services and hygiene.

*Comisión de Deportes y Festejos; Comisión de Cultura.* These are
concerned with the coordination of cultural, traditional and recreational
activities, and also with basic education through libraries, exhibitions, etc.

[1] This is sometimes taken to the national level. All civil servants were
'invited' to contribute one day's pay as relief for the 1957 flood damage
in Valencia. Sympathy was felt for Valencia, but 'not that much', they said.

[2] Sometimes by design on the part of parishioners, who have been
known to bypass the district authorities and directly petition the City
Mayor; e.g. 'round robins' stimulated the removal of tramlines and
certain dilapidated houses in the parish.

that it is impossible to consider one without the other. The 'we-feeling' of the rural community is insignificant at urban parish level, and we must look for it among smaller groups and associations.

As we have seen, one reaction—patronage—to the web of authority operates at all status levels. Individual reactions through breaches of the civil and criminal codes will be discussed later; but we may cite here a few group procedures resorted to with the tacit approval of the community when recognized rights are infringed or endangered. The 1948 revolt in Ramosierra in defence of Pine Luck rights is one example. Similarly, in Madrid, in February 1957, there was a collective boycott (which subsequent arrests proved to have been planned in San Martín) of public transport as a protest against an imminent increase in fares.[1] The great majority in the city sympathized with this act of passive resistance, though some took part in the boycott only from fear of their neighbours' criticism. On the first day buses and trains ran empty and the streets were full of silent walkers and wary policemen, who intervened when students blocked the road in San Bernardo and forced the few 'blacklegs' to alight. But on the second day interest faded. Spaniards rarely walk for pleasure, or for duty's sake if they can avoid it. Yet there was general surprise at the success of the venture, an unusual example of concerted action on the part of a majority of the public. In the parish exaggerated comparisons were drawn with the uprising of May 2nd, 1808, against the French tyranny, starkly depicted in Goya's paintings.

Other more segmentary group sanctions are apparent in the industrial strike[2] and demonstration. Strikes are prohibited by law and are regarded, as one party leader put it, as 'the springboards from which political mountebanks perform their capers'. In the official view, therefore, they have become political acts of

[1] Small, easily-concealed-in-the-hand leaflets appeared some days beforehand addressed to 'Madrilenians' and declaring that 'workers, employees, students, intellectuals, civil servants, business men and industrialists are protesting against the (economic) policy of the Government, which is leading the country to ruin'.

[2] The General Strike of 1917 was also organized from the street of Desengaño in San Martín by Largo Caballero, later premier of the Popular Front government in 1936.

treachery, just as what might be mere divergence of opinion in other European countries has here become 'disloyalty' to the leader, regime and country. Strikers are thus 'rebels' not only against the State but also against their labour unions, which are controlled by the State. There are consequently no strike funds, and a man must be very angry indeed to resort to this measure of protest, for he is almost sure to be imprisoned. The wave of strikes caused by inflation since 1955 has only slightly affected Madrid owing to its lack of heavy industry. News of them comes through the 'grape-vine' in bars and cafés, and reactions to them in San Martín reflect the measure of sympathy for or antipathy to the regime. The 24-hour general strike on June 18th, 1959, called by the Communists, failed not only because the other opposition groups withdrew their support, but because of political illiteracy. Other factors helped: the students were on vacation, so their energetic support was lack-ing; the effectiveness of a strike without violence is not yet under-stood; and a long-standing apathy has led people to prefer foot-ball matches to politics. Fear of official reprisals resulted in a lower absenteeism from work than ever.

Demonstrations, however, particularly by students in the San Bernardo area, may sometimes force the parishioner into a clash with the authorities against his will. The protest march and 'siege' in the University in February 1956 was directed against the domi-nant influence of the Falange in student unions. A lighthearted beginning developed into violence; two students were shot, many more injured, and 500 arrests made. Police, shoulder to shoulder across the street, cleared the area; street stalls were packed up, shopkeepers complained that customers could neither enter nor leave their premises, and bystanders were caught in baton charges. The general attitude of the parishioners was a near-frantic desire to keep out of trouble, even to avoid discussion. 'Moreover,' said old Concepción, the black-market cigarette vendor at the corner of Pez Street, 'the students are always a nuisance; they might spend their time better doing a decent day's work, like us.' A wounded Falange student who hovered on the brink of death for days was visited in hospital by members of the Government, proclaimed a martyr by the press, and later given a medal. The far-reaching results of the affair were not only the cessation of classes and the dismissal of the Rector and the Minister of Education, but also the suspension of legal safeguards and a drastic limitation of civil liberties generally. Each outburst of this nature has been marked in the past by arrests of individuals charged with corrupting youth and fomenting political unrest on behalf of 'a Communist association'. Fear of Communism fast became a phobia in the post-Civil War years. In effect it is an inflated manifestation of an individual viewpoint, found at all levels, that 'those who are not with me are against me'. This leaning towards totalitarianism of opinion tends to thwart and dishearten the would-be moderate; the result is often a rather deliberate indifference. It is true also that the predominantly male values of *hombria* (manliness) and *pundonor* (which makes of every issue a point of honour) play a great part in the framing of attitudes both between Spaniards themselves and towards foreigners.

Students cross-cut all other status groups within the community. Traditionally regarded with indulgence, they are also recognized as future leaders and as vociferous champions of any 'cause', especially that which meets external threats, imaginary or real.[1] In the Franco regime's former political attacks against France (over Morocco) and Britain (over Gibraltar), occurring at regular intervals and often coinciding with domestic unrest, the Falange, through the student bodies, arranged demonstration marches of solidarity in the main streets and to the respective embassies. Although with few exceptions only students participated, the notable effect was to create among all sections of the parish marked antipathy and suspicion (but not discourtesy) towards *all* foreigners. Many of the working people in the parish later confessed complete indifference to and even ignorance of the political issues. A similar antipathy was evident during the visits of the British and Yugoslav football teams in 1956.

Group solidarity is also apparent on a smaller scale among the hostile crowds which quickly gather whenever foreigners (particularly Americans now) become involved in street scenes. The growing number of resident foreigners in the city (estimated at 20,000 in 1956) brings the world around closer to the parishioner and provides his hypersensitivity with a handy target for criticism. 'Colonization by the *Yanquis*' is the current cry heard in bars,

[1] February 9th is a part holiday in memory of the first (Falange) student to be shot on the eve of the Civil War.

whenever those liner-like cars purr by. There is a special slang word for these automobiles, and the Government's efforts to disguise them by normal-looking registration numbers has proved singularly ineffective; for who but an American or a politician would own such immense machines? The traditional enmity with France dating from 1808 is also still celebrated yearly on May 2nd, which is a national holiday.

Except on the rare occasions cited above as special cases of overt reaction to the civil authorities, the police as a body are remarkably unobtrusive. To supervise the 30,000,000 inhabitants of Spain there are not more than 100,000, of whom half—the Civil Guard —are in the country districts. All are armed with revolvers and those in uniform also carry batons. Most of them live with their families, and two of the three corps of police (providing individuals are not officious) seem to be on good terms with parishioners, both in or out of their distinctive uniforms. They mix freely in the bars and cafés, openly buy black-market tobacco and are ready to exchange jokes, even about the Government. Their daily duties integrate them closely with the people; traffic policemen may be quick to levy fines for contraventions of the Highway Code, but they are also ready to give directions or even help to repair a breakdown. The many presents piled round their feet while they are on duty over the Christmas period indicate their comparative popularity. The municipal policeman likewise, though he may fine a housewife for hanging out washing in view of the street, will also sit down and give advice on official procedure such as the completion of complicated census returns or housing permits. All this tends to oil the wheels of the authoritarian machine.

On the other hand, the military corps, divided into Security, Vigilance and Special Service branches, has the task of curbing the rebelliousness in the Spanish character. They are the strikebreakers, they make all the arrests of miscreants, undesirables and political agents, they supervise the movements of foreigners. They are feared because coercion is their business, and they thus disturb the egalitarian values of the community which permit only 'honourable' subordination. Fear is not manifested by cowering under the system of legal authority—that is far from being the case; dread of criticism and change, and of uncontrolled passion and pride plays an important part in general behaviour attitudes. It underlies the declaration by the Republican Gabriel Alomar in 1931: 'The greatest enemy of democracy is demagogy, and demagogy always begets "praetorian" bosses (little Caesars); this is our greatest political shame and unfortunately seems part and parcel of the Iberian race.'[1] All revolutions in the past have been dramatic impositions of power by means of a 'rising' and a 'pronouncement' of a new order. It is fear of the iniquity of power groups that produces an ambivalence in the popular mind— a studied indifference to government affairs at one moment and a belief in solving troubles by violence at the next. For long now the people have stressed 'the superiority of society to government, of custom to law, and of the neighbour's judgment to legal forms of justice'.[2] Laws are nominally obeyed but not really fulfilled. The individual is a bundle of prejudices made up of sympathies, apathies and antipathies, with the past locked up and put away in his mind.

Once the porter fastens the front door at 11 p.m. the streets are virtually under the control of the *sereno* or night watchman, i.e. they are 'serene'. He is perhaps more important sociologically than the policeman. Very few people use or own front door keys which, for the older houses, are enormous. To get in at night, therefore, they must clap their hands and call for the *sereno* who has rows of keys strung on his waistcoat. This furious clapping and these long-drawn cries in the hushed night, the *sereno's* answering shout of '¡Voy!' ('Coming!') and the tap-tapping of his heavy stick, make nonsense of the present campaign for silence. Though he is a traditional character in the Madrid scene, his is not an official post. The pitch or beat is often passed down from father to son, or bought with the goodwill of the area attached, for the *serenos* depend entirely on tips from the neighbours. On their own initiative they have formed a union to protect their interests, and their role is recognized by the State; this invests them with a certain authority and they often co-operate with the police by arresting disturbers of the peace. Apart from the heavy iron-tipped stick, they frequently carry a concealed pistol.

[1] Consider the disorganized growth of *chekas*, or unofficial punitive courts, during the Civil War in Madrid.

[2] Gerald Brenan, *The Spanish Labyrinth*, Cambridge, 1943, p. xvi.

Between them, the porter and the *sereno* constitute a mine of information concerning the movements of neighbours, but their function, which depends entirely on the will of the community, is therefore sanctioned by it. I have seen only one article in the press advocating the disbandment of the *serenos*; it suggested that as modern houses have small locks fitted they are becoming superfluous. But they continue to flourish, for they perform a variety of tasks incidental to the main one, and these I shall refer to in a later chapter.

If, as Peers suggests, the material guarantee of unity and order in the present regime is the Army, then the spiritual guarantee is the Church. But the Church has played a more traditional role; representing by its religious ideals a unifying influence which strengthens the egalitarian values to be found everywhere in Spain. In that sense only, it is the great leveller still. The parish is a community based on the conception of believers that over them and non-believers alike a divine and supreme authority reigns. The priest is, therefore, armed with the dignity and importance of this suprasocial principle which, in effect, should give him a lasting 'father-figure' status—a leadership too often found lacking in the State. Nevertheless, he is theoretically subordinate to those whom he leads, i.e. to his flock.

Questions of faith or past history need not divert us here, except where they colour general behaviour attitudes. As an institution the Church cannot be ignored, for in its sociological effects it has no rival. Alfonso VII in the twelfth century used to hold courts of justice seated in the porch of the monastery of San Martín. Its close ties with the municipality are still symbolized in the City coat of arms, which shows a bear next to a strawberry-tree; whilst the coat of arms of the *Cabildo* or Diocesan Chapter shows a bear standing in pasture land. This represents the fourteenth-century agreement between the parishes and the city council on the division of forest and pasture land. Present spheres of influence between civil and ecclesiastical authorities are delineated in the Concordat of August 1953, an extension of the previous tentative agreement of July 1946.

There is no mixing of municipal and parish functions or posts. Relations between the parish church and the district council are very friendly and co-operative, but quite unofficial at this level. The present Bishop of Madrid is, however, a member of the Council of State, the Cortes, the National Council of the Falange and the Royal Academy, and President of the Spanish Institute. The Abbots of the Benedictine and Mercedarian Orders (both with monasteries in the parish area) are also members of the Cortes and carry the title of Grandee. Clergy are not directly prohibited by Canon Law from holding State positions, but they fill no high judicial, economic or administrative posts, though there are monks from religious orders in the parish who hold university appointments. Liaison between State and Church is effected by a Director for Ecclesiastical Affairs, a State post. In return for free and full use of spiritual power and the exercise of public worship, the Church offers up daily prayers for Spain and the Chief of State. Parish and district authorities act in unison during public processions such as at Easter, when the Sacred Host is carried to the homes of the sick and disabled. The parish priest in a State coach is followed on foot by the city mayor, the municipal judge, the police and the Catholic Action groups.

San Martín has nine priests (including one Irish chaplain) who all receive nominal salaries from the State. As in Ramosierra, the general business of the parish is conducted in the sacristy or church office, and the priests see their parishioners there instead of visiting them at home. Fourteen masses are said on Sunday mornings and one at 8 p.m. for workers, besides weekday services. The church in Desengaño Street seats 3,000, and 500 commonly stand at the last 'sinners' mass at 2 p.m. But Rosa, the old odd-job widow, like many others who are very poor, does not attend the popular masses because she is ashamed of her clothes. Conversely, social climbers and ambitious business men consider it essential to be seen at church services.

Canon Law gives the parish the exclusive right to administer the sacraments of baptism, confirmation, marriage and Extreme Unction. A certificate from the parish priest is necessary in many of the parishioner's secular dealings with official bodies or business enterprises. But scores of parishioners prefer to go for services to the monastery (founded in the sixteenth century as a poor house and infirmary) of the Mercedarian Order in Silva Street, so that at times the parish priest has to go to the monks to check up on a parishioner's conduct. Many couples also have wanted to be married by the monks and cannot understand why the parish church should hold the exclusive right.[1] A further rift between priests and monks is created by the many parishioners who call on the monks in an emergency to administer the last sacraments to dying relatives, a growing tendency not viewed kindly by the parish church.

This issue is only part of a greater tension between the secular priests and the religious orders which has important sociological consequences. Unlike priests, monks renounce all social distinctions under Canon Law; like minors, they have no status as 'persons' in legal contracts. They take vows of poverty and live in disciplined communities maintained by funds derived from their teaching and cultural activities, from donations and from the richer religious houses of America.[2] They have therefore no pressing need to earn money from purely religious services, unlike the secular clergy who often live with their families and engage in business as a sideline. The parishioner is not slow to draw comparisons.

Although the wish is there, the parish church has never become the social centre it is, for example, in England. In the main the people have preferred the monks as confessors, advisers, family friends and mediators. The true leaders of the masses (even at times in their revolutions) have been the monks, as is also true of Latin America. This is partly the result of their successful invasion of the cultural and intellectual fields and their reputation for greater asceticism and saintliness than the priests.[3] Their socio-religious activities in the parish, in schools, in ex-alumni groups, in associations like the Third Orders of the Mercedarians

[1] Complete civil rights of marriage are granted on presentation of a certificate of matrimony, which must be issued by the parish. The State also recognizes the exclusive power of ecclesiastical courts to grant legal separations or to annul marriages. In Madrid, in 1952—a normal year—there were 150 cases of legal separation and eighteen of nullity.

[2] In 1912 the Jesuits were reputed to hold one-third of the capital wealth in Spain. See Brenan, op. cit., p. 48.

[3] The cynical anti-clericalist will say that the modern 'housekeeper' is often the equivalent of the mediaeval priest's *barragana*, a concubine with special dress and rights, tolerated by bishops and sanctioned by the pueblo.

and the Opus Dei, as well as in relief work and missions, has a greater influence on good and bad Catholics alike, since it is more disinterested and effective. Practically all those who have studied for a career owe some debt to the monks and maintain friendly contacts with them. Thus the monk has easy access to many influential people in the government, professions, business and the arts. Many families therefore seek the help and advice of a monk, probably both confessor and friend, on matters apparently far removed from the religious sphere. In this way the monk also fulfils a 'father-figure' role in the social structure to which the parish priest cannot aspire. He is, moreover, the centre of a web of patronage of another sort based, for him at least, on spiritual rather than material gain.

The role of the priest in the urban parish has thus tended to be largely a monitory rather than an apostolic one; emphasis is laid on the prohibited instead of the approved. The social function of parish sanctions which affect believer, agnostic or foreigner alike, is typified by the strict censorship imposed on books, the press, lectures, cinema and theatre, and teaching in general. In this matter the Spanish Church is considered 'more papist than the Pope' and goes far beyond the Vatican's Index. A mixed commission of laity and clergy deals with the written word; its policy is to prohibit heresies or 'procacious obscenities' and all that speaks against the Church or the regime.[1] Violence in print does not seem to be particularly censurable, and there are also signs of a greater general tolerance now. Four years ago, Cela the novelist was often forced to publish in Latin America; in 1957, he was admitted to the Royal Academy and is now considered 'respectable'.

There are 109 cinemas in Madrid and parishioners patronize them as much as twice or thrice weekly. A commission representative of religion, constituted by the State, divides films and plays into those suitable for adults of eighteen or above, and others. This ruling, like the English certificates A and U, appears in every place of entertainment. Far stricter, however, is the semi-official commission known as *Asociación de Padres de Familia* (made up of family heads), which has a normative effect and carries only the

---

[1] *La Cordoniz*, a humorous weekly which is read by a similar sort of public to that which in Britain reads *Punch*, has often been fined and temporarily closed down for such breaches.

moral sanction of the Church and officialdom. Their rulings, which appear daily in the press and in every church porch, are graded upwards for children, young people, adults, and 'prepared' adults; a further category is termed 'Gravely Dangerous', and the last group is considered so immoral that it is graded 'Without Classification'.[1]

In general, their censure falls even more heavily on the revue or variety hall and the theatre. Undoubtedly, many families take serious note of such rulings especially where their children are concerned, but young people are apt to pick on the 'worst' classifications as their first choice for an evening out. Censorship, too, on the dialogue of foreign films (all dubbed into Spanish) sometimes has the ludicrous result of turning divorced characters into siblings, with the consequent implication of incest. To the thinking parishioner censorship is a constant source of irritation, though it is respected as a safeguard for immature minds. It becomes correspondingly stricter for the country districts.

Since the parish church cannot wholly exercise control by preaching from the pulpit or in the Confessional, or by *novenas* and Lenten retreats, it looks to its associations to spread its influence. Of these, the most important today are the Catholic Action groups which are given *carte blanche* under the Concordat to pursue their apostolate. A former member of Catholic Action rose to be Foreign Minister, and the groups themselves regard their activities in just the same light of a crusading campaign against evil as General Franco regarded his campaign against Communism during the Civil War. In San Martín there are four branches for the men, youths, women and girls. Yet total listed membership was not more than 245 in 1957, i.e. approximately one per cent of the parish.[2] In status and proportionate numerical strength they are comparable to the two main *cofradías* in Ramosierra, but their religious mission has now become divorced from any sociological function they once had.

[1] Some of the films or plays which fell into the last two categories during 1955 were 'Gentlemen prefer Blondes', 'Death of a Salesman', 'Sinuhe the Egyptian', '20,000 Leagues under the Sea', 'Madamoiselle from Paris' and 'The Lady of the Camelias'.

[2] In theory the age-bracket for the youths is between 17 and 30, but in practice, on marrying, they immediately pass in to the men's branch.

The women's groups are the most active; they are more numerous and slightly more practical, as in their sewing circles for the poor. They are rather mockingly known as 'las beatas' in the parish, and are accused of hanging on to the priest's skirts that they may get into Heaven quicker. They are the ones who dress and adorn the statues of the Virgin and saints, and are sometimes known as *santeras*. Their role as informants to the priest is less effective in such a large parish, but they constitute a further little web of patronage by being virtually in control of organized charity in the area. Old Rosa, the desperately poor odd-job widow, complained that she really couldn't afford to spend so much time in church but she 'had to keep in their good books'. All aspirants for gifts of food and clothing, which are made to the parish by private or official organizations such as Caritas, must bear a *vale* or authorization, recommended by Catholic Action and signed by the parish priest. This is always restricted to parishioners.[1] Charity is thus controlled and canalized, and rather cold. Free medical treatment is also provided at the parish church, especially for those on the margin of the social security services, such as waitresses, maids, theatrical artistes and the aged. Local doctors voluntarily attend for several hours a week, and the women who help them and keep the records belong to Catholic Action. The doctors in an emergency will visit the poor in their homes, but the accent throughout is on simple 'patching-up' rather than prevention or permanent cure. This small dispensary was begun four years ago by the enterprising parish priest and equipped from donations or parish collections. Nothing of its kind had ever existed before in the parish. It was considered a great boon by the few who benefited from it.

There are nine other religious associations, *cofradías* and *hermandades* whose activities are centred around a regular cult of a patron saint and who, with their statues, play a leading role in

[1] The Secretariat of Charity, taking Saint Martín, who shared his cloak with the poor, as their model, had 521 persons listed as needy in 1957 on a points system (similar to that employed by the Syndicates) which indicates the number of children, aged dependants and so on. Of these, 450 were helped weekly by parcels of milk, cheese and beans which come through the Caritas organization; 26 were given a daily meal of eggs and vegetables, and the rent of eight others is also paid by the parish.

processions during Holy Week and on important feast days. Of these, the two most popular are those dedicated to the Virgin; their earliest records date from 1576. Catholic Action again forms the nucleus of these associations whose membership is not large and is no longer confined to the parish. Once more, the greater social effectiveness of the monks' church in Silva Street is demonstrated by a brotherhood, founded in 1597, whose members carry both material and spiritual aid into the homes of the sick poor within the wider ancient limits of the old monastery of San Martín. Membership has always been limited by statute to twelve monks and seventy-two of the laity. It offers a clear example of the union of the sacred and the secular in an association which, in the eyes of parishioners, is effective and worthy of support (apart from the cult of the Virgin)[1] only if it is beneficial to the whole community in this world as well as in the next. It also provides a source of competitive rivalry between the various cults in the parish manifested in differing devotions and beliefs.

Final mention must be made of the *Sociedad Sacerdotal de la Santa Cruz y del Opus Dei*, commonly known as *Opus Dei*, which was founded in Madrid in 1928 by a Marist monk. Again, it is an alliance of sacred and secular callings, marked by strict obedience to vows of poverty or chastity and distinguished by a pledge to God of all professional talents. It is the first secular organization of its kind to be given official recognition by the Pope and it has since grown to international proportions. There are four classes of membership, stratified according to social status, and the majority of the unmarried live in special residences contributing all their income to the organization. Women are eligible for all classes. Its importance lies in its penetration at all professional levels—three members of the reshuffled 1957 Cabinet belonged to Opus

---

[1] Some say that the cult of the Virgin grew since the Middle Ages as a reaction against the Reformation. Many images were indeed brought to Spain from England and Flanders. However, the cult was very strong during the Moorish wars, as witness the many victories attributed to the Virgin. There is reason to believe, therefore, that many cults simply declined with the advance of the Moors and were revived during the Christian conquests. Protestantism was thought by one girl in the parish to differ from Catholicism only by 'their not believing in the Virgin'. It is interesting to note here the preoccupation of Mediterranean Christianity with the Virgin and that of northern Europe with Christ.

Dei—and its many enemies call its members 'White Masons'. Though it denies any political ambitions, the organization makes a far more active and conscious use of patronage than do Catholic Action groups. Moreover, its movements are surrounded by an air of disciplined secrecy.

# 3

## A PLURALITY OF PROFESSION

MADRID is a city with skyscrapers where water is still sold in the summer. More than any other European capital it is the home of opposites. Earning a living there is usually bound up with a high degree of specialization—a distinctive feature of the city; yet Madrid is full of people who own to two or more paying occupations. (This, I would suggest, is also common to most 'Mediterranean' cities.) There is no common patrimony in San Martín like that which binds the Ramosierra villager to his community and ensures his livelihood. The urban economy supports a leisured rentier class whilst barely maintaining large numbers of the desperately poor.

The economic pull of the city over the country districts in general is reflected in the regular inflow of migrants and in a minor seasonal migration in spring and summer. From about May 15th (the feast day of San Isidro, patron saint of the city) wandering street traders, musicians, beggars, confidence tricksters and bullfighters with their retinues all make their appearance in Madrid. The Spanish tourist is also much in evidence from this date onwards, and *los Isidros*, a term used to describe the country visitors who once came in hordes on cheap excursions to the saint's shrine, has the alternative meaning of rustic or country bumpkin.

The spring and summer fairs are also linked to saints' days— the *Virgen de la Paloma*, beginning on August 15th, is the last and most popular, as in Ramosierra. Thus there is a certain familiar dependence on the seasons, marked by the ceremonial calendar, which is reflected in the hours of work and rest; even the Government moves to the north of Spain for the summer, and most of the smaller shops close down for three weeks or a month. Yet although the rural migrant has probably paid many visits to his provincial market town, he finds the city noisily awesome. The culture-shock he experiences is all the greater in a country which is still undergoing an agricultural and industrial revolution. *Paleto* is a word frequently used by the Jehu taxi-drivers in Madrid to describe the awkward, ingenuous rustic, conspicuous by his rough clothing and sunburnt, surprised expression.

In 1950 Madrid city contained 84 per cent of the total population of Madrid province. Figures for 1955 showed about one-third of the city's inhabitants as active earners: approximately 22 per cent of these were in industry,[1] 44 per cent bureaucrats or domestic servants, and 14 per cent engaged in trading and commercial activities. The ratio of men to women workers is about three to one. Of the remainder many of the professional class and some of the clergy have some sideline in business. San Martín in this respect follows the general pattern and cannot be singled out as specializing in any one trade or industry, except, perhaps, clothing. But a high proportion of the parishioners, especially those with sinecures or government posts in the mornings, devote themselves to some additional form of gainful employment in the afternoons and evenings. Perhaps the most obvious exceptions are craftsmen and the permanent staffs of shops and factories. My own porter was also a postman in the same area; a minor railway official became a swimming-bath attendant in the afternoon; and many, if not holding down a specific afternoon job, act as commission agents. This widespread plurality of occupation naturally tends to divide loyalties which might otherwise be directed towards a single employer. It should also dispel the popular illusion that Spaniards are congenitally lazy—an illusion fostered by the fact that much business is conducted over coffee in bars and restaurants.

A fine stratification in professional status is a marked feature of the economy. One example is the *practicante*, a kind of inferior medical practitioner who has his own practice and performs minor operations such as lancing and injections. The highly fractionalized specialization of crafts to be found in the side streets is connected with the mentality of 'repair' rather than 'replace'. Sunday morning shopping in the 'Rastro', the flea-market equivalent of London's Petticoat Lane, is a favourite

---

[1] Madrid has little heavy industry and is concerned mainly with the manufacture of goods from imported raw materials; glassware, munitions and chemical by-products are the most important.

'I came here from the pueblo because I was fed up with working on the land.'

pastime. Products in the urban parish are made to last, to be passed down to future generations rather than scrapped and replaced when old. A tailor shook his head doubtfully at a request for real buttonholes in the sleeves of a jacket and asked: 'How shall I be able to shorten or lengthen these when you give it to your son?' A surprising number of rich and poor alike have their suits and overcoats (which elsewhere would be thrown or given away) completely 'turned'. It is a poor family indeed which cannot afford to go to one of the tailors or dressmakers who abound in the parish of San Martín. Labour is cheap. Handmade goods are still widely sold at low prices by multiple single-product retailers, and many are made or ordered specially for the customer. There is therefore a greater *rapport* between buyer and vendor here than on the main streets. The personality of the family business or craft in the Pez area is revealed by the shopkeeper's reference to his regular customers as *parroquianos*, the word used for 'parishioners'. It shades off into the impersonality of the Gran Vía department store. The word used in the Gran Vía is *clientes*.

But changes are apparent. Ready-made goods and manufactured articles are gradually driving the family business into bankruptcy, or more and more into the comparative oblivion of the side street. Daily one sees 'Liquidation of Stock' painted in white on shop-windows, or handwritten notices warning neighbours of removal. Craftsmen too are switching over to wholesale production. So the range of economic relationships is being extended far beyond the parish limits and in the process is being depersonalized. While the number of establishments devoted to the sale of staple food products shows a normal rise owing to the generally increased commercial activity, Madrid stores dealing in ready-made clothing, haberdashery, footwear, jewellery, hardware, toys and pharmaceutical products nearly all at least doubled in number between 1942 and 1954.[1] Only dairies and greengrocers diminished, for they are gradually being absorbed by larger combines such as the multiple store or supermarket. The latter announce 'Prices to make you laugh' and thus undercut their weaker neighbours.

The huge department store employing hundreds of girls is also a feature of the post-Civil War era. Here, as in the market, the

[1] See the economic supplement to the daily newspaper *Pueblo*, February 26th, 1957.

customer can see everything without being pestered to buy, and can moreover make all his purchases within a limited area. The first moving escalator in Madrid was installed in the Galerías Preciados store in San Martín in 1955. For weeks it caused feminine shrieks of nervous excitement and provided a harmless form of amusement for both young and old. The covered market in the Plaza Mostenses also grouped many former street traders all under one roof. Unlike the new supermarkets it conforms to the traditional pattern. During 1956, five new American-named cafeterias sprang up in San Bernardo Street alone, and many old ones were titivated with neon lighting. Though stool-at-the-counter service is their speciality, they have preserved the tables and chairs section of the traditional café.

In the rural parish of Ramosierra choice of occupation was strictly limited by ecological circumstances and controlled by value sanctions. In the urban parish of San Martín two important differences must be emphasized. Here migrants from various regions tend to adopt occupations suitable to their character, tradition or capabilities; moreover, women are being employed in ever increasing numbers.

Sun-tanned labourers expertly swinging picks on road repairs have often just migrated from the country districts, as have the dumpy maids who fill the markets in the morning, and the cheaper harlots who haunt the bars at night. A high proportion of men originally from Galicia wear the key-laden waistcoats of the *serenos*, trundle around their knife-sharpening kit on barrows, or take a personal interest in their customer's choice in family-type restaurants. Shrewd Catalans with the latest price lists at their fingertips strengthen the Madrid ranks of business men, bankers and salesmen. Red-cheeked girls from Asturias mingle with other waitresses born in the parish in the new cafeterias and in the summer drink stalls selling *horchata*.[1] The dark wiry Andalusians figure strongly in the arts of dancing, entertainment and bullfighting. Touts who furtively sell 'Parker' pens and 'gold' rings in the tourist-ridden main streets are usually gypsies from the south. Thick-set Basques are renowned for their activities in professions or sports requiring strength and skill. It is the garrulous taxi-driver, mechanic, porter, messenger, hatter or tailor who has more

[1] A soft drink made from *chufas*, the root of the edible cyprus.

likely than not been born and bred in Madrid itself. The few migrants from Ramosierra do not seem to favour any special occupation in the city, although many of them are found in the catering trades.

Girls hurry along to their new jobs in stores, laboratories and offices; older, poorer women have long sold tobacco at busy street corners next to the blind man (or woman) who bawls out the luck of his lottery tickets. About one-seventh of the women in Madrid now spend much of the day at work away from their own homes, and domestic service accounts for two-thirds of these.

The live hand of the State has a finger in all branches of the economy. But the State economic controls evidently do not have the moral sanction of the community; interference or shortcomings are offset by alternative—sometimes clandestine—action on the part of the community.

Only the railways and the roadways (1941) have been national-ized. But the present National Institute of Industry is a govern-ment profit-making concern, and the State subsidizes organiza-tions such as the film companies and the Pegaso automobile plant in Madrid, which produces heavy trucks and expensive cars.[1] Nevertheless, transport in general is unreliable, and the delays in communication have created a whole army of messengers, and of middlemen and speculators who specialize in quick buying and selling. Few can afford the glossy national Pegaso car—a prestige vehicle—and anyway most prefer the variable personality and intimate service offered by the taxi-cab.

Government controlled provincial associations operate the 1,228 generating stations which supply 82 per cent of Spain's hydro-electric power. Madrid lies in the arid area which covers 72 per cent of Spain and, although there are sharp rains about the vernal and autumnal equinoxes, there is periodic drought in the summer; the number of cubic inches rise and fall in the reservoirs still makes headline news. Until 1956, official cuts in electricity occurred at least twice a week; unexpected cuts, however, were more frequent and, in the same year, water-meters were installed in all the houses of the parish. But just as the fountain at the street

[1] In 1954, Spain had four cars and three lorries per 1,000 inhabitants. Compare the U.K. figure of sixty-three cars and twenty-two lorries. *Economic Survey of Europe*, United Nations, Geneva, 1957.

corner has always been a surer source of cool water than the tap, so too every household maintains a supply of candles, and cooking is still largely done on old-fashioned coke or coal stoves.[1] When the electricity fails, therefore, there are merely a few pungent remarks made about the great advances in modern science, or the family take their chairs a little earlier into the street, as is their custom anyway.

Since 1939 prices have been officially controlled and, in periods of inflation, enforced by sporadic fining campaigns. Price control decrees require the display of notices in shop-windows such as 'Prices of August 1956'. Yet, inside the haberdasher's in January 1957, the customer was met with a shrug of the shopkeeper's shoulders and the wry explanation that, although the price was the correct one, the measurement of a metre of cloth had shrunk a little 'because of the cold'. Other storekeepers simply state that times are bad and frankly charge a higher price, thereby risking a fine. 'Some sell at last year's prices and others sell at next year's prices,' remarked a cynic. In 1955 rumour of a wave of smallpox spreading from the Pyrenees sent the price of serum soaring. In most cases, the law is nominally obeyed (that is, the notice goes in the window) but is not fulfilled, and the natural law of supply and demand continues to operate with a nice disregard for State intervention.

Workers in similar occupations are associated through the high degree of stratification imposed by syndicalism, which has given workers social service benefits and insurance. Theoretically it should have resulted in a greater interdependence between work groups, but the opposite seems to be true; the various branches of professional and commercial activity appear to isolate themselves from one another.[2] No doubt syndicalism has provided a great impetus to the country's economy in general—a seventy per cent rise in commerce in the last-twenty-two years in Madrid—but in the process it has heavily burdened the already vast bureaucratic machine.

Every time a parishioner buys cigarettes or a can of kerosene

[1] Coal has always been scarce, too; coal merchants are often men of great wealth.

[2] Like the old guilds, in fact. Each branch of a syndicate still has its own patron saint on whose feast day religious services and organized secular leisure activities are held.

he does so by favour of State monopolies established in 1939—matches only ceased to be a monopoly in 1957. But in a land of scarcities 'grey' or 'black' market operations have never been viewed as immoral;[1] these are our Anglo-Saxon terms for what in Spain is an essential part of the patronage system. So widespread are these operations at all levels of society that profiteers and paupers alike benefit.

American-type and domestic branded cigarettes are officially sold at the State monopoly stands, *estancos*, which also sell stamps and postcards. Weekly quotas arrive on Wednesday, but by Saturday only the cheapest and darkest national brands remain. 'Monopoly of a thing,' a father satirically explained to his enquiring son, 'means the exclusive right of one organization *not* to have that thing.' Yet at almost every street corner at all hours of the day and night kindly-looking old women in black supply (for an extra peseta or two) all types of cigarettes, including English brands which are not officially available. They owe their comparative immunity from the law partly to their evident poverty[2] (and consequent inability to pay fines) and partly to the fact that the service they provide is complementary to the State monopoly's. In most of the larger bars and cafés the resident bootblack openly offers the same service to the community; the distribution of contraband tobacco in the parish is highly organized through a thousand waiters, messengers and nightwatchmen, and is cheerfully taken advantage of by all, including the police.

When the parishioner buys a lottery ticket, or imports or exports any article, he further swells the coffers of the State, which derives a large part of its total revenue from these rigidly controlled transactions. As with cigarettes, so with the sale of tickets for the special Christmas and Easter lotteries; when the State stalls run out unofficial sources freely offer the eagerly sought tickets. Even churches have notices in the porch announcing lottery tickets for sale. So too with the much coveted import and export licences,

[1] Though not through lack of trying by governments. Consider the rationing period in the immediate post-Civil War years when rewards (40% of the fine) were offered to informants who were allowed (under the *Ley de Tasas*) to trade with profiteers in order to secure a conviction. See Allison Peers, *Spain in Eclipse*, London, 1943, p. 187.

[2] Their daily earnings rarely amount to more than 20 or 30 pesetas—about three or four shillings (42 or 52 American cents) in 1957.

for it is considered only right and proper to help a relative or friend to jump the long waiting list. It is not a question here of saying that one may be entitled to these things by right, for between what is one's right and what is possible lie a thousand indifferent shrugs of the shoulder.

These and other practices such as the 'commission for friendly services' at high bureaucratic and business levels tend to infuriate the more earnest American capitalist seeking to establish a company or make a contract in Spain; he regards them indignantly as a misuse of money which his own tax payments have helped to provide in foreign loans and blocked funds for building bases.[1] Nevertheless, they (and other foreigners) have little hesitation in using bogus (Spanish) patrons or men of straw as a means of introducing more foreign capital than is legally permitted into a new commercial venture. Nor are they shocked, it appears, at the old Spanish custom of maintaining a special set of books for the tax collector.

Capital is only gradually becoming more fluid; raw materials remain in short supply and internal purchasing power is still lower on the average than in any other European country. Family budgets, whatever the breadwinner's occupation, cannot therefore reflect economic and social values to the extent that they do in Britain. Low purchasing power encourages fractional retailing, a traditional thrift in making-do, and a real capacity for being content with bare essentials. At the family level it is evident that the desire for consumer goods has not greatly outpaced the limitations imposed by income; the Madrilenian has as yet neither the opportunity nor the desire to live on credit.

It is a truism of economists that wages are always chasing prices. Official figures show that in 1957 the average working family in Madrid was living on a little less than 2,000 pesetas (about £19) a month, and that the worker had to labour over seven times as long as his American counterpart to be able to procure equivalent consumer goods. The professional economist is now regarded with

---

[1] The failing economy of Spain in general and Madrid in particular was initially bolstered up by a $100,000,000 American loan in 1950 and by several others since. The operation of the air bases under the later pact of 1952 provides relatively easy employment for many parishioners of San Martín at attractively high wages.

some respect, and his exhortations to 'foment the will to cooperate', to 'organize', to 'serve in a responsible manner' in order to increase productivity and better the standard of living appear in more and more daily editorials. Since 1939 government economists have stressed the importance of transferring part of the rural surplus population to expanding industry.

The minimum daily food budget for a family of three (supplied by my porter's wife) is more revealing than impersonal national statistics:

|  |  | Prices | |
|---|---|---|---|
|  |  | 1936 | 1957 |
| Chick peas | ¼ kilo | 40 céntimos | 3.00 pesetas |
| Bread | 1 ,, | 65 ,, | 7.00 ,, |
| Egg (for child) | 1 | 15 ,, | 2.50 ,, |
| Meat (for stew) | ¼ kilo | 45 ,, | 8.00 ,, |
| Potatoes | 2 ,, | 25 ,, | 4.00 ,, |
| Wine | 1 litre | 50 ,, | 5.00 ,, |
| Milk | 1 ,, | 60 ,, | 4.00 ,, |
|  |  | 3.00 | 33.50 |

It is significant that since 1939 women's wages have risen much faster than men's, and apprentices' wages almost twice as much as those of trained workers. Wage claims are in theory initiated by the syndicates and are always related to the 'national interest'. In fact they are now often stimulated by columnists in the national press, or by letters to the editor from groups of individual workers such as the staff of the Madrid City Council. In other cases they may be the result of unrest or illegal strikes— one such caused a general twenty per cent increase in April 1956.[1]

[1] A month earlier there had been a headlined announcement from the Chief of State that 'there is no economic crisis', and that 'the peseta is oscillating in some markets because of the ambition and lack of patriotism of some bad Spaniards and foreigners established here'. (See the newspaper *Hoja del Lunes*, March 18th, 1956.) Lack of confidence in the peseta was further revealed by the arrest of 369 Spanish citizens in March 1958 on the charge of having maintained unauthorized deposits in Swiss

The gruelling struggle of the majority to earn a living (*ganarse la vida*) is closely associated with a professed disdain for this mortal life (*menosprecio de la vida*) and the things of this mortal life. It was expressed by the man who described his wage as 'not enough to live on, but one might die with dignity on it'. The struggle to live is seen in the minute calculations of rich and poor alike in order to extract full value from each peseta, while the disdain is expressed in conspicuous and honorific expenditure. The struggle to live largely accounts for the multitudinous divisions in the economy, the multifarious activities of every worker, the ritual of bargaining, the ambitious schemes which too often fail, and the love of gambling. Disdain for life paradoxically seems to encourage the show of generosity, building for display, the lavishness of uniforms, titles and religious ornaments, and the heavy courtesy formulas.

In addition there is an instinctive reluctance to associate in cooperative groups, behind which seems to lie a fear of being bound by ties curbing the individual personality. This fear partially accounts for the lack of enthusiasm for technical work—for technique *does* bind men to machines. The Madrilenian kicks his motor-bicycle when it breaks down and professes indifference towards Sputniks and hydrogen bombs. We have noted elsewhere that labour is not considered an end in itself. No 'do-it-yourself' kits are sold in the shops. There is no feeling that work is a 'noble art', and consequently no desire to work just for the sake of it. There is therefore a clearer distinction in the urban parish between rich and poor, since differences in income and material possessions are sharply reflected in spending habits and in available leisure time.

The numerous street traders, perhaps more in evidence in Madrid than in any other European capital, earn a precarious living. Their trade depends on strictly personal relations with the parishioners, and in this way helps to define parish limits and loyalties. In San Martín shoemakers used to station themselves

---

banks. Total fines amounted to approximately £1,000,000 and individual fines to as much as £18,500. (See *New York Times*, March 10th, 1958.) In 1959 a new policy involved devaluation of the peseta, credit squeezes, cuts in public spending and a general domestic austerity plan. (See *New York Times*, June 29th, 1959.)

in the porches of private houses until the turn of the century.[1]
Nowadays an occasional editorial deplores the growing number of
street vendors and stalls, which seem to appear overnight and are
beginning to choke the pavements. But while purchasing power
remains low they fulfil a very necessary role by fractionalizing
parts of the retail trade. Pitches are licensed and jealously guarded
by their owners, usually women or old or disabled men. Some set
up home-made portable stalls at vantage points, often next to the
blind vendor of lottery tickets, to sell the popular pine-nut seeds
(*piñones*) and as little as one caramel or one cigarette at a time.
They are there throughout the year, often for as long as sixteen
hours a day. In the winter, shapeless in innumerable coats or thick
black shawls, they sometimes have small coke stoves and sell chest-
nuts. They are joined in the summer by stalls selling football-sized
melons; their owners sleep in the cool street. Others hawk icecream
(in six or seven 'American' varieties) and cool drinks like *horchata*.

Pitches for temporary stalls on the Gran Vía during the first
week of the year are costly. These specialize in toys, trinkets
and small gifts of all kinds for the essential present-giving on
January 6th—the day of the Three Kings. They remain open until
there are no more customers—as late as 3 a.m. on the day of the
Epiphany. On one other day of the year, dedicated to the 'National
Fair of the Book', stalls, trays and even perambulators appear with
books for sale at a discount of ten per cent off the cost price.

There are also the regular but unlicensed pedlars and hawkers
such as the knife-sharpener with his weird, time-old call on a
Pan-like pipe, and the rag-and-bone man with his mournful cry
and rarely filled striped sack. At 7 a.m. only head-scarfed women,
garbage collectors leading donkey carts,[2] and black-veiled ladies
on their way to early Mass disturb the otherwise deserted
streets. As the summer heat increases out comes the water-seller
carrying a large two-spouted earthenware jug (*botijo*) on her
shoulder, the brightly dressed gypsy peddling cheap saucepans and
crockery for old clothes, the persistent flowerseller shadowing the
young couples outside the fashionable restaurants, and the vendor

---

[1] It is said that they were the carriers of all the gossip and acted as a
kind of male 'Celestina'. See Mesenero Romanos, *Escenas Matritenses*,
Madrid, 1851.

[2] Only in 1956 did the municipality completely take over their function.

of flaky waffles (*el barquillero*) weighed down with his heavy circular box, which has a wheel of chance to beguile the juvenile buyer. In a corner of the local market the lame salesman of *aleluyas* sings samples of the illustrated popular songs, each with a heartrending moral in countless verses. Winter forces the men to join the army of messengers, become waiters or do odd jobs, while the women scratch a living by helping a relative or by cleaning and mending.

Two important figures from the sociological viewpoint are the bootblack and the itinerant lottery seller. A bootblack is attached to one or more café-bars, which may include an outdoor pitch, and a few of his kind are learning English at language academies to deal better and more profitably with American tourists. He wears a dark uniform overall, cleans and may often make small repairs to shoes, sells black-market cigarettes and cigars, provides State lottery tickets, and performs a variety of small personal services for customers, which may boost his monthly income from tips up to 6,000 pesetas or more in the summer.[1] These *limpiabotas* of Madrid have their own guild and patron saint.[2] Many of them are the confidants of their customers, and it is said that their knowledge made them dangerous men to cross in the Civil War.

Less frequent but no less important in the life of the parish is the peripatetic lottery seller. He may also carry a stock of cigarettes in the voluminous pockets of his lounge-suit, but he specializes in the State lottery and has his own privately printed lottery tickets (which fractionalize those issued by the State). Much of his business is done on credit and he is entirely dependent on the goodwill and tips of his customers. He is a well known figure in all the bars, mean and elegant alike, within the parish where he has a definite beat. Like the bootblack he shares many secrets; but he also lends money, and his roaming mission makes him the acquaintance and servant of a wide circle of people who regard him as a possible bearer of good fortune. He is 'the man with a million', an essential harbinger figure in a highly competitive society where gambling may bring a form of messianic reward.

[1] About £36.
[2] The Virgin of the Immaculate Conception. December 8th is a holiday for them, and a special Mass is celebrated in San Martín Church for guild members.

Moreover, like the taxi-driver, he is an important channel for the flow of gossip, price movements and the news which never appears in print.

A fervid belief in luck in one form or another is strikingly apparent in the city parish. It is true that the quasi-personal character accorded to facts and things—the animistic value attributed to mascots and talismans by more primitive peoples—is in this society largely channelled towards religious figures and saints. But there has also been a spread in the urban setting of a faith in the efficacy of special numbers, in the fall of the cards, and in horoscopes. Veblen speaks of this as an animistic habit 'which acts in all cases to blur the appreciation of causal consequences'.[1] It therefore increases in intensity with the specialization and depersonalization of work in the semi-industrial urban parish. The vast popularity of the lottery, introduced into Madrid in 1763, seems to support this theory; it is far more widespread among all income groups than, for example, the numbers game in New York or football pools in Britain. An obsessional state of expectancy pervades the city before the big Christmas draw, and a monthly dream world (which Calderon would have recognized) maintains a regular optimistic tension—a theme for a modern playwright.[2] A faith in decision by lot seems to be general. Compare the Pine Luck division in Ramosierra and the choosing of young men for the military draft, both by lot. Most examinations contain a definite element of chance. Each candidate must blindly pick a ball from an urn, and the number on the ball refers to the subject on which he will be tested.

This gambling urge is turned to account by various charities which publicly raffle desirable articles such as sewing-machines, ice-boxes, motor-cycles or scooters, as well as household gadgets. These *tómbolas* are often organized by the diocesan or syndicate housing committees. Enormous stands are packed with prizes supplied free by well-known manufacturers. Daily takings in the larger raffles, which last about a month, are as much as half a million pesetas, and the *tómbolas* generally serve as an important means of advertising for the bigger commercial companies.

[1] See Thorsten Veblen, *The Theory of a Leisure Class*, New York, 1899, p. 285.

[2] See Antonio Buero Vallejo, *Hoy es Fiesta*, Madrid, 1956.

Other more modern methods of advertising pioneered since 1939 by the powerful soft-drinks companies are also largely based on the desire to gamble and the belief in luck. Bottle tops provide the lucky drinker with anything from a five-peseta prize to a whole apartment. Local Spanish firms are following suit—the department stores and branded food producers are the most active—vying with one another on radio programmes and in the monster stores on the Gran Vía to give away the most in campaigns of conspicuous generosity. Thirty to thirty-five per cent of commercial radio time and press advertising space is taken up by the big *almacenes*. Some of the smaller shops in the Pez area also banded together in 1956 to offer jointly a ten per cent discount on selected goods. Another group of forty-four producers in the Fuencarral area offered, in 1957, a 'dream holiday' in Paris and forty-four different articles of clothing to lucky customers. Nevertheless, despite the ballyhoo of big-scale advertising, the local market and the smaller shops in the parish still seem to retain the loyalty of their regular poorer customers.

As yet 'the accusing finger' of modern advertising is not common, and little or no emotional unease is felt by the failure 'to have a second bathroom', to use deodorants, and so forth. However, although campaigns are adapted to local tastes, there is a noticeable tendency for the ideal types depicted on hoardings and in newspaper advertisements to be un-Spanish in physiognomy and to follow rather the characteristics found in the American cinema star. There are no sandwichmen, but sometimes motor-scooters act as brilliantly-painted advertisements for wine firms. I have on occasions seen a weirdly dressed figure on stilts scattering handouts, but the Spaniard is generally loath to make himself appear ridiculous even for profit.

Again, advertisement encourages 'snobbish' tendencies in speech, drink, clothing, entertainment and in the home, especially among the moneyed, leisure class; but these perhaps are based more on what the fashionable Englishman, Frenchman or German is thought to do. Language academies have mushroomed under the management of foreigners since the Civil War, but only a minor percentage of the pupils learn for purely practical reasons. Whisky, foreign wines, and *cocktels* are now an essential and expensive part of any fashionable reception. English cloth is highly sought (although Edwardian or other outlandish styles for men would be ridiculed) and women eagerly scan French or German fashion magazines in all the expensive hairdressers. Stationers now sell quite large quantities of religious and secular Christmas and birthday cards—a move towards foreign customs: January 6th and the name-day are the traditionally important feasts in Spain, not Christmas Day and birthdays. Golf, polo, and tennis are common at the best clubs, and the players may return to homes decorated in modern styles. Yet this is the exception. Generally, homes at all class levels are furnished in an old-fashioned style with plenty of heavy furniture, often passed down from father to son. The general impression is one of a rather solid Edwardian cosiness. Preference scales for spending in the urban parish are as wide as the pocket book (and the minimum canons of good taste and morality) will allow.

The 'rich' are those who never directly go shopping for food. They order goods by telephone; and their maids, unaccompanied, buy the fresh meat and vegetables in the market. Moreover, they conspicuously seek prestige through donations to charities or by acting as patrons to the arts or higher learning. There are few misers in this society. The richest man in Spain—and he is extremely rich—came from a modest background, but recently endowed the most remunerative scholarships and awards ever founded for scientific or literary merit. What passes comparatively unnoticed, however, is the immense amount of charitable work which many of the wealthy effect through personal relationships. Between them and their employees, servants and dependants there still exists a familiary tie of almost mediaeval strength which makes a personnel manager in the factory needless. But one cannot generalize in the urban parish; there are good and bad employers, mean and generous rich people. The anonymity of the city swallows up both virtue and vice. As a generic term, the rich are those who do not need to work, those who can indulge in conspicuous leisure. They are all that the adjective implies—'noble' (*ricohombre* means a nobleman of the ancient nobility of Castile), 'opulent', 'pleasing' and 'select'. As a class, therefore, they are to be envied and are the enemies of the poor;[1] as individuals, they are to be

---

[1] Treatment of the poor—an indefinable term—must be left to a further work. But see Chapter 5 for a discussion of the divisions of the society, and in particular, the beggars.

respected or despised according to their generosity or meanness.

The attitude to money can be seen in the question of payment and generosity. Cash, and the actual handing-over of it for goods or services received, is regarded as a regrettable necessity. Drinks and refreshments are paid for only when the person has completely finished and is about to leave. The new hire-purchase systems are popular because they provide a friendlier arrangement, apart from facilities for payment. Loans and credit on a gentleman's agreement are still common practice.

In like manner, generosity is related to honour and personality. Charities or public appeals have to depend largely on donations from corporate bodies rather than from private individuals who prefer to personalize the relationship between donor and recipient. So it is that even the tip becomes a gift, not necessarily a matter of course but a dignified exchange between two persons of equal merit, which creates esteem. There is no servility in the idea of service. Even among intimate friends the payment of the bill for lunch becomes a point of honour, and the waiter is often placed in an embarrassing position. This attitude makes it impossible for a foreigner to share his taxi or buy someone a drink unless he extends a formal invitation. However, when the parishioner offers you his house or his food, the invitation is not to be taken literally; it is simply an expression of his generosity which must be manifested in a traditional, albeit nominal hospitality. How far this ritualized sense of hospitality serves to remind a stranger of his status as an outsider need not concern us here.

# 4

## THE CITY FAMILY

NO SINGLE family occupies a whole house in the parish of San Martín. The fortunate who can afford it rent or own a complete floor, but it is more common to find two or three families, each with its own private entrance to its home, sharing a floor. Often they have no binding ties with each other but are migrants from different provinces. These L-shaped *pisos* ideally, but in practice rarely, provide a separate front room for each of the children and a back room for the maid, if one is employed.[1] Fifty years ago the staid *sala de visita* or reception-room, crammed with knick-knacks, was a respected feature of a house. It gave way after the first world war to the more comfortable *cuarto de estar* or living-room, which modern observers complain is now rarely lived in since the family increasingly spends its leisure time out of doors.

Composite households of the three-generation type are the rule rather than the exception. They consist of the basic family and often one set of grandparents. Temporary residents sometimes include a close relative, a migrant from the country who will remain as a non-paying guest until he sloughs off the status of *paleto* (country bumpkin) and finds both a job and suitable accommodation. Commonly found odd additions to the normal grouping are unattached (and usually unemployed) siblings or cousins, who contribute little but the charm of their company to the household. This is not, however, wholly self-sufficient for, with other households in the buildings, it shares common dependence on the services of the porter below and on the landlord's goodwill.

---

[1] National average density of occupation is about 1·1 persons per room. But 20 per cent of the population are housed at a density of more than 2 persons per room. Large cities as a rule have fewer dwellings per 1,000 inhabitants than the national average, but this is outweighed by the greater average size of the city room. (*Censo de Edificios y Viviendas*—Madrid, 1953.)

Consideration for neighbours necessarily enters into the mode of living; for instance, the neighbours' permission must be sought for any special celebration that may lead to unaccustomed noise, and in modern buildings roof-terraces and courtyards, as well as the heating plant, are shared in common. A rather general attitude towards neighbours was tartly expressed by old Manuela who, besides being the porter of her condemned building, ran a newspaper kiosk outside: 'They're just a nosey lot because they've got nothing better to do, especially that number 16.' She told me later that she much preferred her new home in the modern *barrio* of Argüelles where 'the others are not peeking in your window all the time.' The strong family independence which, in the rural parish, offsets close habitual village contacts is weakened in the urban parish. The latter cannot provide the same interdependence and sense of community, with the result that, despite an enforced proximity, neighbourhoods form less well-defined groups and have less voluntarily in common to bind them.

Here one cannot speak with the same assurance of a 'typical' family, though the social values and basic norms of the pueblo hold good in the city. The father is still the household's head and master, whose manliness and sense of honour make him leave household drudgery to women and minors. Though he may be retired from gainful employment he still dominates the home, even when his grown-up grandchildren are living there. Where the father is dead this role is assumed by the eldest son if he is of age. Often, however, the head of the family is not its sole supporter, and in the urban parish there is no family plot of land or right to a common patrimony. Moreover, he is usually an employee whose work outside the parish may keep him away from home for most of the daylight hours, though it is true that the majority still hie home for their midday meal.

Let us take the extreme case of José Ramón, a RENFE (national railways) office employee aged 59, with ten children. Out of his salary of 2,750 pesetas a month he pays 150 pesetas rent for nine small rooms on a floor of an old house in the Pez area. A further 1,000 pesetas a month is earned by his eldest unmarried daughter, chief seamstress to a dressmaker. José gives all his money to his wife, who returns him an allowance for fares, tobacco and other miscellaneous items. Their commonest meal is the popular *cocido*, a dish of vegetables and a few scraps of meat; they keep no maid and the women make their own clothes. José admits that 'life is difficult', but says he 'gets by' with the help of odd commissions and because of State aid which not only pays his children's school fees but also exempts him from taxes.

Three points drawn from this example should be borne in mind: the wife is the manager of the budget in many working-class families; daughters have become important contributors to the household's income; and the State acts as a kind of *padrino* to the family. Allowing for the dangers of generalizing from a particular example, the case given is typical of such large families. Generally speaking, the further away the family is from the continual worry of subsistence living, the more secretive the husband becomes about his total income, and the more often it is he who makes his wife an allowance.

A small family of three at a similar level of poverty is typified by the case of X, a 25-year-old glassblower who supports his infirm and widowed mother and his young sister on a basic daily wage of twenty-five pesetas. He began in the workshop as an apprentice at 14 and complains: 'How can I think of getting married under such conditions?' Lack of money is, it seems, the greatest single reason for delay in setting up a new independent family unit.

One could, of course, quote other examples from higher income levels where the father remains the sole provider and the family lives under no pressing economic difficulties. But the point must be stressed that, the greater these difficulties, the more the wage-earner falls short of the ideal pattern of the father's role. In all senses he is still the legal and moral head of the family. Even in the few cases where a wife gets a legal separation the husband keeps control of her property, and until 1958 his permission was needed before she could obtain employment or a passport. But other influences such as support from the State rather than the kin group, the growing independence of his womenfolk, and his long hours of absence from the home all tend to reduce a man's status and authority within the family. He will most probably have to work to a greater age than he might in the pueblo, where he would be kept in leisure by his children; pensionable age is a nagging worry for many a father. Nevertheless a father's judgement is still sought on all matters affecting the family; he is still the champion of its rights and defender of its reputation, commands respect from all its members, and is a law unto himself. *Llevar la vida padre* ('to lead a father's life') in colloquial language means to lead a very comfortable life indeed. When he dies half his property goes by law to his wife and the other half is shared equally among his children. When the widow dies her half of the inheritance passes automatically to the children. This is Castilian law, the law of the land.

A wife complements and supports her husband's role; as a mother, too, she is the internal guardian of the home. Her role is designated by the official term for her occupation (*sus labores*), which ideally limits her to household duties. For the city women who cannot afford a maid the essential daily tasks begin about 7 a.m. when she goes out to buy the milk for preparing the light breakfast. After seeing the children to school and cleaning the house she no doubt listens to the food prices on the radio (found in the poorest homes) before going to market, with a sharp eye on the scales, to return home triumphantly or disgustedly to cook the lunch. Once this is over and the men are out of the way, she usually spends the late afternoon and early evening bent over her sewing by hand, collecting the children from school, and in preparing the snack for tea (*merienda*). Probably she listens enthralled to a melodramatic serial on the radio while awaiting her husband's return, and spends a quiet time with him before dealing with dinner. Housewives are constantly urged and tempted by the commercial radio to buy this soup or that chocolate but, though company profits show that they are, individuals will rarely admit to being influenced by advertising. It is almost as if they distrust the disembodied voice from that small box. By midnight the housewife is thinking of going to bed, though in summer reluctantly.

Her week is divided up into special daily tasks. Mondays are given over to washing at the ribbed stone *pila* in the kitchen sink where the clothes are still 'bucked' with lye; washing powders are now advertised on a grander scale, but most housewives and servants continue to use the *lejía*, or lye water boiled with ashes. Tuesdays and Wednesdays are devoted to the drying and repair of linen. Thursdays and Fridays are the days for careful ironing, an important activity in the city where appearance counts for so much; the massive coke-filled iron is the housewife's standby. Saturday she devotes to a more detailed cleaning of the house and kitchen, for 'cleanliness is next to godliness'; and she will use the short-handled besom for sweeping.[1] Finally, Sunday is truly a day of relaxation and of personal care in clothes and adornment.[2]

I do not suggest that there is anything singular in this description of a housewife's minimum duties; perhaps its value lies precisely in the fact that it shows a total, unvarying preoccupation with the home. In these tasks maids never completely replace the mistress of the house, who is continually supervising. Pride in the home, good cooking and fine needlework are still considered a glory for their own sake, and not as tiresome drudgery. Moreover, these duties must still be performed by the housewife who goes out to work. She remains the focal point of the home, and the mediator between the children and their father. Her parents may have provided or found the *piso*, and any relatives staying with the family are usually hers.

In an atmosphere of respect and affection for his parents the son grows up sure in the knowledge that he is the potential heir to the father's authority. He is not necessarily named after his father or grandfather (as is usual in the pueblo), but his Christian name is always a saint's name and tends, in Madrid, to be one of those of the twelve Apostles. Jesus and Angel are also common names, and are used with no trace of self-consciousness. As in the pueblo, the patron saint's day is an important occasion for present-giving. At school and in play the boy swiftly becomes separated from his sisters and emulates the manly role of his father in regard to the home. The segregation of the sexes is not, however, so marked as in the rural parish. Secure in the oft-demonstrated love of his parents, the boy, in particular, still submits to a strict family discipline in which physical punishment becomes largely unnecessary and is even abhorred.

The ritual dressing-up in a miniature monastic white habit

[1] Compare also the Madrid street-cleaner and his dainty, knee-high bin. This accords with Foster's observation (see G. C. Foster, op. cit.) on motor patterns and the preference for short-handled implements.

[2] Recent national figures show that 79 per cent of the total number of dwellings have electricity, 34 per cent have running water and 11 per cent have baths. Rural dwellings particularly lack basic amenities. Madrid is *not* one of the three out of the twenty-four large cities where as many as half the dwellings have running water. (*Censo de Edificios*, op. cit.)

or in the popular admiral's uniform, for the first Communion and Confirmation instil in him a respect for the parish and the ministers of the Church, as well as lending significance to the crucifix which hangs over his bed. He may be a wage-earner at 12 years old; but financial difficulties in the home, or in many cases the long academic training for highly competitive professions, coupled with his stint of military service, often result in the boy's reaching social adulthood in marriage at a later age than his village counterpart. This does not mean that he may not be saddled with responsibilities as head of the household at an earlier age. He often is, as soon as he comes of age at 18. However, the son is usually the first of the family to seek escape from the street in which they live, and parents in the poorer areas of the parish greatly lament the new liberty evident among young wage-earners. This appears to be accentuated when son and father follow different occupations.

The daughter of the house is a future wife and mother, and all her training in the home is designed to that end. Imitating her mother, she automatically adopts the same protective feeling towards the men of the family. Again, the daughter is not necessarily named after mother or grandmother. Highly favoured are names usually associated with the Virgin Mary such as Purificación, Visitación, Maria de los Dolores, and Concepción.

In her eighth or ninth year the daughter is 'married to Christ' in a white bridal gown at her first Communion in the parish church and, like her mother, she steadfastly maintains traditional religious practice from that day on, particularly through retreats in Lent and services on the many feast days. She is probably one of forty others in her grade at school, where she is taught by nuns; but her progress in formal education is viewed much more leniently than that of her brother. She will no doubt go through a phase of wanting to be a nun. Unless it is absolutely necessary for the welfare of the home she is not expected or permitted to become a wage-earner; but there are indications that this attitude is undergoing a change. However, daughters of 'good families' that employ two or three maids may find leisure hangs heavily on their hands; often, they are decorative but (as regards household tasks) useless additions to the home. Of all the internal relationships in the home, the bond between mother and daughter is the strongest, and this bond is strengthened vis-à-vis the men when the grandmother too forms part of the household. It becomes particularly marked, of course, at the age of puberty.

As a group the family rigidly adheres to meal-times, which are nevertheless more flexible in the city because of the men's more demanding exterior duties. Breakfast is a light meal of coffee, buns or fritters. The labourer often makes do with a warming glass of unsweetened *anís* on his way to work 'to kill the little worm', but he will munch an enormous sandwich at eleven o'clock or thereabouts. One to two o'clock is the rush-hour for the Metro and buses, because between two and four in the afternoon the city takes its midday meal leisurely and peacefully, as is evidenced by the almost deserted streets. Cooked on a coke- or gas-stove, thick broths in winter, hors d'oeuvres in summer, fish or eggs or vegetables (eaten separately), a meat course and a sweet are the minimum dishes for the majority, except the very poor. Meals are always served hot, and it is a sign of humiliating poverty indeed to have to eat 'cold'. Even the district soup-kitchen provides three courses at separate, cloth-covered tables for the resourceless derelicts.

Rich and poor alike will enjoy the typical Madrilenian *cocido* of boiled bacon, chick peas and potatoes, though those who can afford to do so will embellish it. *Chorizo*, highly spiced pork sausage, is found in every home, and sliced tripe in piquant sauce is a special favourite in Madrid. Mutton and beef are the cheapest and most popular meat, usually sharpened by wrinkled red peppers and pungent garlic; and the servant eats as richly as her master. Wine invariably accompanies the meal of the humblest, and large quantities of fresh bread rarely leave the luncher hungry.

In the blanketing heat of the summer, offices and shops open from 5 to 8 p.m., and even the flies indulge in a siesta after lunch. A brave attempt to introduce the American working-day timetable in 1956 had to be abandoned and, despite a journey daily made memorable by a seemingly impossible crush, the worker will always prefer to come home to lunch. The *merienda* (evening-snack) consists of either chocolate or coffee with bread, jam or sliced sausage; tea is drunk rather self-consciously by some of the modern-minded parents. The last meal of the day—dinner— which is just as heavy and formal a meal as lunch, is taken as late as 11 p.m. Only in very unusual circumstances will any member of the family be absent, and if anyone goes out afterwards it is most often as a member of the family group on a Saturday night.

Generally, there is greater variety in the urban diet yet, despite the splitting-up of meals into various courses, the poor eat considerably less than the ordinary villager. Meals are taken much later in the city. Moreover, there are fewer occasions on which formal feasts are held for related kin in the home.

Children are never left by themselves, and baby-sitting as a paid occupation is unheard of. Grace before meals, Sunday Mass as a group and, less frequently, family prayers at night are still activities which are the rule rather than the exception. Most homes have at least a picture if not a small statue of a religious patron, usually the Virgin, who is the source of all favours; and this urban household cult to a certain extent supplants the traditional lares of the village household. Life is thought of as something within, not outside, oneself. Relationships within the family are not quite so harmonious as the romantic ideal likes to suggest; but this is thought quite natural—pure harmony is the product of several and opposed sounds. Meals in the home establish unity precisely by providing excellent occasions for the discussion of disuniting subjects, and as a matter of course guests are excluded who are not part of the accepted family circle.

The intimacy of the family table is characteristic of the many *pensiones* or boarding houses in the Pez area of the parish which advertise for permanent boarders (*estables*). Very few provide lodging only. The owner or his wife presides at the head of the table and the paying guest is treated as one of the family. (A contrasting formality can be found in the *pensiones* of the Gran Vía which cater for more temporary boarders.) To a lesser degree this spirit explains the popularity of the family-type regional restaurants which abound in the side streets, with a regular clientele exchanging news from the provinces over their meals. A family rarely eats out as a group; these restaurants are a haven for the summer 'bachelor' (familiarly known as 'Rodríguez') who has sent his family away to escape the heat.

Three out of every five women who work in the city of Madrid work for other women in the home. As part of the household, maids are drawn into the family circle. They live in, but the problem of keeping them in has become increasingly acute, and cleaners employed for a number of hours only are slowly replacing resident servants. They are usually older married women and are known as *asistentas* since, like charwomen, they only 'oblige'. The average wage for a maid in 1956 was 350 pesetas (about £3 3s.) a month with her keep, but the higher wages offered by American families and the competing attractions of factory or cafeteria work (where a girl has more opportunity of meeting a suitor) are raising this figure every year. In most families the *chacha* or *tata* (both affectionate terms) becomes in addition a nurse to the children, a chaperone to the young daughter, and an accepted non-kin member of the household, though she does not eat with the family. The governess in aristocratic homes is rarely accepted with the same affection, since her duties do not touch on the domestic welfare of the home. Language reflects the human element; the word for 'servant' is little used—much preferred is the word *criada*, someone who is reared and developed in the household.

Servants are the responsibility of the head of the household—they are not covered by the system of social insurance—and, when they fall ill or reach retiring age, the family is expected to care for them. The maid thus becomes wholly dependent[1] on the good will of the master and mistress, and outwardly considers them as beneficent patron figures. She is expected to *sisar*, i.e. filch trifles, especially on the shopping accounts, and most families will be content to keep this within reasonable limits.

Rich families may also keep an *ama de leche* or wet-nurse, who enjoys special status and privileges in the home, for the baby's physical well-being is thought to be bound up with the contentment of the *ama*. An acute observer of domestic life in Madrid[2] claims that they are usually strong mountain women whose vitality is transmitted with their milk to the child. Many still wear a mixture of their regional costume and the striped apron, white stockings and starched cap of the traditionally depicted *ama*. With the children in perambulators they fill the parks and squares in the mornings, gossiping among themselves or furtively flirting with soldier admirers.

Parishioners declare that the faithful servant type is a common

[1] Some attempt is made by the parish church of San Martín in evening classes to teach illiterate servants the 3 Rs and 'general culture'.
[2] See Maura Laverty, *No More than Human*, London, 1944.

enough phenomenon in this society; most of them certainly appear to be well treated and fiercely loyal to their masters.[1] One wonders, however, to what extent this is a comfortable myth created by benign employers.[2] Some maids are not above filling the role of the old *correveidile* (a mixture of tale-bearer and procuress) in its more harmless current form of go-between for young daughters and ardent suitors. Nevertheless it would be uncharitable and misleading to disregard the evident two-way loyalty and mutually respectful recognition of status. In the mornings when mistresses are out the courtyards resound with local gossip and with bursts of the latest popular songs.

One might suppose the sanctions surrounding courting to be inimical to the perpetuation of society. But since these sanctions, indicative of a rigidly monogamous society, restrict the choice of a life partner, courting is in some ways facilitated. Pritchett once said that in every Spanish girl's gaze there lies marriage and eight children.[3] One can see this cool, bold (but not shameless) gaze cast every evening during the *paseo*[4] on the men as they pace up and down the Gran Vía.

A word now used among the Madrid youth, but never in the pueblo, is 'flirt'. It suggests that with the loosening of family control and multiplicity of contacts, distinctive features of the city, courting has become frivolous and uninhibited. This is patently untrue, but the word does denote an experimental stage in courting procedure which would not, and could not, be manifested in the pueblo. Nor need this stage be ephemeral; to have a 'flirt' (the person, not the activity, is referred to here), may sometimes lead to a more stable footing when the *novios* are said 'to have

[1] An extraordinary exception was a maid employed by an American family who was in the habit of hiring out the American baby for two hours or so, while on a Sunday morning stroll in the park. The baby-hirer was a gypsy woman-beggar who clothed it in a ragged blanket for effect, and tenaciously solicited alms outside the church. She made the mistake of approaching the actual parents, to whom I am indebted for this account.

[2] Compare the 'naturally happy Negro mammy' servant myth questioned by Harriet Martineau in *Society in America*, London, 1837, vol. 2, pp. 152–54.

[3] V. S. Pritchett, *The Spanish Temper*, London, 1954.

[4] As a fashion it was originated by the seventeenth-century monarchs in Madrid who were pleased to wander the length of the avenue Paseo del Prado, near the present park of that name.

relations', i.e. are committed to the recognized formality of courting which will end in marriage. It is significant, however, that the
flirt is usually of a lower social status than her boy friend.[1]

A girl is almost always accompanied by a chaperone on any
social excursion from home until she is about 18 or 19, when she
is allowed to go about with girl friends of similar age and status
who are known to the parents. The amount of freedom from that
age on varies according to the social position of the family.[2] No
'decent' girl, however, would be seen alone with a man in a car or
after dinner unless she is his *novia*. Professional and occupational
demands are slowly liberalizing this attitude. Moreover, girls
now attend the university (mainly in the arts and pharmaceutical
faculties) or language and general culture classes in commercial
institutes. Girls in their 'teens from the urban parish, since about
1948, are also to be found studying abroad and (far more infrequently) girls from pueblos travel alone to Britain and other
countries to work in hospitals or as family helps. Nevertheless,
cases could be cited of unmarried women in their late twenties who
would not be allowed such independence by their parents.

A girl counts on attracting a *novio* at least during one of the local
fiesta fairs, when parental control is relaxed. On June 13th, at
dawn and during the early hours thereafter, there is a long queue
of girls outside the shrine of San Antonio de Florida, whose cupola
is decorated by Goya. There they stand, each clutching twelve
pins which they will drop into the holy water font with a prayer
that the saint will help them find a *novio* or keep their existing ones
faithful.

Boys tend to go about in groups at an earlier age, but seldom,
among either the rich or the poor, start serious courting until they
are 25 or older. Many must complete their long *carrera* (i.e.
studies for their career) before marrying, and the poor have the
extra difficulty of providing for dependants and finding a *piso*
to live in. Courtships are not as a rule long drawn out, but few
men, rich or poor, venture on matrimony before the age of 28 or

---

[1] The term may also be used for the older married man who is having
an indiscreet fling; as well, of course, for the old lecher.

[2] In general, a greater freedom is allowed the daughters of upperclass
families. Moreover, the telephone in the city allows them more opportunity for courting.

29, and some much later, unless parents or wealthy *padrinos* resolve their immediate financial problems.

Compared with the pueblo, there are abundant opportunities in the urban parish for prospective *novios* to meet in relative privacy. Selection of a mate is not, however, a casual procedure. If for the moment we arbitrarily divide the city into the three social groupings of (a) high, (b) middle and (c) low, we can see that young people of (a) meet at sports clubs, *cocteles* (i.e. cocktail parties), private house parties, 'snob' cafés such as are found in the Calle Serrano, and at favoured summer resorts such as San Sebastián or El Escorial; those of (b) meet in offices, at university or institute classes, through associations such as the Falange and Catholic Action, or in the evening *paseo*; the most numerous (c) groupings meet their partners by more direct approaches in the factories, shops or cafeterias, in the parks or plaza, or at the *verbenas*—the local fiesta-fairs.

Behaviour in public is at all levels very correct and formal, though there is a certain amount of the horseplay type of flirting among soldier-maid couples. Yet, normally, a strong sense of propriety governs courting relationships. One couple I observed for months did their courting at the entrance of the girl's hotel; the boy never stepped into the porch, she never stepped out of it. City life is such that the relationship may be unknown to the parents until the *novio* seeks them out and asks to be considered as a formal suitor. If he is accepted the couple will hold hands in public rather obviously and will be seen and invited everywhere together. Nevertheless, parents still exercise considerable control over the choice of a spouse, and those who are conscious of their social position will ensure that their children do not marry beneath them. 'Casa tu hijo con tu igual, y no dirán de ti mal' ('marry your child with your equal and they will not speak evil of you'), runs the saying.

There is no serenading by individuals in the urban parish, but groups of male students from various faculties in the university go about in colourful period costumes playing stringed instruments. 'La Tuna', as they are called, play under the balconies to selected girls (who may have requested the privilege) and are then invited into the house for refreshment—all forty or so of them.

When the young people are in a position to marry, the procedure between the parents and close relatives is the same as in the pueblo, but a normal engagement ring worn on the third finger of the left hand now tends to replace the traditional bracelet as the betrothal gift. The city girl now often marks this event by the gift of a watch to the man. At the marriage ceremony the plainer ring placed on the bride's right hand is known as the 'ring of alliance', and the groom will also give her thirteen pieces of money known as *arras*—a further symbol of contract and of equal sharing of goods.[1] A white veil is extended over the head of the bride and the shoulders of the groom to signify the symbolic submission of the woman.

We have already noted the extent of parish control over a marriage. It must take place in the bride's parish church; there is no civil marriage in Spain. The banns must be read on several consecutive Sundays in all the parishes in which either of the pair has lived in the past. Tuesday is not a popular day for weddings— as the proverb says, 'en martes ni te cases ni embarques' ('neither marry nor embark on a Tuesday'), and May or October are the most popular months. A formal photograph of the happy couple usually appears in one of the innumerable photographers' shops in the side streets or, if the families are rich and well known, in the press or the glossy magazines. Broken engagements are very rare indeed.

In the choice of where to live there is a definite tendency to find a *piso* in or near the locality of the bride's mother. Many wealthy parents buy a separate *piso* for their son or daughter on marriage. Mothers eagerly encourage the matrilocal preference by persuading their husbands to buy whole floors of a building where their married sons and daughters may later live as part of a three-generation family group.

That the housing shortage is a telling obstacle to independence is illustrated by this story. A man of 30 married an invalid widow of 87. He was the sub-tenant of her *piso*, which he inherited on

[1] Formerly the *arras* was recognized as a dowry, and was a sum not exceeding a tenth part of the man's fortune given to the wife for her maintenance after his death. In 1528, the Cortes moderated by law the value of dowries given by the bride's father on the grounds that humbler families would never otherwise marry off their daughters. See Federico Carlos Sáinz de Robles, op. cit. Even on entering the more exclusive convents today a prospective nun will take with her a large dowry.

her death a month later, the arrangement having been agreed to by both before the marriage.[1] There is a limit to relations' hospitality, and the desire to set up one's own separate household is at times very strong. Antonio, the garage hand, originally came from Andalusia and lived with his wife and small child under very crowded conditions in his brother-in-law's home. One night he and a group of friends took a lorry-load of bricks to the outskirts district of Vallecas and, by dawn, they had built a rough shanty[2] amongst the many others there. 'Once it's up,' he told me, 'the police won't touch you, but they will prevent you putting it up if they catch you.' With the furnishings, he thought that it had cost approximately 4,000 pesetas, or five months' pay. Every newly-married couple, incidentally, insists on entering a new home with at least some new furniture.

When the couple cannot count on parental help, they must often accept State aid which, under the decree of February 1941, acts as a form of State dowry. Providing they are both practising Roman Catholics between the ages of 25 and 30, and the man does not earn more than 12,000 pesetas a year, he receives a loan of 2,500 pesetas. The woman is granted 5,000 pesetas only on condition that she promises to give up any gainful employment. No interest is charged, and the loan is repaid at the rate of one per cent a month. However, part of the loan is waived on the birth of each child, and the loan is entirely cancelled on the birth of the fourth. Many more receive regular family allowances from the State, beginning with the second child and increasing with each successive one. A growing dependence on State aid is indicated by the eightfold increase in such payments between 1939 and 1945.[3]

Apart from family allowances, there is a premium for childbirth, granted once a year; 50,000 pesetas for the Spanish couple with

[1] Daily newspaper *ABC*, February 16th, 1957.

[2] These 'moonlight shacks' can be found on the outskirts of any 'Mediterranean' city.

[3] The scheme was given great impetus when General Franco 'created' it on July 18th, 1938, the day of San José, protector of the family, and issued the first allowance. It really sprang out of the system of social insurance begun in 1908. This latter scheme is obligatory for all employers, who contribute 5 per cent of the worker's salary whilst the employee contributes one per cent. See P. Florentino Del Valle, *Las Reformas Sociales en España*, Madrid, 1946.

the greatest number of children and fifty provincial awards of 15,000 pesetas each. Widows and orphans are also covered under a comprehensive scheme, which provides old-age and invalidity pensions, injury insurance, and health and maternity benefits. The socialistic tendency of the welfare State is obvious, but in the case of health insurance it is too impersonal and ineffective for most families. Rafael, a clerk aged 30 and earning about 2,000 pesetas a month, pays seventy pesetas a month under the national health scheme and another sixty pesetas to a private scheme. 'Very efficient,' he says of this last. 'When I had to call the doctor in the middle of the night for the birth of my baby, there was none of this "We don't open till 9 a.m." business.' He also added that it guaranteed him a 'second-class' funeral. Nevertheless, attention should be drawn to the intrusion of the State, especially at crises, in the life-cycle of the family, and to its taking over of responsibilities which were once those of the wider kin group.

This results in the family being driven more within itself without the corresponding sense of community found in the rural parish. A higher proportion of both sexes remain unmarried, and there is a greater concomitant degree of social isolation of the individual without family group ties, as in most cities.

*Compadrazgo* (godparenthood) and spiritual sponsorship at marriage help to provide new ties as well as reinforce existing ones between kin. The usual pattern of the father of the bride and mother of the groom as *padrino* and *madrina* at a wedding breaks down in the city, and uncles and aunts figure strongly as wedding sponsors and godparents. One case was found where the altar boy had to act as *padrino*, but this argues an unusually high degree of social isolation. Ashamed of unsophisticated parents and the impression they may give, the type of groom who gets married in a tuxedo may choose younger, more presentable persons— brothers or friends—as wedding sponsors. Nor are the *padrinos* at a wedding often found as baptism *padrinos* of the children of the marriage, as was the case in Ramosierra. Many cases of siblings acting as godparents were recorded. But the frequent appearance of 'friends of the house' as godparents suggests that the habit of choosing an influential (and preferably rich) friend or employer is fast increasing. This, of course, happens far more often than is possible in Ramosierra, and *compadrazgo* in Madrid must be considered as one of the most important links in the chain of patronage. Yet the advantages derived from an influential patron are sometimes gained only at the expense of a social separation imposed by class barriers between co-godparents. And since there is a limit to the number of godchildren whom a godfather can conscientiously care for, *compradazgo* at times becomes a mere formality.

The high infant-mortality rate of 187 for every 1,000 live births in 1900 had been effectively lowered to 53 by 1953 (compared with 29 for every 1,000 live births in the United States); but the decline has not been a steady one, and the rate was still as high as 143 per 1,000 in 1941. Women are only just beginning timidly to attend maternity centres set up in Madrid by U.N.I.C.E.F.[1] There is now a scheme afoot to make available milk-bottling facilities, under the auspices of the W.H.O., to supplement the powdered milk donated by the U.S.A. and given daily to two-and-a-half million children in Spain.

As, only a generation ago, the chances of a baby dying were almost one in five, one expects and finds the usual superstitions during pregnancy. Many believe in the connection between 'cravings' and the naevus mark (*antojos*), though the educated woman will dismiss such ideas as being pueblo women's tales. One does not, however, find the converse belief that pleasant impressions during pregnancy will have a beneficial effect on both the expectant mother and her baby, as was once apparently the case in the United States.[2]

In spite of the implied revolt against social mores, many women do not consider child-bearing to be their only duty and ideal. Though contraception and abortion are both strongly condemned by State and Church, on the grounds that a possible life is destroyed, both are evidently practised in the city. Information on these matters is not easily obtained; but the old woman with crude

---

[1] See UNESCO report E/ICEF/L642, August 26th, 1954, in which it is stated that approximately 10 per cent of pregnant women attending maternity centres in Madrid and Barcelona had some syphilitic condition. From this was drawn the quite unwarranted estimation that one in ten of the population at large had syphilis.

[2] See George G. Nathan and H. L. Mencken, *The American Credo*, New York, 1929, p. 109: 'if a woman about to become a mother plays the piano daily, her son will be born a Victor Herbert.'

implements or special concoctions (she is sometimes known as a *sabia*) and the fashionable doctor in his modern surgery will lend their illicit services, providing the right friends effect the introduction. Women whose husbands can afford to let them do so spend much of their time now in beauty-parlours or at their favourite hairdressers; and some of these, I was assured, cloak the activities of abortionists.

Illegitimacy still bears a heavy social stigma, but approximately six out of every 100 children are born out of wedlock. This is an average figure over a twenty-year period.[1] Under the short-lived constitution of 1931, illegitimate children were given legitimate status. In 1951, of the 7,546 women who entered maternity homes in Madrid 1,056 were unmarried and forty-two were widows. Nowadays, if the child is not legally recognized by the father (a more frequent occurrence here than in the pueblo) it will bear the name of the mother and, though baptized in the normal way, will experience a number of difficulties in later life such as being refused admittance to certain private schools. If recognized by the father, then the child will bear his name and receive all the ordinary rights. By no means do the parents always marry,[2] nor does the child always remain with the unmarried mother. When the grandparents are living, it is they who frequently care for and educate the child. In the same way, orphans are assimilated into the family circle by grandparents, and, in these cases, the bonds of godparenthood will also exert themselves.

Death emphasizes the sense of kinship and coherence of the kin group. One still finds the grandmother in black who daily studies the large obituary notices ringed with heavy black lines in the newspapers. For her it is a social duty, and she may be vexed to read of a 'private funeral', which she considers a modern impertinence. Apart from the *esquela* or obituary notice inserted in the press by the family, there often appears another inserted by the business or cultural entity on behalf of a late respected member. Whole pages, for five or six days, publicly express the mourning of

---

[1] The highest figures for this period are; 37,413 illegitimate births out of a total of 598,089 in 1944; 29,347 out of a total of 561,193 in 1951. See *Guía de la Iglesia en España*, Madrid, 1954.

[2] The consensual union or common-law type of marriage, so widespread in Latin America, is now rarely found in Spain.

colleagues or fellow artists if the dead man was a well-known figure; and subscriptions are quite often opened (but rarely pursued) to raise a public monument. When this type of person dies the balcony windows of his house are shuttered, and for nine days the half-open door mutely invites sympathizers to list their names within. Their action is later gratified by the receipt of a black-edged card from the widow. Relatives make their condolences in person and have usually been present for the last rites and at the *vela* or wake which follows. Burial next day at one of the cemeteries near the shrine of the city's patron San Isidro is attended only by the men; the women remain to 'accompany the immediate family in their grief'.

For a Spaniard making his will, the important part has always been the religious ceremony, namely the special mass and offering, the appointment of a guardian to keep alight the candles during the ceremony, the arrangements for distributing alms at his death, and so on. Only when all these conventions are complete is the testator tranquil; the actual details of the will are often a tiresome necessity to be gone into with the notary. A modern illustration of this personal defence of a man's own right to salvation was forcibly portrayed in the most successful play in the Spanish theatre since the Civil War—*La Muralla*, by Joaquín Calvo-Sotelo—which was produced in Madrid in 1954 and ran for an unprecedented length of time. It told the story of a man doomed to die who wished to make retribution for a past offence at great material cost to his family, and who fought unsuccessfully against 'the wall' of opposition set up by his kin.

It is still a common act of faith for relatives of a dying man to make (when the doctor has given up hope) promises of penance, such as offering candles or some silver object to the parish church; some even promise to walk barefoot to the Cerro do los Angeles shrine ten miles outside Madrid,[1] or to wear chains and carry a heavy cross in the Holy Week processions.

Fifty years ago, when wakes were *de rigueur*, the food and wine supplied were said to represent the sins of the deceased, which were

---

[1] Such a promise was made by my maid if the district council granted her a *piso* instead of the tumbledown shack her husband had built on the outskirts. She got her *piso*, but her husband prevented her from carrying out her promise because of her ill-health.

absolved by the act of consumption. The feeling of obligation to take part in the wake has weakened but it is still strong.[1] The older generation declare that they remember the *lloronas* or *plañideras*, professional women weepers keening at funerals in some of the villages of Madrid province before the Civil War. The number hired indicated the wealth and social status of the deceased. This never seems to have occurred in San Martín. Yet a man's rank may be measured even now by the degree of flamboyance of his funeral and the number (and rank) of mourners who walk behind the hearse.

All spinsters, and boys up to the age of 17 or 18, are buried in a white coffin, a symbol of their supposed innocence. Few people are buried under the civil rites—only fifty-four in 1952 out of a total of 15,249—and, where this occurs, the fact is glossed over in conversation or in the press. Much annoyance is caused by the official desire to disinter dead 'heroes' and re-bury them ceremonially elsewhere. A recent example is provided by the monstrous monument known as the Valley of the Fallen near El Escorial, in which it was proposed to re-bury the dead of the Civil War and, eventually, General Franco. Though burial rights were magnanimously extended to the fallen of the losing side, family protests were so violent that no further action was taken, and it now appears that General Franco remains the only candidate. Funeral processions in the city, which are always attended by at least three lugubriously chanting priests in their robes, and altar-boys swinging censers, hold up the traffic and disperse only at the end of parish limits; thus is signified the final control of the parish[2] over the mortal frame.

Custom, not Church or State, demands various grades of mourning according to the relationship with the deceased. Complete black is worn for one year in memory of a parent or close relative;

[1] One woman I knew accidentally received a black eye from the corner of the coffin as it was borne from the room. She explained it, only half in jest, as a last 'kick' from her first cousin for not having participated in the wake.

[2] A current popular saying even now is that 'he never had anywhere to drop dead'. The parish association, San Vicente de Paúl, does guarantee the needs of indigent families and acts as a burial-aid society like certain *cofradías* in Ramosierra; yet, in the city, this is a matter of shame for the surviving members of the families.

thereafter, men will wear merely a black tie, or a black strip on their lapel, while women will wear a sober grey dress for the three to six months of half-mourning (*medio luto*). During this time no public entertainments should be attended or formal invitations accepted, yet in the city this largely depends on the individual conscience, and is often relaxed, especially by the men, after a few months.

Old people guard these norms more meticulously, and a husband may wear black for the rest of his life when his wife dies, and vice versa. Black is worn habitually by many in the villages, since someone is always dying in the upper age groups of their large families. Younger people, in general, now tend to make only a token display of traditional mourning standards, though the two most conservative groups are the nobility and the very poor. Mourning is still, however, an external mark of family cohesion typified in a formal manifestation of grief.

On the first of November, All Saints' Day, the approaches to the cemeteries are crowded with stalls selling flowers, sweets or fritters, and the gaiety of the mourners in the street contrasts sharply with their respectful and sombre attitude in the graveyard. This is a special day for visiting the graves of deceased relatives although, throughout the year, alms, prayers and masses are offered to relieve their souls from suffering in Purgatory. In November, too, it has been the fashion in Madrid for the last fifty years or so to go to *Don Juan Tenorio*, a nineteenth-century play by Zorrilla. Don Juan, who has murdered the father of a girl he has recently ravished, is redeemed after death by the innocent love of one of his victims. In the sixteenth-century play on the same theme—*El Burlador de Sevilla*, by Tirso de Molina—Don Juan is condemned to hell fire. Most people know some of the more florid and melodramatic verses by heart. It is yet another indication of an ever-present preoccupation with the cult of death and mortal decay—'We are nobody', they say—so evident in their art and, therefore, in everyday life.

Death does give a melancholy edge, an urgency, to life, and folk songs are full of verses such as:

*Cada vez que considero*
*Que me tengo que morir,*

*Alzo los ojos y digo*
*'Mi Dios ¿por qué nací?'*[1]

But continued deliberation on the thought of death argues a thirst for immortality, a 'longed-for reality of eternal beatitude'. Even the funeral card bears a message from the dead: 'Do not lament my passing, those whom I have loved, for I rest with the Lord and I ask Him to reunite us all in Heaven.' Mourning practices are in fact designed to perfect and reinforce ties of human and supernatural love. Grief, therefore, is to be openly and dramatically expressed, not controlled by a tight-lipped reserve, for pure emotion in a sense bridges the gap between life and death. Brenan draws attention to the lack of 'religious' texts on graves in the Madrid cemeteries[2] which, for some reason, reminded him of pagan tombstones in Italy. Some of them are mere pathetic exclamations such as 'My Daughter!' If God is thought to be the great creator of everything, then it is logical to presume that only in Him can all things be perfectly reconciled. It was a Castilian mystic, Saint John of the Cross, who summed up this impatience for immortality in the phrase: 'I die of not dying.'

[1] Every time that I consider
That I must die,
I raise my eyes above and ask,
'My God, why was I born?'
[2] Gerald Brenan, *The Face of Spain*, London, 1950, p. 29.

# 5

## SOCIAL POSITION AND IDEALS

IN A PREVIOUS chapter I tried to link the pueblo idea of status with the concept of morality. Now, in dealing with urban status, I shall endeavour to show how it has become separated from ideal patterns of behaviour reflected in the family. In so doing, I shall again be concerned mainly with an analysis of ideal role which, in so far as it is embodied in overt behaviour, is the dynamic aspect of status.[1]

Why this concern for role here? In part, because a notable lack of works on social history[2] in Spain already hints at a national unconcern with merely social divisions. It is test enough to see the puzzled brow of a parishioner in San Martín when asked to place himself in a social class. Yet he does make certain distinctions in social rank by pointing to the role a man plays in life, and these distinctions can be followed up by means of the same criteria as were used in the pueblo. In this way I hope to plot not only a hierarchy of status groupings—again I have called them leaders, controllers and servers—but also the social distance between them, which reflects class consciousness.

The conventional division of urban communities into high, middle and low classes has undergone a change at the hands of modern sociologists. Both the Middletown[3] and the Yankee City[4] studies evolved hierarchies of six classes partly based on government statistics (themselves founded on arbitrary socio-economic classification) and partly on personal placings by the individuals

[1] See Ralph Linton, *The Cultural Background of Personality*, London, 1947, p. 50.

[2] Two possible contemporary exponents are Julio Caro Baroja and (the late) Doctor Marañon.

[3] R. S. and H. M. Lynd, *Middletown in Transition*, New York, 1937.

[4] W. Lloyd Warner and Paul S. Lunt, *The Status System of a Modern Community*, New Haven, 1942.

interviewed. Current market research in Britain favours five divisions. Not only has a points system[1] been devised as an index of the family social status, whereby possession of a refrigerator merits five points, but attitudes also are now measured statistically. The passion for fitting people into pigeon-holes grows with the search for working tools.

Yet these laudable attempts to evolve finely stratified hierarchies have more success in highly industrialized societies. In Spain, particularly, the lone research worker must trust to his sense and to the 'feel' of the community in which he has integrated himself. Spaniards are not willing subjects for research, and their governments are not usually disposed to allow it. The scene—so common in Britain and America—of a social scientist armed with a questionnaire, knocking at a door and engaging a not unwilling housewife in a lengthy interview, is quite unfamiliar as yet in Spain.

Let us first consider differences from the pueblo pattern found within family status as regards age and sex, and see how these affect the family in its dealings with the society as a whole. Life in the capital is a losing fight against anonymity, which the continued strength of the family units (often jammed cheek by jowl in tenement-style buildings) still does much to alleviate. Though not so sharply as in the pueblo, a person's role is nevertheless well defined.

A child has a role cast for him from the very start. A minor until 18, he remains under the authority of the head of the household legally until he is 21, morally until a later age depending on the personalities involved. The status of boys under 18, and women of all ages was clearly indicated in 1940 when for a period tobacco was rationed and its sale forbidden to them.

Children appear to be spoilt by doting parents, who endeavour to spend the maximum time possible with them and shower much obvious love on them. Yet most Spanish parents view with alarm what they would call the excessive liberty and folly of the 'free education' enjoyed by many a North American child. Bookshops do not sell tomes on 'How to bring up your son'; and Carnegie's best seller, *How to win Friends*, gathers dust on the shelves. Respect for his elders comes easily and naturally to the child, and so

[1] See F. S. Chapin, *Experimental Designs in Social Research*, London, 1947.

NON-INTERVENTION. 'After all, at first sight one doesn't know who is in the right!'

does his acceptance of a mutually helpful circle of kin as the true and only useful frame for life. Adolescence as a problem in Spain has not yet arisen in any marked form.

Nevertheless, a capital city which trebles its population in fifty years can also treble its vices. The growing permissiveness towards children is reflected in the widening rift between them and their parents, partially fostered, in some instances, by the intervening role of the family maid. One of the more potent reasons for this estrangement is a new status that the son (and to a lesser degree the daughter) acquires through the power of knowledge. In many cases this knowledge, if of an academic[1] nature, barely takes him beyond the stage of literacy, yet it is a stage his parents perhaps did not reach. The poorly-educated working youth, who has just mastered the art of reading, is quickly noticeable in buses and trains, finger to print and thoroughly engrossed in a paper-backed novel. Of recent years, it has often been a knowledge of languages, equipping a young man for a better job dealing with tourists or with the resident Americans, that has taken him into a different social world and salary scale. Or the parent-child status gap may be widened by that peculiarly sharp experience of city ways, to which the young adapt so much more rapidly.[2]

Though the adolescent delinquent as a member of a street-corner gang is not a marked feature of city life in Madrid this is not to say that he does not exist. Yet it is evident that there has been only a slight increase in adolescent crime in the last twenty years and that the important rise is amongst the 21-25 and 26–30 age-groups. It is at these ages that we meet the hooligan, a further indication of the arrested social development of the young

[1] The parents of college undergraduates are now often forced out of their living-rooms by the 'study bull session'. Bands of students who neither know how nor want to study alone 'invade, in teams, one house today, another tomorrow, with resulting damage to the household's stocks of oranges, coffee, cigarettes and cognac'. See the *New York Times*, June 27th, 1959.

[2] Consider, for example, the extraordinary number of *botones* (hotel or restaurant page-boys) who are employed as young as thirteen years of age; their work quickly gives them a worldly-wise experience lamented by their parents. Generally, one notices a greater sophistication among Spanish adolescents than, for instance, among similar age-grades in Britain.

male in the city. *Gamberro* is a new word which originated about 1955 and is now noted with frequency and alarm in the press. It is used to describe a vain and truculent bully, who originally began by venting his surplus energy and manliness in minor vandalism, or in blasphemy and sheer noise for its own sake. Of late, he has turned his unwelcome attentions to women, and aged or weaker men, annoying and sometimes maltreating them. Their activities—for hooligans are always found in groups—are known as *burradas* (literally, 'droves of asses', but the expression is applied also to stupid actions or sayings) and are really 'dares' which constitute a challenge to all kinds of authority. Although bitterly criticized, such conduct is encouraged by the ordinary citizen's disinclination to interfere actively in any unpleasant situation. The 'Teddy Boys' in Britain are an obvious parallel, but the *gamberro* is usually much older, is in no way distinguishable by special dress, and may belong to any social class; for example, the *señorito*, the son of well-to-do parents, is sometimes found in their ranks. Sanctions by public ridicule, as when local justices made them wear a placard and sweep the streets, have seemingly proved inadequate. Fines have merely raised the status of the budding *gamberro* to that of a veteran who now boasts of his clash with the authorities.

Passing from age groups to sex, we find that another deviation from the pueblo's ideal patterns of behaviour lies in the existence of prostitution and houses of assignation (*casas de cita*) in the urban parish. Article I of the government decree of March 4th, 1956, states: 'In line with the vigilance over the dignity of women, and in the interests of social morality, prostitution is hereby declared an illegal traffic.' Brothels and 'houses of tolerance' (in the sense of tolerating what cannot be approved) were to be closed under this decree all over Spain. Special protective measures under Article 447 of the Penal Code were also applied to women between the ages of 16 and 23.[1]

Whereas formerly the professional prostitute was noticeable only in bars or night clubs, especially in the Gran Vía area, since the decree she has also stationed herself at the darker side-street

---

[1] This is not the first time the municipality has intervened. Compare the formation of a brotherhood—La Ronda del Pecado Mortal—a kind of eighteenth-century Salvation Army.

corners in the parish. The girl, who also expects dinner from her client, generally appears at about 9 p.m.; later, she will try to catch the cinema and theatre crowds at about 1 a.m. She usually appears again between 4 and 5 a.m., when the cabarets close down. She is aided by the collaboration of the less scrupulous night-watchmen or taxi drivers, to whom she pays commission. The former gives her entry into the now illegal brothel or house of assignation, and the latter supplies the essential late-night transport to the more disreputable places of entertainment on the outskirts of the city. She appears to be an individualist: the systems of working syndicates, call-girls, or employer-pimps are not yet common. But to some extent she does depend on the good will of the nightclub proprietor for whom she may act as unofficial hostess, or on the owner of the bar to which she habitually brings custom.

Houses of assignation are not only used by the prostitute but are meeting points for clandestine lovers. Rooms are let by the hour or by the night, and the notice *Pension* on the door should be taken at times to mean bawdy rather than boarding house. The fact that they flourish[1] suggests that urban standards tolerate, if not condone, infractions of the moral code because of a protective anonymity impossible in the pueblo. It is one more illustration of the saying 'the law is obeyed but not fulfilled'—part of the covert reaction to authority. The *sereno* explained it by a shrug, adding: 'Life is difficult—one must live somehow.'

When discussing ideal types in the pueblo we saw that, as part of the cult of manliness, the female expects the male to be a light-hearted gallant in matters of sex provided he does not threaten the stability of the home. Here in the city a man finds opportunities denied him in the pueblo, although his boasts of conquests should be accepted lightly. Thus the status of women in general is lower, and the well-born 'mistress'—she is called 'a friend'—is discreetly accepted outside the home. The offensive insult *cabron* is used more indiscriminately (though the reaction to it is just as fierce), and the wittol—the husband who 'wears horns'—is a common object of scorn. In the pressing subway crowds the so-called 'Metro Romeo' is able furtively to take his fleeting pleasure. To a certain extent

[1] Of the twenty-six houses in one small street in the Luna-Pez area, two were accorded this title by the night-watchman, one of which had begun to operate since the decree.

these urban attitudes to sex explain the comparatively lenient view taken of venereal diseases,[1] cures for which are openly and largely announced on doctors' signs in the San Bernardo area. Tuberculosis, for instance, is regarded with rather more prejudice and fear.

Nevertheless, it would be wrong to assume a drastic difference from pueblo ideal patterns or, indeed, to regard the Madrilenian as specially libidinous—a fallacy which goes with the belief that the sun is sexually exciting. The man still accords the woman a chivalrous attention even when she is past child-bearing, and the prostitute or indiscreet mistress is regarded as a 'fallen woman' with much the same connotation as the word 'strumpet' or 'hussy' conjures up in English.

Marriage is still the desired vocation of all who do not feel the higher celibate calling of the Church. About one in 200 does in fact answer this latter call, which for some has a professional rather than a vocational ring. The avowed bachelor or spinster is, therefore, a social curiosity, and is made to feel that somehow a duty has been neglected. 'Las beatas', who surround the priest, are deemed to have failed in a double sense, for they lack the courage to join a nunnery.

To some extent, the teaching profession now provides an outlet for such women, because next to having children of one's own the best thing is the care of other people's.[2] Many have accepted this new role with relief; and women are now found in sole control of the pre-school and a few mixed classes. Legally on an equal status with men—their salary scales are in fact the same—they are usually denied advancement to higher educational appointments because of prejudice; only 170 such posts out of a total 3,079 in 1956 were held by women.[3] In general, a woman is still not accepted in public

---

[1] These affected 2·75 per cent of the population of Madrid in 1950. Compare the 0·25 per cent for Soria. See *Guía de la Iglesia en España*, Madrid, 1954. One suddenly becomes aware of the few homosexuals, too, in the city, where they congregate in particular bars, restaurants or studios. They are often referred to as 'those from the opposite sidewalk'.

[2] Hence also the universal-aunt type of spinster who often becomes a baby-sitter, chaperone and housekeeper all in one.

[3] Ninety per cent of the rural teaching staff in 1951–2 were women, and their numbers rose to 35,215 out of a total 60,637 in public primary schools. The only woman holding a university chair at present in Spain is the Professor of Pedagogic History in the University of Madrid in San

or governmental affairs and, in the few prominent places to which she has penetrated, her reception has been decidedly cool. Allowed to study for many careers (pharmacy is a popular one) on a level with men, the women complain that after they receive their degrees or diplomas opportunity is prevented from even tapping at their door.

It is not for us to judge whether or not the breakdown in prejudice will be accompanied by a breakdown in family life. But this is what the thinking man fears, quite apart from the competitive threat to his domain. Nevertheless, there are already outstanding women in the arts and professions; the invaluable secretary-typist and the laboratory assistant are firmly entrenched; female factory hands are cheaper to employ; and the attractions of the shop-girl and cafeteria waitress are manifest. Slowly but surely men are showing a greater if begrudging acceptance of the urban women in her not entirely new role. Women fought in the militia for the Republicans in 1936-8. Augustina de Aragón was the famous defender of Saragossa against the French, Saint Teresa was a leading mystic, and Spanish history is full of the energetic activities of queens and princesses. Yet it is still unusual to see a woman driving a car, and the even more uncommon sight of a girl stoutly managing a motor-scooter drew the indignant comment from a mature, educated man: 'What in the world are we coming to?'

Although women are supposedly not permitted by their menfolk to go out to work unless it is absolutely necessary to prevent hardship for the family, we find that about one in every seven women in Madrid is in fact gainfully employed. Yet the State will not grant a marriage loan to a girl unless she promises to give up working. There are, therefore, two types of women who continue to work after marriage. One (and she is in the minority) does not need the money but has an exaggerated sense of vocation or independence; the other needs the money for her family and has no choice. The husbands of both will be the butts of a neighbourly but unveiled criticism; the one because he has a wife who must be rather eccentric; the other, because of his shortcomings as a provider. Both criticisms reflect on the men's honour which is

Martín. See the report on Doña Maria de los Angeles Galino in the daily newspaper *Ya*, March 17th, 1957.

incapable of preserving their wives' ideal role (and, by extension, their sense of shame) intact.

A good wife who does not need to work but who is not blessed with children will be many times a godmother, and may dabble in charitable works under the direction of the parish church. Similarly, the flag-selling stalls of the Red Cross and the boards of orphan schools are graced by aristocratic or wealthy wives and spinsters, whose enforced leisure or lack of family ties drive them to seek a new status of their own, or a prestige which will add to that of their menfolk. In this way a man's status is raised by the institutionalized activities of his wife or immediate female kin.[1] Even so, a good wife and a good mother in the home is still the ideal; by the influence she wields there she makes up for her lowly status compared to the man.

The status of the family vis-à-vis others is largely judged on how it measures up to these ideal patterns which the more active role of the woman in the urban parish is obscuring. An emotional strain evidently takes its toll, as the rather higher figures for mental illnesses among women suggest. Yet strangely enough it is the family woman rather than the working girl who is most likely to commit suicide, according to the statistics. In the tangle of urban relationships there lies the vague feeling that those in a high social position are to be excused their indiscretions, whilst those in a low social position are not expected to know or act any better. Somewhere in the middle, therefore, with 'las beatas' at one extreme and respectable home-loving parents at the other, are those who would like to be considered guardians of the moral code. It reminds one of the lower-middle-class morality of Shaw's Doolittle.

Does pride of birth give us a clue to status? If I say that the hidalgo[2] and the *chulo*—the true Madrilenian—can and do meet

---

[1] A Spanish woman may also hand on the status of her nationality to a foreign husband, if he so desires. Many refugees during World War II took advantage of this; viz. *Civil Code*, Article 17.

[2] In 1956, there were 368 listed grandees, 249 of whom were living in Madrid. Approximately 2,300 others used some kind of noble title. See *Heráldica Guía de Sociedad*, Madrid, 1956. I use 'hidalgo' as a general word to incorporate all titled nobility. It is in fact the lowest in the status hierarchy of nobles; the highest are the grandees (dukes, marquis, counts) and between them come the *caballeros* who were at one time all members of the four principal knightly orders.

each other with a warmth and naturalness which would make a socialist sing, I merely draw attention to the distinction the Spaniard in general makes between personality and social position. The point is that they rarely do meet in this capital city, which provides a number of diverse social and professional environments claiming the interest and time of its various component groups.

Since the liberalist epoch of the Second Republic, the fortunes of the nobility have declined both materially and morally. Many tactfully shed their titles in 1931, swiftly if mistakenly relating the Spanish word *liberal* to the politically extreme left. Yet with the official revival of interest in a return of the monarchy, the aristocrat is once more associated in the popular mind with a future court circle, and with the power and patronage he will enjoy. In this sense, he is as much a typical figure in the Madrilenian scene as the *chulo*. But the bland faces of the monarchists who peer out from their casino-club windows of La Peña in the Gran Vía gaze on a younger generation[1] who demand from them more than just the social utility of their rank and a leisurely or sentimental interest in charitable works. Hence the recent consolidation of their privileged position by alliances[2] through marriage and politics with the wealthy and powerful, who on their side gain prestige.

Whilst only the dual surname of the man (the patronyms of the paternal and maternal grandparents) is used for all official purposes, as many as four surnames on the distaff side are quoted on admittance (through a *padrino* sponsor) to exclusive societies such as the military orders of Alcántara, Calatrava, Santiago and Montesa, or the noble order of the Golden Fleece. In the parish of San

[1] The association of the Falangists (at least in their own minds) with youth, the worker and a 'national revolution' has caused much uneasy public comment concerning them and the monarchists. See the daily newspaper *ABC*, March 1st, 1957.

[2] The nobility of Madrid are exclusively associated in the sixteenth-century corporation known as *Real Cuerpo de Hijosdalgo*. *Hijosdalgo* is the same as hidalgo, which literally means 'sons of something', i.e. landed property. All mayors of Madrid are now honorary members of this association and nobles' wives become *damas*. It should not be forgotten that the woman retains her patronym on marriage and passes this on to her children. Grandchildren thus have an equal claim to inheritance from both sets of grandparents. The woman may also pass on titles which are not specifically of the male line.

Martín, an ancient religious brotherhood of a militant nature known as *Archicofradía de María Santísima de las Mercedes* also demands multiple surnames of high rank as a condition of membership. Generally, the greater the preoccupation with one's genealogical tree shown by a meticulous use of multiple surnames, the more the person will merit the socially distinctive term *gente muy fina* or *gente muy bien*, i.e. 'very fine folk'. Where this prestige is linked with power and influence (which automatically brings wealth), a further distinction is made in the popular idiom by describing them as *gente de categoría*, i.e. people of rank.

These points are all exemplified in the case of the present Chief of State. Francisco Franco Bahamonde is a man of humble parentage from Galicia whose brilliant military career quickly made him the youngest general in the army. He has no son, but he married his only daughter to a marquis, and now has one grandson and two grandaughters. In order to preserve the name of Franco a special decree was passed in the Cortes. The grandson is now named, first, after his maternal grandfather and, secondly, after his father and paternal grandfather, a reversal of the normal procedure which is regarded with some amusement in many circles.[1]

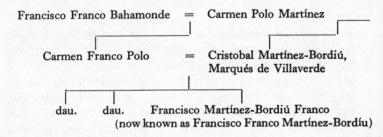

Francisco Franco Bahamonde  =  Carmen Polo Martínez

Carmen Franco Polo  =  Cristobal Martínez-Bordiú, Marqués de Villaverde

dau.    dau.    Francisco Martínez-Bordiú Franco
(now known as Francisco Franco Martínez-Bordíu)

*Gente fina* also set the fashions in dress, speech and mode of living in the capital and, by extension, in the provincial cities. Their sons are called *señorito*, respectfully by the servants and scornfully by the general public if they are idle and conspicuously manifest their freedom from financial care. Disdain for menial labour and for earning a living has long been proverbial among

[1] General Franco has also created titles which are not recognized by the diehard monarchists, and are sometimes pointedly not used by the recipient.

well-born Castilians. Yet perhaps one of the greatest social changes in the last twenty years is the new willingness of the young *señorito*, freshly graduated from law school, to pay his own way on visits abroad by washing dishes and the like. *Gente fina* and people of rank go to their country estates at week-ends in their chauffeur-driven cars, and regularly take a summer vacation, perhaps at Biarritz or San Sebastian—the summer seat of the government. They are the people to whom tradesmen deliver, and on whom the artisans and professional class, such as the barber, the tailor, the doctor, the lawyer and sometimes the priest, are summoned to attend at home. Others who try to ape their fashions or manners, and thus falsely assume their social status, will incur the derogatory use of the word 'snob' (now incorporated directly into Spanish) or the critical adjective *cursi* (mannered) because of the airs they adopt.

In his own inimitable way, the *chulo* is also an aristocrat, for he is the traditional picaresque character from the low quarters of Madrid, a true *hijo* or son of Madrid. As such, he owes allegiance only to his family and to his locality, unlike the hidalgo who may not have been born in Madrid and has wider loyalties and responsibilities. His typical dress, which died out at the turn of the century, was something like that of the London Cockney: narrow trousers and short tight coat, a cap or bowler, and a 'choker' scarf. Like the costume of the Pearly Kings, it is still worn at local fairs, and even at smart fancy-dress balls by such as hidalgos. The *chulo's* shuffling walk and harshly enunciated slang challenge the world to question his claim to the title of *castizo* (from *casto*, pure), or pure-blooded Madrilenian. By no means does he speak the purest Castilian, but he injects a special waggishness into his speech which evokes admiration and has the power to produce laughter; in other words, he has *gracía*. Quick-witted, knavish and artful, sharp to jest and to anger, he is the natural successor to Goya's *majo* or *manolo*[1] whose feminine counterpart worked in the cigarette factories of old.

---

[1] See Mesonero Romanos, op. cit., for a full description of this type. *Majo* is still much used as a complimentary adjective meaning 'spruce' or 'handsome'. It was the *manolo*, in nineteenth-century costume largely copied from the Andalusian, who carried a ready knife in his waist-band and was notorious for his wild arrogance, illiteracy and antipathy towards all that was not of his locality and habit.

Though the *chulo* has become something of a music-hall character, the word lives on in popular parlance. Once carrying prestige, it now often has a derogatory and unpleasant ring (apart from its alternative meaning of 'pimp') and may stamp a man as vulgar and cheaply arrogant in his behaviour. When applied to the man who imagines himself to be a 'masher', it implies that he is also shameless. If not employed jokingly, therefore, it can be a cutting insult.

The importance of the *chulo* lies in his special link with the locality in Madrid. Galicians, Basques and Catalan migrants preserve their regional identity to a much greater extent than the others, and pass their strong sense of separatism on to their children. They keep firm the ties with their natal homelands, which they refer to as 'my land' or 'my village', and rarely attempt to become *castizo* even in the third generation. Migrants from other regions tend to lose themselves in the personality of the city and—like the *chulos*—adopt its norms and its pride for their own.

Nevertheless, from this short comparison of the hidalgo and the *chulo* we can see that their peculiarities of character and status do not arise so much from the fact that they are found in Madrid, as from the fact that they are both Castilian. They are both *arrogante*, which does not carry the same pejorative value as 'arrogant' in English; a closer translation would be 'spirited'. Ideally, both are 'honourable' types, for it is manliness which afterwards justifies an impetuous action, whereas honour provides virtuous grounds beforehand for performing it. Hidalgo and *chulo* are conservative and complementary characters; the idealism of Don Quixote is matched by the proverbial realism of Sancho.

One is not surprised to find that they collaborated in 1520 as *comuneros* — revolutionary councils formed to protect traditional rights against the encroachments of Carlos I; three streets bear the names of the martyrs to this day. Similarly, to meet another external threat, they combined in 1808 against the French in the streets of Madrid.

Occupation and wealth are two very important criteria when considering status in the Spanish urban setting, for they provide a measurement largely independent of that of the family. They are, however, less valuable as general indices of class when the two are not necessarily and intimately correlated. At the highest level *los gordos*—the 'fat' ones, i.e. the wealthy and influential— cannot be easily defined by profession or occupation, for they own to many and various. Lower down the scale, syndicalism has done much to fix salary and wage scales for recognized professions and occupations, but the delineation of socio-economic groups in the labour force as a statistical concept has as yet hardly developed. A glance at the official classification for Madrid will show the grouping together of allied professions with little regard to a scheme of class hierarchy; engineers are lumped together with mechanics, skilled manual craftsmen with labourers, truck drivers with aircraft pilots. Moreover, the issue is confused by the common plurality of occupation, which constitutes a double or even treble status rating for the individual concerned. Some indication of the man's own estimation of these is apparent in his declared choice out of the two or three occupations he pursues. For example, a man is an Army captain first and a restaurant-owner second, for though his military duties may be only part-time, he feels they give him a higher prestige. Again, a civil servant is a *funcionario*, who supplements his income in the evenings as a commission agent. A reversal of this feeling may occur where the incomes from the two occupations are greatly disparate. In general, however, permanency of tenure, a regular income and a pension scheme are what the man most earnestly seeks. These are all to be found in some form of government employment, and for these reasons the sinecure is as highly desirable as it is common, since it also allows much freedom of movement. As long as an appearance is made from time to time, especially as pay day draws near, there is little danger of losing the post, particularly if it has been obtained through patronage or nepotism. Up to ten years' leave of absence may be given in some lower-grade positions.

A further general distinction might be drawn between the labourer who draws a daily wage (*jornal*) and the worker who is paid a monthly salary (*sueldo*), but the class-consciousness that exists between the factory hand and the white-collar worker in Britain could not be assumed in Spain.

Social divisions in this 'open-class' society seem to depend less on occupation and on function than on the principle of caste. By this I mean the principle of restricting certain jobs to the 'right' people, as well as designating status on the basis of birth, and circumscribing social contact between different groups the members of which tend to marry among themselves.[1] This is surely a feature of any society where a highly-developed system of patronage creates exclusive spheres of influence. It is an aristocratic principle, and the traditional preoccupation with a sense of honour does much to maintain it. To describe how these spheres of influence interact would be a study in itself, but certain institutionalized attitudes between broader divisions of society do reflect a type of class-consciousness.

From the survey given in preceding chapters a three-fold division of society again most easily suggests itself, as it did in the pueblo. Some might object that this is merely the conventional division of classes under another guise; but the terms 'leading', 'controlling' and 'serving' do more adequately express the existing corporate class-consciousness. In the following table I single out only certain roles and occupations, some of which have already been discussed:

*Leaders:*    The Party Chief. The Monk. The Hidalgo. The Army General.

*Controllers:*  The Lawyer. The Priest. The Doctor. The Banker. The *Técnico*. The Rentier. The Civil Servant. The Teacher.

*Servers:*    The Policeman. The *Sereno*. The Porter. The Street-Vendor. The Messenger. The Maid. The *Chulo*.

The list is by no means complete, nor can these broad divisions serve as more than a mere guide to social class as such. For instance, the controllers are themselves split into separate strata; some play a passive rather than an active controlling role.

Outstanding among the leaders is the Army General, because of the special part he has played during the last hundred years in changing his country's destinies. A peculiar admixture of soldier and saint in the Castilian character produced the Cid, the Grand Captains, the conquistador, the mystic Saint John of the Cross,

---

[1] See R. M. MacIver and C. M. Page, *Society*, London, 1949, p. 358, for a discussion of the caste principle in an open-class society.

and the aggressive Dominican, Las Casas. The impassioned monk-leaders of popular movements, the generals who are king-makers, and perhaps the guerillas, are more modern examples. It should not be forgotten that Isabella was expelled and the Bourbon dynasty terminated in 1808 by Generals Prim and Serrano; that it was a General—Martinez Campos—who restored the dynasty in 1874; and that the two most powerful figures of this century—Primo de Rivera and Franco—have both been Generals of the Army. It is the Army which is said now to be the real representative of public opinion and the real repository of sovereign power.[1]

Political fortunes do not concern us here, but we cannot ignore the claim that the old *Juntas de Defensa*, composed of Army officers, sprang in the main from the so-called Liberal middle class of the last century, many of whom were revolutionary in spirit. This certainly accords with the view held of them now by the 'fine folk', while the minor ranks evidently do not figure high in the social scale. Yet both the military politician (the essence of heroic patriotism) and the monk (the educator and confessor) stand out in the society, for they represent solid social institutions, national in scope, amongst a people who tend to resist their growth beyond the local level.

All members of the leading group command an elevated status, for entry into the group depends on the power and influence (and, consequently, wealth) that one can wield. They are those most likely to effect changes in the social, political, economic and religious structure of the whole country. They are the envied, the 'estimable folk'. And everyone wants to be a *jefe* or chief: the love of pompous titles, the continuous exchange of courtesies, the fondness for uniforms—all reveal this clearly. So it is the desire of members from all other groups to associate themselves in some way with a leader-patron and benefit from his favouritism. Such are the obligations of patronage that often it is not so much a question of selecting the right man for a job as of having a job for the right man.

Amongst the controllers, it is evident at once that in the upper strata the social distance between the lawyer and his client, the priest and the faithful, the doctor and his patient, is basically much

[1] See Sir George Young, *The New Spain*, London, 1953, p. 69.

greater than it would be in the pueblo. These are highly regarded not only because they hold monopolies of essential services and thus control the destinies and welfare of others, but also because of their ability to mix freely with the leaders. It is common enough in countries where industrial and commercial development has been slow for those achieving higher education to show a preference for studying law. This preference in Spain goes with a general litigiousness at all levels—a corollary of the mutual distrust prevailing in a highly competitive society. Though it would be impossible for all those who study law to practise it, the dilatory pace of legal proceedings ensures that many are permanently employed in their profession, and it is a commonplace point of honour to refer to 'my lawyer'.

Similarly, in a 'shoestring' economy where ambitions greatly outrun means to fulfil them, the banker plays a specially important role, commanding all the respect due to the power implied by his control of wealth. For wealth enables a man to be idle and generous (not only in judicious charitable donations)[1] and thus win social esteem. It also inevitably leads to the acquisition of property and the ability to live entirely from rents, which is everyone's dream.

Again, under the pressure of increasing industrialization, engineers, architects and high-grade *técnicos* enjoy a status which is mocked, but perhaps envied, by those engaged in the liberal and fine arts. Multitudinous academies and institutes turn out hundreds of other *peritos*, or so-called experts, who are less concerned with their technical professions than with the added prestige and income that their titles will afford them. Whilst others who have studied for a career at a university are automatically granted an elevated rank, only those who apply it to achieve a position of influence and wealth can command general respect; for only then do they fulfil a controlling or leading role in the community. Students, marginal to both groups, demonstrate their impotence by their public acts of rebelliousness. Universities are ever the home of lost causes, and a lecturer's salary is rarely more than that of a garage mechanic.

Many educated Spaniards bemoan the lack of solid middle-class

[1] See the criticism of the daily religious practice but lack of real charity amongst the wealthy, by the Bishop of Saragossa, quoted in the *Universe*, March 21st, 1958.

consciousness of the sort found in northern Europe. Various attempts have in fact been made in the past by the monarchy to offset the power of the nobles and the Church by encouraging the rise of a lettered middle class.[1] Under the recognition of the strains on the economy during the last fifty years, what I shall call the intermediate controlling group has itself been split. The upper strata, which include the newly rich (such as the import-export merchants), increasingly tend to imitate the nobility and seek to ally themselves to them. The lower strata, overwhelmed by the unequal struggle against the rise in prices, and the desperate need to keep up appearances, are reduced to a standard of living sometimes below that of an agricultural labourer.

A case in point is that of the minor civil servant or chief clerk known as *jefe de negociado*. He is the one who must wear a tie, appear at Mass with his family, and at all costs give his daughter a white wedding in the proper style. The modest businessman whose shop is being swallowed up by the giant store, and the teacher whose pupils become prosperous, are similar examples of people who feel they have a certain position to maintain and are reduced to telling lies about the summer holiday they could not afford. Their personal tragedy is that they are maladjusted to the social structure, and are losing their position of control over the destinies of others. Their economic position is no longer commensurate with their status, and their influence wanes. For those who are not prospering must necessarily keep up the appearance of being richer than they are, though few will categorically admit to being rich. There is a general trait in the national character at all levels which demands a certain care in understating one's resources. It is a form of propitiatory understatement also found in the pueblo, a sense of being much at the mercy of the supernatural, exposed to one's neighbours' envy, and therefore vulnerable. Anthropologists will be familiar with this attitude in many primitive societies, too. Extreme divisions of wealth only add to the corporate class-consciousness at either end of the scale.

[1] The seventeenth century divisions of townships into *abolengo* and *realengo*, and the *golillas* (those who wore the ruff) were evidence of this. In the nineteenth century they wore the Prince Albert type of frock coat and were known as *gente de levita*, implying that they were 'respectable folk'.

The servers are those most likely to be referred to by other groups as *la gente ordinaria* ('common folk'), or as 'low class'. Many of them are recently-arrived migrants from the country districts, who find it difficult to slough off their pueblo manners and withstand the jibes of the true Madrilenian. Controllers and leaders recognize, however, that servers provide essential if menial services to the community; it is, after all, the dustman who follows the ambassadorial procession, and unskilled labour in the city is at a premium. These are the men who in the Pez area trudge through the streets to work in the early morning, whose pay (spent mostly on food) is by the day, and whose budgets are invariably strained.

In this urban society where honour still plays so vital a role the only really casteless individual is the gypsy who, to the caste-conscious *chulo* of Madrid, is a shameless foreigner.

Yet, occupying a marginal position in the social structure approaching the realm of the untouchable in all senses of the word, is the professional beggar. His physical[1] or social deformities have driven him beyond the stage of possible reintegration in society. Unlike the unemployed worker, he need no longer struggle to keep up appearances. In a sense he is lost to the community, for he has become isolated from any intimate contact with either leaders, controllers or servers. Socially immobile, unqualified for social security benefits, patronless and frequently cut off from ordinary family relationships and a supporting kin group, he can meet others only with the social gap of charity yawning between them. Yet, although he no longer fulfils a useful function in the modern urban setting, his presence, like that of the rich, is accepted as a necessary fact; he is simply a *desgraciado*—a 'de-graced' person, a hapless wretch.

Everyone stoutly maintains that poverty in itself brings no disgrace, and there is a manifest pride in the beggar who says: 'I am a poor man,[2] yes, but decent and honourable like others'. By this he means that he has not reduced himself to the exhibitionism

[1] Physical deformity alone need not be a handicap to steady employment. Many blind people sell lottery tickets at street corners, and I know of one boy with two hooks for hands who runs a newspaper kiosk in the Gran Vía.

[2] There is a significant difference between 'I am poor' (*Soy pobre*), and 'I am a poor man' (*Soy un pobre*); the latter would only be used by a beggar.

of the sleeve-plucking and whining 'shameless' beggar; for even among beggars there is some hierarchy of status depending largely on the presence or absence of honour. Sardonic but un-cringing, he never deigns to sing, sell matches or offer any service (as does his northern European counterpart) for the charity he expects by right. Hence his traditional plea, 'Alms for the love of God!' was customarily answered, 'Forgive me, brother!' by the almsgiver, for one could never be too sure that one day the positions might not be reversed. The modern beggar uses the same plea with a certain dignity, but perhaps with a diminishing confidence in his once institutionalized role. He salutes a giver with the words 'May God repay you!' but his pleas are now often impatiently brushed aside. Moreover, the city police carefully remove him from the more fashionable streets in the parish—away from the view of the curious but more easily shocked foreign tourist.

Even so, officialdom recognizes the shred of honour retained by the beggar (which keeps him just within the social structure) by the distinction it makes in the term *pobres de solemnidad*, i.e. poor people in real distress, and the special *hospitales* or almshouses it maintains for them.

It may be a subconscious sense of solidarity with the poor, common enough in mediaeval times,[1] that leads the aristocracy to aid them, provided they are poor but also honest. Looked at from another viewpoint, the poor provide an ever-handy means to a rich man's salvation. The parish organization known as 'The Spanish Action for the Cultured Word and Good Customs of Madrid' was founded in 1916 on the lines of a religious brotherhood to campaign against the rash of blasphemy; in 1930 its function changed to that of social welfare, and it was extended all over the city. But this was evidently not socialist enough to prevent the director from being jailed by the Republicans during the Civil War that followed. Among its active patrons on the board are members of the Bourbon royal family; and duchesses and countesses hand out clothes and toys at Christmas to those armed with the appropriate certificates from the parish priest. In the same way, it provides clothes for the slums and prisons throughout the year, and sponsors 'Cam-

[1] Princes washed the feet of beggars and frolicked hand in hand with paupers in the universal Dance of Death. See Pierre Schneider's, 'The Minimum Man', in the *Listener*, December 8th, 1955.

paigns for Kindness' and free night-schools for the working poor.
A reformative element and a certain missionary zeal are always
present in these dealings with the poor. Even prisoners can earn
remission of their dramatically long sentences and support their
families by work in the jails. Those active in this type of charitable
works are usually leaders, whereas membership of the parish church
associations is made up largely from among the controllers.

Can further indication of status be given by forms of speech?
This poses a difficult problem. Nicknames, so common in the
pueblo, lose their force outside the kin or work group in the
anonymity of city life, for they are only effective where common
ties are recognized; but the diminutive and affectionate form of the
Christian name is general. Again, the definite article plus the
Christian name is enough to describe someone of a certain notoriety
in the street area; but, among the common folk, it is usually linked
with the man's profession or some physical characteristic to make it
clearer—for instance, Pepe the shoemaker. Politicians, however,
are natural targets for widely-known and often uncomplimentary
nicknames, which are at once a form of social satire and a definition of status. A more harmless example is 'El Cuñadísimo' ('the
super brother-in-lawman') applied to Serrano Suñer, General
Franco's brother-in-law, when, as Foreign Minister just after the
Civil War, his influence was powerful.

As terms of social distinction in speech, *Don* and *Señor* are
widely used. The general pattern of respect which underlies them
in the pueblo is valid also in Madrid, but the use of the terms is
more liberal. Most employers or superiors are called either *Señor*,
or 'Don Antonio', 'Don José' etc., and the formality of diverse,
non-intimate relationships in the urban setting demands their
constant employment according to the social distance implied.
(For instance, my porter called me 'Don Michael'—pronounced
phonetically—but in the pueblo I merited neither *Don* nor *Señor*.)

In the same way, the use of the respectful third person is supposed to be the rule rather than the exception that it is in the
pueblo. This is not true of the young, however: some say that
they must know each other quite well nowadays before they learn
each other's surnames. Moreover, the intimate second person is
studiously utilized by the priest preaching to his flock and by the
Party leader exhorting his followers. In this sense it establishes

a closer contact, and God is thus addressed in prayers. But when it is used by employers to their workers, by elders to youths, by the *señorito* to the taxi-driver or beggar, or when it accompanies an insult, it becomes the obverse side of a flaunted superiority.

The insult is an essential by-product of the city, where manners become separated from morality, and indifference rules. The comparative absence of proverbs and adages—so common in the pueblo—is matched by the frequency of the rumour and of direct abuse aimed mostly at the parentage or inhumanity of the recipient. Such terms as 'imbecile', 'idiot', 'animal', 'clown', 'beast', are common references either violently abusive or, of course, at times intimately affectionate. Their force is much greater than their English translation suggests, as their florid use by taxi-drivers indicates. Uglier insults involving parentage are used only by the 'common folk' (or so one is led to believe) until tempers fray and rank is forgotten. Gossip becomes rumour in the city, and abusive terms used about, rather than to, a person mainly concern sexual indiscretion; the wanton will be described as 'mad' or 'a so-and-so' (*fulana*), both words heavily censurable. Frequent insertion of the diminutive will often, however, tone down an ironic saying or expletive.

Conversely, urbanity favours the weighty courtesy and the sesquipedalian phrase in which both government decrees and football reports alike abound. It goes with the constant handshaking amongst all classes and the chivalrous handkissing of married ladies by the socially conscious male. The *piropo* or compliment paid to the female sex is not unwelcome to any woman, when charmingly put, even in the main street; so that '¡olé tu madre!' (literally 'Well done, your mother!') is the highest possible flattery, for it is a compliment to the mother as well for producing such a beautiful creature. On the other hand, urbanity here does not lend itself to euphemistic language such as 'noctician' for night-watchman or 'sanitary engineer' for dustman; the sense of reality is too sharp for that. The flow of formality must be viewed as a protective cloak for hesitancy in action and spontaneity in emotion, not as a reasoned expression of calculated thought. It is common politeness which makes a man offer an onlooker his food before eating, yet even this once general formula is now being abandoned by leaders and controllers. These groups increasingly tend towards new fashions in speech which are perhaps more urbane than humane, and are typified in the bored and mannered language of the *señorito*.

It is seemingly a paradox that the spirit of individualism does not extend to dress and appearance. Attention was drawn earlier to the extreme conformity in this respect born of a fear of ridicule, and of censure implying ill-breeding.[1] This feeling consequently requires dressing down to an inoffensive sobriety,[2] which is considered good taste. It is apparently stronger among the young, for it was they (not the elders) who, at a certain ambassadorial ball, curtly disapproved of their parents capering about in fancy hats and false beards.

Servers show an inclination for heavy stripes in their suits, and among them a man might consider it the height of fashion to wear a dinner-jacket to his wedding; leaders, on the other hand, would always wear morning dress, as would most controllers. There is no group like the A class of British market research who can afford to dress shabbily. A fine appearance is essential at all times and at all levels. Only a manual labourer walks about in his shirtsleeves, and even he must put on a jacket to enter the cinema; for him, of course there would be a distinction between his working dress and his 'walking-out' suit.

Men never wear bowlers or carry rolled umbrellas, rarely wear caps (though those fresh from the pueblo might wear a beret), and only carry sticks if they are lame or blind. That once aristocratic symbol of bishops and kings, the glove, is worn by the humblest soldier and Customs official. A generation ago only actors, priests and bullfighters regularly shaved, and these were considered 'common folk'. Now, a beard is a Bohemian eccentricity, and actors, priests and bullfighters are perhaps the most flamboyant characters in the Spanish scene, accepted even by 'fine folk'. A carefully-groomed air is facilitated by the tailored suits and hand-

---

[1] This was the cause of a successful revolt in the city during the reign of Carlos III whose Italian minister, Squilache, tried to force a new dress on to the population by sending constables and an attendant tailor to pursue objectors in the streets. See Sáinz de Robles, op. cit.

[2] Young men do demonstrate their personality by covering their new motor-scooters in emblems and flags, whilst the older, more important, members of the leading group fly their authority on the bonnets of their official cars.

made shirts (which are not luxuries) with tasteful monograms at the chest; but this is intended for outdoor display.[1] Within the house comfort is the rule and, as the summer heat develops, modesty is slowly jettisoned until the pyjama stage is reached.

The wiles of women ensure a greater variety in appearance, but this is at all times governed by a becoming modesty appropriate to their sex. It certainly involves no shapelessness in dress, except among those wearing the mauve of the penitent. But good taste ensures that no woman would appear in public in trousers, for example, unless she were bound for an excursion to the mountains. Every church porch bears a notice entitled 'Norms of Christian Modesty' giving explicit instructions on the proper form of dress to be worn in church, even for girls up to the age of ten. Mantillas are now reserved for formal church ceremonies, but shawls are frequently worn as a daily garment, especially by the poor. In general, women do not slavishly follow fashions from abroad. Maids may try to imitate their mistresses in matters of dress, but a *marquesa* will dress up like her maid if she wants to look smart. Long and meticulous is the preparation for the *paseo* in the evening, when the woman displays herself; for she, too, must always present a 'fine' appearance.

[1] Its apogee was reached by the eighteenth-century *petimetre* or fop, under French influence.

# 6

## LEISURE

AT ALL TIMES in the urban parish there is a higher proportion of individuals at leisure than in the pueblo, where leisure is generally more strictly regulated and becomes the concern of the whole community. In the city ephemeral fashion, etiquette and convention influence uses of leisure which, in the village, tend to be dictated by unchanging custom. Moreover, entertainment in the parish of San Martín is fast becoming a commodity, whereas it is still largely an individual activity in Ramosierra.

With these three differences in mind, let us examine what the urban parishioner does in such time as is not taken up by the demands of business, occupation or mere hurry. I shall first sketch the more traditional leisure patterns, and then trace the effect on them of modern invention and the media of mass communication. Within this framework I shall make a distinction between *active* leisure, wherein people provide or join in amusement of their own making, and *passive* leisure, wherein they watch, listen to, or read about entertainment which is provided for them.

A Madrilenian in London for the first time shivers a little at the unfriendly climate and is amazed at the purposeful bent of the few people he sees about in the evenings. 'There is no life in your streets,' he complains. This is not to say that he depends on the activities of others for his amusement, except to the extent that he relishes an audience. His leisure is not planned but spontaneous, and relies on the moving pattern of ordinary life. He has little time, in general, for the educative use of leisure, so that the useful hobby or purely intellectual pastime is not widespread in Madrid. Why should he 'do it himself' when the highly fractionalized economy provides an army of people who will do it for him more cheaply and efficiently? Moreover the ties of family life are not irksome bonds to be broken at the slightest opportunity.

Simmel sees 'a Spanish pride and contempt for labour developed from the fact that for a long time they had the subjugated Moors for their labourers.'[1] But idleness should be distinguished from mere indolence; there is no air of fatigue but, rather, a whole-hearted vitality in the parishioner's use of his leisure hours. He makes a firm distinction between the routine drudgery of earning a living and h s spare time. But a rigid punctuality (except for bullfights and football or other matches) is foreign to an imaginative and spontaneous character much given to experiment. Although every man wears a watch he is not governed by it. 'We are not trains,' he says.

This attitude is illustrated by his lack of bustle when walking—he frequently stops to emphasize a topic graphically; and by the innate punctilio with which a Spaniard accompanies his guest on his departure to at least the corner of the street. Later, during the endless and stately procession up and down the Gran Vía or Calle Serrano[2] between 7 and 9 p.m., people look at each other rather than at the shopwindows. Their stroll is punctuated by time-old salutes of 'Go with God!' Or they halt, embrace and chatter with much animation. The *paseo* is essentially a pre-courting procedure and a training in deportment, so that there is a settled, even melancholy, air about the older married folk who watch indulgently from the many cafés dotting the route.[3] Life inside the café however has long been the prerogative of the more mature man. The *tertulia* or evening coterie is a substitute for the exclusive club. It became fashionable in the seventeenth century when chocolate or sherbet were drunk instead of the coffee and cognac of to-day, and recitals of poetry or of German or Italian music were the vogue. From private houses it spread to the old glass-walled cafés, and with it spread political intrigue. But the 'café politician' is

[1] Georg Simmel, 'Superiority and Subordination as a Subject Matter of Sociology', in the *American Journal of Sociology*, Vol. II, pp. 1896–7.

[2] The Gran Vía is gradually replacing the old *paseos* in Alcalá, Recoletos and the Prado. It is the haunt of the newly-rich, the tourist and the busy professional class; Calle Serrano is the favoured spot for the *señorito* and the fine folks' daughters who now casually smoke and drink wine at the elegant outdoor café tables.

[3] In 1950 there were approximately 1,500 taverns and over 1,000 cafés in Madrid.

now as harmless as his counterpart in a British saloon bar, and a good deal less politically minded.

In these cafés cliques were formed, perpetuating themselves as professional rather than cultural groupings. Today, a budding or successful artist, actor or writer must be looked for in the Café Gijón. The walls of the Café Varela in the Santo Domingo area are plastered with the poet-clients' favourite verses. Bullfighters discuss their next appearance in another café, and even some of the brotherhood of San Roque from Ramosierra, resident in Madrid, meet on Sunday mornings in their chosen café. On Sunday afternoons, however, all the cafés are crowded with parents and children eating cakes which they may have brought with them from home. Their large ante-rooms are often used for wedding receptions or for the many luncheons given in honour of public figures. The café is, therefore, a social necessity in the main streets and squares where, seated in the shade in summer or on upholstered couches in winter, friends can be met, business discussed, and the world passed in review.

The *tasca* or tavern, each with its regular clientele, is much more the haunt of the server, and is found in side streets. It has no divisions reflecting class structure, like the various bars in an English public house. Taverns usually bear the owner's name, and if he or the barman is a migrant, sometimes act as centres for provincial news and gossip. A 'no-treating' rule is tacitly recognized; but a man may buy another wine after invitation, or pay for a round on the result of such games as *chino* (guessing the number of coins in the hands of the group), *mus* (a fast game of bluff with Spanish playing cards), dominoes or dice. Tipping is unusual, but the few coins given to individual waiters or barmen are put in the *bote* or communal staff box. The serving of wines and aperitifs is conducted at a furious and skilful rate during rush periods, and business goes on until the small hours of the morning. But drunkenness is unusual, and disorderly behaviour rarer still, except perhaps in the 'low quarters'. Overt aggression as a means of resolving arguments is not common. Spaniards are quick to anger but slow to fight, although this is due to no fear for personal safety. Most of the taverns now provide a small dining-room and a full kitchen service at economical prices, and it is to those which acquire a certain reputation for well-cooked food that occasionally the wives of the controllers (and less frequently, the wives of leaders) are now brought for 'atmosphere'. Before 1936 no woman, except the lowest type of harlot, was ever seen in a tavern.

There is little or no entertaining in the home and more leisure than ever is now spent out of doors, so that the family may only meet as a group at meal-times in the home, which is often more like a private hotel or dormitory. A curious effect of this and of the new estrangement from children has been to drive the older parents (especially of the leading and controlling groups) into going about in bands. Whereas a man dutifully but sporadically took his wife out to a theatre or café in the past, they may now go out regularly on Saturday evenings to dine, a habit almost un-heard of before the Civil War. At one time cafés were full of taci-turn, elderly couples seated alone—the husband glancing enviously at the men's heated discussion groups, the wife eyeing a courting couple in the corner. But it is now not uncommon to find six or eight married men and women in a party. Their common tie is that of age and friendship, though some of the women may be related. On this regular Saturday outing they are dedicated to enjoying themselves and to spending money which, in the past, they would have religiously saved for their children. There is an oddly nervous, even melancholy, air to the somewhat febrile enjoyment mani-fested by these ageing, portly groups during their weekly round of pleasure, as they drink freely in their chosen café and then surge on to a cabaret or, at dawn, to another tavern in the 'low quarters'. One may overhear them in the days that follow animatedly reliving their night out with their intimates. Writers in the newspapers lament the decline of filial love and respect on the part of much occupied children, which (they imply) is responsible for these bands of lonely parents.[1]

Tourists also are discovering the charms of the *tasca*, and the locals regard this foreign invasion with somewhat ill-disguised resentment. Thus, as the premises and prices of 'Casa Manolo' or 'Casa Pepe' become modernized, the erstwhile regulars move away into the backwaters of the poorer Pez area.

The cafeteria with its chrome fittings, strip lighting and Ameri-can name, has mushroomed in the main streets since the arrival

[1] See Antonio Díaz Cañabate and Manuel Halcón in the daily news-paper *ABC*, July 12th, 1957 and July 19th, 1957.

of the American base workers in 1952. It attracts young people to its stools, and the courting couple or modern-minded family to its discreet back tables. Here, too, tourists and resident Americans flock in droves, for it supplies the drinks and dishes they are accustomed to. Cafeterias are adding to the new element of bustle in the urban parishioner's life by converting him to the quick snack or sandwich, and luring his custom by the prizes offered by the makers of the new foreign soft drinks. Their sharp glare of gaiety and their pretty waitresses attract the cinema crowds, and pander to the habit of idle, late-night wandering, so beloved of the Madrilenian, which various governments have unsuccessfully tried to curb.[1] The official State bulletin of November 26th, 1940, denounced this habit as a fashion imposed by 'a lazy minority', and ordered theatres and cinemas to close before midnight and bars before 1 a.m.; midday meals in hotels and schools were to be finished by 2.30 p.m., and the evening meal by 9 p.m. It was another bold but useless attempt to reform the city and, incidentally, to procure a much-needed saving on electricity and in food consumption. Life in the café, tavern and cafeteria is gay and ebullient on ordinary days; it is doubly so on holidays.

The public pageant and other forms of 'passive' leisure must, if the Madrilenian is to feel a sense of affinity and be able to associate himself with the proceedings, conform with the characteristic fondness for individual display and ostentation. The most important are the religious fiesta and the lay spectacle. When a man spends up to sixty hours a week working, and another twelve hours travelling uncomfortably to and from work, he is in a favourable mood to be diverted on Sundays or holy-days. Periodic extravagance and fine array have a particular appeal to people renowned for the normal austerity of their life, in accordance with the sobriety of the Spanish temperament.

Religious fiestas in Madrid (apart from the regular Sunday devotions) are directly related to the cult of patron saints or the celebration of outstanding events in the life and death of Christ.

---

[1] Even in 1631 there were complaints by Viennese diplomats about the late-night habits of Madrid. See *Biblioteca Nacional M.S.* 2363, folio 293, Vienna, March 10th, 1631. The introduction of public street lighting in 1871 only encouraged the custom.

It is on these occasions that the parish as a cohesive unit can most easily be defined, since they become a focus for parish or district loyalties. They may be divided as follows:

*Local:*  (i) Popular cults of a small quarter, e.g. Our Lady of Mercy in Silva Street, the Virgin of Atocha, Jesús de Medinaceli, etc.

(ii) The patron saint of a parish, e.g. San Martín.

(iii) The patron saint of a district, e.g. Our Lady of the Dove for La Latina.

(iv) The patron saint of a guild, e.g. Santa Lucia for seamstresses.

*City:*  The patron saint of Madrid, i.e. San Isidro the Labourer. (Rural districts of Madrid province may have two patron saints, as does Ramosierra.)

*National:*  (i) The patron saint of Spain, i.e. Santiago.

(ii) The patron saint of a guild, e.g. San Martín for tailors.

(iii) Religious festivals of Holy Week, the Epiphany etc.

The brilliance of the three major feasts—Holy Thursday, Corpus Christi and the Ascension—is now a thing of the past. They lost public interest when the Church suppressed their pagan element; for example, the 'Tarasca' of Corpus Christi in the eighteenth century. Although the ritual calendar is full of fascinating feast days and practices, I shall confine myself here to a brief description of the Good Friday processions.

Even Holy Week in Madrid has lost much of the magnificence that marked its sixteenth-century processions (known as 'The Processions of Blood') which are still carried on in Avila, Cartagena and Seville. Since 1939, however, there has been a revival of solemn pageantry, and many parishioners now take part with their favoured images borne by brotherhoods, followed by penitents barefoot and carrying heavy crosses and chains. These dignified, silent processions on the night of Good Friday are so ordered as to represent, by the succession of images, the journey to Calvary. When I joined it, all the participants[1] from San Martín wore black

---

[1] It would be fair to say that the majority of the participants are leaders and controllers; the majority of the spectators are servers. In

robes and cone-shaped hoods emblazoned with a blood-red cross at the breast, and carried ancient, tall candles or small crosses. There are no recognizable personalities except the organizing officials, who carry pilgrims' staffs topped by silver crosses, and brotherhood members who wear pendant crucifixes. Many famous men consider it a duty to disguise their rank under a penitent's hood. No women participate; but many who are attached to the brotherhoods have the envied task of adorning and dressing the statues. Any parishioner is entitled to join the procession on payment of a small donation.

The two floats (*pasos*) supporting the images from San Martín were mounted on rubber-tyred trailers supplied by the Ministry of Transport. Outside the parish no great fervour surrounds these two life-size figures—the one a prostrate wax-like Christ specked with painted blood, in a glass coffin; the other a 'Virgin of Loneliness and Great Sorrow', her eyes shedding glass tears. Spectators are, however, moved to clapping (quickly hushed) at the sight of the legendary Jesús de Medinaceli image[1] resplendent in a twenty-foot embroidered robe and followed by 1,500 penitents. The facsimile statues of the 'Christ of the Great Power'[2] and 'La Macarena' of Seville, both carried by resident Andalusians in Madrid, often inspire *saetas* (pious ejaculatory songs) from fervent bystanders and spectators on balconies. All images are heavily flanked by pear-shaped electric bulbs in glass bowls as well as by flaming candles and heaped vases of flowers. Through the sounds of bugle and drum, the dragging of feet, and the signalling thud of the officials' staffs, there comes the faint tinkling of these candelabra. Costly jewels, necklaces and crowns make up the Virgin's ornaments. Most of the many thousands of spectators kneel as float after float[3] falters by. There is a simple but terrible beauty about the whole scene.

1957, approximately 120 parishioners took part but, in all, the number of penitent participants for the whole of Madrid was in the region of 50,000 and the number of nazarene brothers about 7,000, according to the press. See the daily newspaper *Informaciones*, March 20th, 1957.

[1] An estimated 20,000 file past this image on the first Friday of every month. There is a special queue for those with invitations.

[2] The original image was given a Communist Party card during the Civil War so that it might be spared to Seville.

[3] The column from San Martín linked up with nine other parish

The more localized fiestas which specifically concern the city
or a district are characterized by a regular form. They not only
celebrate the actual day of the patron saint but (as in Ramosierra)
may cover longer periods sometimes lasting, in Madrid, up to three
weeks. Their *raison d'être* is sacred: their celebration is, on the
whole, profane. They begin with the warm weather, and the most
popular are those at the height of summer.

In the first days of May, heralds, trumpeters and kettle-
drummers in full eighteenth-century costume proclaim the feast of
San Isidro[1] the Labourer, patron saint of Madrid. Wags are fond
of saying that he is the ideal patron for the city, since he prayed
whilst a visiting angel did the ploughing for him. But his true
association with Madrid lies in his power to bring rain; and his
shrine is marked by a fountain reputed to have health-giving pro-
perties.[2] It stands on a small hill overlooking the River Manzanares and the bridges of Toledo and Segovia.

In the dusty meadow below, after taking the waters, picnic
crowds of families sit amidst the thick smell of oil-fried fritters,
with a happy disregard for the dead in the two large cemeteries at
their elbows. The fair that occupies their attention afterwards
and lasts for several days is perhaps the biggest, noisiest and
dustiest of the whole year. But it is not the most popular, because
the weather is unsettled and there are unpleasant memories of the
site's use for executions during the Civil War. For all that, while
few parishioners from San Martín seemed to visit the site regularly, many make a point of going to the fair.

Mass is celebrated at the shrine on the morning of May 15th
and various fruits are offered up to the saint. In the afternoon,
there is a professional bullfight followed by the classical dance
of San Isidro, which includes competitions in the *chotis* (schot-
tische). During the evening the image of the saint, accompanied
by another of the Virgin, is taken in procession through the streets
from the cathedral, and further gifts of fruit in his honour are

---

columns at the central square of the city and then filed through the
parish in a procession which lasted, in 1957, from 11 p.m. to 4 a.m.

[1] Born 1082; died 1170; canonized 1622. Legend has it that he struck
a rock with his goad to produce water because his plough-team of oxen
was thirsty.

[2] Madrid claims to have the finest drinking water in Spain.

presented by the Town Council. A public dance and fair follow in the main square of the old city. One notices that the pattern of ritual and festivity is, in essence, the same as that in the pueblo. This also applies to the many fiestas throughout the summer; the chronological log below will show the modern accretions to the basic pattern.

*Morning*

1. Reveille (*Diana*) by drums and fife, fireworks, and church bells in the early hours.
2. Publication by the common crier. This now often takes the form of a public discourse (sometimes by radio) from a well-known literary figure.
3. Tour of the district by giant-headed carnival[1] figures, or by locally elected beauty queens in old-fashioned gigs with retinues, to make offerings to the patron saint or Virgin.
4. Muster by a brass band (often military) of the local mayor and councillors, the military chief of the district, the municipal judge, and procession to the parish church for solemn High Mass, with a sermon by a guest preacher.
5. Inauguration of art exhibitions, performances of puppet shows or other traditional art forms.
6. Distribution of food parcels to the poor, from the town hall.
7. Midday concert by the brass band in the most popular local square or cinema.

*Afternoon*

8. A bullfight, football or 'pelota' (Spanish variation of jai alai) match, or such competitive activities as sack races, motor-scooter trials, 'hunt the chicken', card games in local taverns, racing for ribbons by men on bicycles. (The multicoloured ribbons are usually donated by girls, and the competition is a recognized prelude to courting. The race is run on horses in the pueblos.)
9. Public refreshment for local children and/or the poor, with gifts of free tickets for local entertainments.
10. Religious procession with the image of the local patron saint

[1] The pre-Lenten carnival is now forbidden, as is the wearing of masks at any secular fiesta; it led to too many old scores being settled incognito.

mounted on fire-brigade carts or municipal vehicles, with the ecclesiastical, civil, and police authorities in attendance. Evening service and benediction in the parish church.

11. After dinner, a firework display, local fun-fair, popular dance or 'kermesse' (admission sometimes chargeable); variety shows with guest radio stars, dancing competitions for the tango and *chotis*; displays of regional folk culture, raffles (with prizes donated by local industry), election of beauty queens and maids of honour by streets or local quarters, and prize-giving for the best adorned balcony, window or communal court-yard.

The extent of these activities is controlled by the funds at the disposal of the fiesta organizing committees, derived from donations by local businesses or from direct levies on the neighbours. District committees are autonomous, and are usually composed of priests, industrialists and Falange officials, under the direction of the local district council. Public expressions of charity are now essential to these fiestas. The poor are either directly fed, or are given food parcels or even small sums in cash; always provided they possess the indispensable certificate from parish church or local council. Scholarships are sometimes offered on these particular days, or dowry subsidies are given to professing Catholic girls of the district. The election of beauty queens or local 'Misses' has now extended to occupations, so that one finds a 'Señorita Metro' or a 'Señorita Cafetería'.

Throughout the fiesta period, especially in the older parts of the city, there is an accent on *castizo* ties with the locality. Costumes of the *chulo* and the feminine *chulapa* are frequently worn at fairs, or in dress competitions. The street decoration, the officially encouraged appearance of organ-grinders, and the presentation of old-time Spanish operettas (*zarzuelas*) are all aimed at evoking the Madrid of the 1890 period. But the strident noise of the round-abouts and 'bumpem' cars at the fairs is anathema to the official campaign for a silent city. One by one the fairs are being removed to open ground away from street areas, and so another link with the locality is broken.

Another aspect of 'passive' leisure is the lay spectacle provided by the national fiesta of the bullfight, and the newer enthusiasm

'... and now Olmeda centres. Azpeita traps it, but Olsen dribbles the ball away from him and passes to Rial

for professional sports. Interest in the bullfight is now waning among all but rabid devotees, and the best seats are packed with camera-laden tourists. Nevertheless, the bullfighter is still an heroic idol who must win or lose his reputation in the Madrid arenas, for the Spaniard is a seasoned critic of his own traditional practice. The working parishioner will probably buy a cigar and attend at the ring; or will at least take a close interest in one of the ten fights during the fiestas of San Isidro, when the best 'swords' are on display. Even now, the aristocrat occasionally participates on horseback in the bullring at a charity show; while the *tienta* or week-end party at a nearby country estate, where young bulls and bullfighters are accustomed to the ring atmosphere, is a highly exclusive gathering. There remains a flamboyance and a thrill in the dignified but dangerous bullfight ceremony which can never be quite replaced in the hearts of handkerchief-waving or hissing crowds.

An interest in league football now tends to outweigh that in all other sports among the younger men. Football was introduced into Spain in 1882 by the English, and most of the operative words such as 'penalty', 'goal', 'offside', are incorporated directly into Spanish. Association matches are held always on Sundays or holidays (as are bullfights), and excite hilarious triumph or deep depression, according to the result. All taverns and many cafés blaringly relay the match by radio. The 1957 victory of the Real Madrid team over Manchester United in the European Cup was featured in headlines second only to 'Crisis in Jordan'; but it is typical of Spanish courtesy and tact that a barman asked his clients not to 'crow', because there was an Englishman present. Women, too, now appear in the banked seats of the monstrous stadiums. Preoccupation with personalities, however, is the striking point to notice. The life-histories, merits and faults of each prominent player, and of some foreign footballers too, are intimately known and violently discussed, so that the professional[1] football idol is a household name. It is, therefore, the individual's brilliance rather than the team's which matters, since it draws the association with one's idol closer.

[1] Falange organizations and syndicate groups now provide sports grounds for accredited amateur members, but physical exertion for its own sake is not, on the whole, popular.

Football, then, is mainly a matter of the individual spectator's identification with a chosen hero. The same individual can, as we have seen, associate himself with the traditional festivals and pageants either as a Catholic, or as a Madrilenian, or as a parishioner of San Martín.

There are, however, other and more modern media of leisure activity which tend to approximate tastes and leisure habits (both active and passive) to new, world-wide and untraditional standards; and foremost among these new media is broadcasting. Since the psychology of suggestion is always most powerful when it is aimed at the largest proportion of the population in their most receptive moments, the volume of radio advertising is immense. Next to the bed, a wireless set is the most essential article in Madrilenian homes, especially those of servers. The wealthy controller and leader will supplement his set with one of the expensive new 'pick-ups'.

Figures[1] show that out of every sixty minutes occupied by the spoken word, approximately fifteen minutes are devoted to commercial slogans and exhortations. Commercial groups now organize 'live' programmes before an audience; their success largely depends on the personality of a loquacious compère and the giving away of valuable prizes in 'double or nothing' shows. They are marked by the growing participation of enthusiastic amateurs who have increasingly adopted the practice (borrowed from professional artistes) of 'dedicating' a song or act to some friend or relative. Such a dedication by a suitor to his *novia* may cut directly across obstacles set up by her family and leap over the recognized steps in courting procedure.

Radio Madrid itself broadcasts for sixteen hours daily and, by such request programmes as 'Know Your Neighbour', provides a link between family groups and communal courtyards. Food prices help the housewife choose her shopping in the morning, and serial plays keep her fast to the radio in the afternoon. Workshops, factories, hairdressers', and department stores operate under the crackle of light music. But programmes must be short to hold the butterfly-attention of listeners, and rarely exceed fifteen minutes in length. Only in Holy Week are religious music, plays, and talks broadcast uninterrupted by commercialism. Television is still

[1] Taken from the *Anuario Estadístico de España*, Madrid, 1957.

in the experimental stage and is a great curiosity, but the few sets available are expensive, and irregular programmes flicker for a three-hour period only in the late evening.

When the parishioner is not parading in the *paseo*, sitting in a café, or listening to the radio, he is probably in the cinema. Madrid had eighty-nine cinemas listed in October 1957, and fifty-three of these gave continuous performances from 10 a.m. or from 4 p.m. until 1 a.m. the next day. They show, in the main, American or Spanish 'dramas', with a high proportion of short documentary or propaganda films. The palatial cinemas in the Gran Vía are covered with brightly vulgar posters, which are as heavily censored as the films they advertise. But the parishioner is either bewildered or amused by the pace and nature of foreign habits depicted on the screen, and is not, on the whole, prone to imitate them. At most, the American film causes an earlier sophistication in the young, and adds another divisive element to the estrangement between parents and offspring. Spanish productions, therefore, compare unfavourably with imported films only when they attempt to step outside the limits imposed by the national temperament and their own technical deficiencies.

The same might be said of the fifteen theatres in Madrid, of which only six or seven regularly produce legitimate plays or visiting ballet. The remainder present variety shows which greatly depend for their success on Andalusian song and dance; or else low quality revues in which the embarrassed posturings of chorus girls are accepted with impatient tolerance. One wonders whether the restrictions imposed by censorship on these media—the cinema and theatre—are any greater than those of the hidebound convention in pre-Shavian London.

Although the cinema habit is widespread, it has not developed into the passionate obsession found in some parts of northern Europe. The vicarious thrills presented to the parishioner in artificial, flickering shadows are too far removed from his experience for him to treat them more than lightly. For example, women are often far more fascinated by shots of an American kitchen than by the heroine's predicament. But, like the radio, the cinema is a counter-attraction to organized communal leisure, and is responsible for stimulating fashions or 'crazes'. Again, in spite of and perhaps because of the great tradition in the Spanish theatre, audiences prefer the dark anonymity of the cinema to the theatre except on those rare occasions when, by the sheer quality of his writing, a modern playwright succeeds in pleasing both the censor and the public.

Other evening entertainment, advertised throughout Madrid, is provided by sixteen *salas de fiesta*, thirteen of which could be classified as night-clubs or tea-dance salons far beyond the server's pocket, whilst the remaining three are popularly-priced dance halls. There are no street entertainers or buskers, with the possible exception of the organ-grinder in typical *chulo* costume, whose reappearance has been encouraged by the City Council: otherwise this type of exhibitionism is left to the gypsy at fairs. The students' orchestra, 'La Tuna', is the nearest approach to the strolling player, and university students are also the only notable enthusiasts of the amateur theatre, which draws heavily on national classics.

One curious survival, however, is the *coplera*, or singer of popular ballads, occasionally to be found at markets in the parish. Accompanied by a male guitarist, she sings the thirty or so four-lined stanzas with no pretensions to tone or quality of voice, but with particular attention to the words. Her primary intention is not to entertain, but to sell the songs afterwards for a few coins. Her efforts are never applauded and are regarded with some amusement. Some of the titles are very expressive: 'The Child Abandoned by its Mother at the Inn', 'The Villainy of a Son', 'The Kidnapped Daughter' and 'The Horrible Crime on the Outskirts of Santiago de Compostela'. All seem to be stories with a heavy moral, told in song; and they are of interest here only because they reflect the degree of sophistication of the small groups (all servers) who listen and buy. They are a folk art-form which represents the transition from sacred to secular song. The similarity between these and the *corridos* in Mexico described by Redfield[1] is striking. Street vendors also sell cheap song-sheets, but these are conventional romantic verses from the south already largely diffused on gramophone records.

In his reaction to the written word, the parishioner's passive leisure is again restricted by the limits of his own desires and by

[1] See R. Redfield, *Tepoztlan—A Mexico Village*, Chicago, 1930, p. 180.

censorship. There are over 1,000 vendors of newspapers in Madrid, some of whom are now installed in solidly-built kiosks with their portable radios and small stoves for winter; but the greater number are ensconced in home-made stalls, or at simple street-corner pitches. Most kiosks keep large stocks of cinema and fashion magazines;[1] comic papers ('TBOs') of the type of 'Roy Rogers— Cowboy' or 'Superman' (translated), small quantities of tobacco and perhaps lottery tickets. They also conduct a busy lending library service in paper-backed romantic or adventure novels (many of them translated from the English), whose borrowers are mostly maids and taxi-drivers.

There are four morning, one weekly and three evening papers which supply the news and the most important lottery results; two others (with the greatest circulation) deal exclusively with crime and sport. Some are controlled either by the Monarchist faction, the Church, or the Falange, but the habit of reading the daily news is not a majority one, for the bulk of these papers is devoted to foreign affairs or advertisements. Foreign correspondents complain that nothing of news value ever happens in Madrid, and attribute it to the national trait of minding one's own business, and the Madrilenians' unproductive leisure habits. Columnists are inclined to give abstract personal opinions rather than facts—there is little deliberate criticism—and this cannot be entirely accounted for by censorship. The parishioner therefore tends to buy a paper for some specific reason, such as the entertainments column or the announcements of flats to let, businesses for sale, and so on. Women are not regular newspaper readers, and there are no 'Aunty Jane' columns to lend advice on personal problems, although letters to the editor have now been introduced. A strong satirical note is apparent in the two main humorous magazines, and many cartoons mirror the frustrating aspects of modern life, and amusingly scoff at the unsolved problems of local authorities.[2]

It is an impossible task to define the reading habits of an urban population, or to do more than single out certain characteristics in so-called cultural pastimes. Public libraries are magnificent but

---

[1] There were 539 publications in 1952. See *15 Years of Spanish Culture* published by the Diplomatic Information Office, Madrid, 1952.

[2] Compare 'Las Fallas' in Valencia at Easter, local fiestas whose central themes are 'guys' satirizing local problems, which are later burnt.

few[1] and do not generally lend books except to students. The librarian, therefore, is not an important figure in influencing cultural choice among the masses. National Book Fairs are held yearly when ten per cent discounts are offered to all buyers, but paper is expensive here compared with Britain, and cheap editions are not common; so that in 1947 a total of only 5,300 books was published—that is, an approximate ratio of one book per 6,000 inhabitants. Nevertheless, new and second-hand bookshops abound in Madrid, although they are by no means the first choice of the gift-shopper.

As one passes an old house where Lope de Vega lived and wrote, or a tavern that Goya frequented, one is reminded that Madrid has some of the finest collections of incunabula in the world and probably the greatest art museum in Europe—the Prado. Like most museums, it is now visited more by foreigners than by nationals.[2] This merely reflects a general movement whereby the gain in popular literature and art is made at the cost of more traditional art forms. But the cultural wealth and art treasures are not generally locked away in glass cases; they are on the walls and shelves of public and private buildings as well as churches, and many of them are in daily use.

It is, however, in the spoken word that the parishioner finds his true choice for active leisure. This does not drive him into exclusive associations of the functional-aim type, except in the realm of sport. Apart from a comparatively minor participation in those set up by Falange, syndicate, or Catholic organizations, he evidences little desire to segregate himself into vocational groups with a separate *esprit de corps*. 'Morale' symbols such as the pennant, badge or pin are conspicuously few and are mostly related to a religious patron or aristocratic order. It is true that there are six major clubs in the city, but four of them provide sporting facilities such as golf, tennis, swimming and polo. If membership throws the parishioner into contact with a group recognized as enjoying a superior social and economic position, this is a secondary consideration for him compared to the advan-

[1] In 1952, Madrid University libraries jointly possessed over half a million books. See the Diplomatic Information Office, op. cit.

[2] In 1951, there were 405,782 visitors, some 50,000 of whom were nationals.

tages the club supplies.[1] It is the unobtrusive association, such as the Opus Dei, with a suprasocial aim, and providing means for mixing in daily life at all levels of society, that is the most influential.

However, the ordinary man has a passion for conversation, and this revolves around his ability to assume several personalities with ease. He is a natural actor but not a natural intellectual, though what he lacks in subject matter is made up for by an enviable command of oratory. Although a widely-read or much-travelled man is the exception, a traditional cultism in his speech and literary background, coupled with a basic Christian philosophy that never wavers, makes the educated man a born conversationalist. Formal gatherings never pass without their quota of laudatory speeches, and at 7 p.m. there is an impressive variety of lectures available to the intellectually-minded public. But it is at the informal gathering over the coffee table—especially at the *tertulia*—that the parishioner, in full discussion with his friends, is in his leisure moments most at ease. For him, then, time is more than money; and, although it is said that leisure is the waste of time (just as consumption is the waste of goods), he will not agree. He may pass the time, he may even 'kill' time, but if he is in company he will not feel that he is wasting it.

Finally, increasing individual transport (like labour-saving devices and tinned foods) is effecting a new leisure pattern for the moneyed parishioner. Easy-purchase payments are also bringing it within the range of a wider income group. The extraordinary rise in the number of motor bicycles means that a new exodus from the city takes place every week. No longer is the country weekend or the summer holiday entirely the privilege of a wealthy few. The young are also freed by this means from parental control, and courting habits are being sidetracked by the motor-scooter. Although a popular and cheap family car has still to be put on the market, the national product 'Biscuter' is gaining in popularity. Its unprepossessing appearance, however, and the fact that the driver when seated is almost at the ankle level of the pedestrian, are not features which easily satisfy Castilian pride. 'It is all right for the Catalans,' they say, 'but it's really a toy.'

---

[1] Some, especially military officers, may be influenced by the fact that the Pretender's son is now a member of one.

New trends in leisure habits are indicative of the social change that the urban parish is experiencing. Young people have more opportunity and a greater range for privacy. City women are invading what were once exclusively male domains of leisure, and many wives now frequently accompany their husbands in leisure activities outside the home. Moreover, because of a greater desire to entertain, especially on the part of leaders and prosperous controllers, the home is being opened up to a wider variety of guests no longer composed solely of kin and intimate friends. Work and leisure in the city are more sharply divided than in the pueblo. The holy-day is becoming a holiday; the fiesta is losing its religious connotation. Perhaps less than ever before in its history, is San Martín, as a parish, a primary focal point for leisure activities.

# *Epilogue*

## THE CITY AND THE VILLAGE

As a detailed analytical comparison of the urban and rural Spanish parish is not possible in this book these few closing comments are aimed at setting in their proper perspective some of the facts given previously.

Neither San Martín nor Ramosierra should be considered as wholly urban or wholly rural in character. Both have a long history as parishes—San Martín since 1098, Ramosierra since at least 1538 (the date of its earliest records). Whatever the original form of its settlement, San Martín is now not just a conglomeration of urbanized peasants and rural ideals; it has characteristics peculiar to all city parishes and a special personality of its own reflected in its five distinctive areas. Nevertheless, there steadily filters into its jurisdiction a proportion of the constant influx of migrants to Madrid; these and the regular rural contacts that the parish daily maintains undoubtedly exert a modifying influence on its otherwise urban way of life.

Again, despite the comparative isolation of Ramosierra in the forested sierras it is not culturally self-sufficient. Dependent to an ever-increasing degree on the provincial capital, it contains elements such as the *élite*, the police and the State employees who not only serve dutifully to bring the national closer to the local but who also wilfully cultivate and value their contacts with the outside world. Moreover, the Madrilenian resident who returns faithfully to his native Ramosierra for the August fiestas is not necessarily pining to return for ever; and every year he brings the breath and the effect of the city with him. So, too, the ex-emigrant rarely entirely severs his ties outside the pueblo which, although they may prejudice his struggle to reintegrate himself into village life after many years abroad, in part help to sustain him. Recently mindful of the virtues (not to say the vices) of town or city life he

233

has introduced some of these (e.g. the drainage and electrical systems) into the pueblo, as well as the vestiges of an urban ethos he once enjoyed. Not least, the young are another element who effect some dilution of pueblo life as a result of turning their eyes and imitative tendencies towards the brighter lights of the provincial and national capitals.

Yet to imagine that changes in the so-called traditional culture are only a recent phenomenon would be to ignore the reality. Ramosierra, after all, was a favourite hunting lodge for courtly nobles in centuries past, and once boasted of six chapels. Wandering pilgrims must have roamed into its confines bringing news and perhaps different customs from far-off shrines since the discovery of Santiago's tomb at Compostela in the ninth century; and who knows for how long the vagabond seasonal labourer has been following the grape harvests to the north and passing through Ramosierra, as he does today? As for the Mesta sheep route which runs so close to the pueblo, no one can quite calculate the cultural effect it had in the past. The picture then of a forest village happy in its ignorance and independence is a romantic but a misleading one. There has long been a curious discontent in Ramosierra underlaid by the feeling that old ways must eventually fade and that new ways are discomfiting.

To an even greater extent, San Martín—at the very centre of the royal court and the capital for so long—has undergone much domestic change and many foreign influences. New perhaps is the North American airbase worker with his tempting dollars and machine culture; but the flamboyant tourist with his clutch of cameras, the foreign student and, for that matter, the impecunious foreign teacher are no more than modern counterparts of figures who have been familiar on the San Martín scene for centuries, as indeed have the foreign diplomat, monk and merchant. Their effect on Castilian society cannot easily be gauged, yet we know that whereas change is often violently imposed from within the society itself it may also be insinuated gradually from without.

To my mind, this variable change has been a constant factor in the urban life of Madrid (and hence in San Martín) since it became a capital, and its effects have probably reached out even to Ramosierra. No doubt both parishes are undergoing a swifter transition now which will presumably increase in pace as the Age of Technology advances, but it would be quite wrong to consider them as having been static before.

Despite this, it is true to say that the concept of the parish as a meaningful unity has persevered in the individual and official mind. That it is synonymous with the *campanilismo* of the pueblo only strengthens its force, for the village and parish of Ramosierra are essentially one and the same. In San Martín, however, parish and neighbourhood are no longer interchangeable terms. Certainly the individual is reminded of the still vibrant force of parish authority at a baptism, at a marriage, at a funeral or, for instance, when he needs charity; even on the many days of fiesta it still has deep significance for him since it helps him to achieve his spiritual reality—an integral part of his general culture. Yet he will grudgingly admit that his sense of actual coexistence with others is probably determined less by parish boundaries than by the effective range of criticism or approval voiced by the tight group of neighbours among whom he lives. This is properly the sense of neighbourhood.

With few exceptions I have purposefully avoided the use of the word 'community', for it is far too ambiguous. It can, however, be broken down into two main factors whose interaction provides a clue to what is usually meant by community. Some distinction should be drawn between what I call a sense of coexistence (e.g. the *campanilismo* of the pueblo) and the sense of loyalty which may or may not accompany it. In the urban setting, one can but rarely make an active choice of the area in which one is to live; one is either born into it or constrained to live there by circumstance of family and of work or by availability of housing. Nevertheless, loyalty to that 'community' (however large or small an area and population its definition may involve) is still a matter of choice— and I do not refer here to a mere nostalgic attachment to locality. The sense of coexistence—strong in the village parish, weak in the city parish—has a permanent static quality. It is based on a constant, territorial relationship. The sense of loyalty, on the other hand, is based on a variable, social relationship and is an abstract senti- ment. Indeed it is but one of many of its type and fluctuates con- siderably according to the role that the individual is playing, e.g. whether it be that of a family head, a worker, a sodality member, a villager, a parishioner and so on. With the increase of the social distance involved in these relationships so its intensity weakens. Thus, whilst the villager in Ramosierra may have many, even conflicting, loyalties it is none the less more likely that these would merge and equate with his sense of coexistence or *campanilismo* more often than would those of the San Martín parishioner merge and equate with *his* sense of coexistence.

One's social stake in Ramosierra as a 'son of the pueblo', greatly fostered by the Pine Luck, is certainly more important than one's social position within the village; for the individual, it is even more important than being a Castilian or being a Spaniard. Under normal conditions, this is quite the reverse in Madrid; the accident of being *castizo* or of belonging to a particular area in the city such as San Martín has little significance these days.

On the other hand, it would be misleading to overstress the practical importance of *campanilismo* in the pueblo and whatever its counterpart may be in the city. For this sense of coexistence, however strong or weak, bows to the respective loyalties binding family, work, social, religious or patronage groups which divide the village into cliques and, in the city, often range far outside neighbourhood or parish limits. In either case the result is not exactly conducive to civic-mindedness or to so-called community services.

It is not surprising to me, therefore, that there are two parallel channels linking town and country in Castile: the one set up by official State and Church structures, the other established by patronage. A fear of abuses by a recurrent series of power groups partly accounts for the ambivalent behaviour of both citizen and peasant; but it is also the outcome of their attempts to resolve the dilemma of segmentary personalized loyalties having to work within, and often against, the nationalizing impersonality of official systems of authority.

# BIBLIOGRAPHY

Aitken, B., 'The Burning of the May at Belarado', *Folklore*, 1926.

Alford, V. and Gallop, R., *The Traditional Dance*, London, 1926.

Arensberg, C., *The Irish Countryman*, New York, 1950.

Brennan, Gerald, *The Spanish Labyrinth*, Cambridge, 1943; *The Face of Spain*, London, 1950.

Buero Vallejo, Antonio, *Fiesta*, Madrid, 1954.

Calvo-Sotelo, Joaquín, *La Muralla*, Madrid, 1954.

Capmany, A., *El Baile y la Danza: Folklor y Costumbres Espagñolas*, Vol. 2, Barcelona, 1931.

Caro Baroja, Julio, *El Sociocentrismo de los pueblos españoles*, U.N.C., Tomo 2, Mendoza, 1954.

Chapin, F. S., *Experimental Designs in Sociological Research*, London, 1947.

Del Valle, P. Florentino, *Las Reformas Sociales en España*, Madrid, 1946.

Elworthy, F. T., *Horns of Honour*, London, 1900.

Evans-Pritchard, E. E., *The Institutions of Primitive Society* (broadcast talks), Oxford, 1954.

Foster, Geo. M., 'An Ethnological Reconnaissance of Spain', *American Anthropologist*, Vol. 3, 1951; *Empire's Children*, Smithsonian Institute, 1948.

Haddon, A. C., *Magic and Fetishism*, London, 1906.

Laverty, Maura, *No more than Human*, London, 1944.

Linton, Ralph, *The Cultural Background of Personality*, London, 1947.

Lynd, R. S. and H. M., *Middletown in Transition*, New York, 1937.

MacIver, R. M., and Page, C. H., *Society*, London, 1949.

(de) Madariaga, Salvador, *Englishmen, Frenchmen and Spaniards*, O.U.P., 1949.

Martineau, Harriet, *Society in America*, London, 1837.

Mesonero Romanos, *Escenas Matritenses*, Madrid, 1851.

Mumford, Lewis, *The Culture of Cities*, London, 1938.

Nathan, George, and Mencken, H. L., *The American Credo*, New York, 1929.

Parry, J. H., *The Spanish Theory of Empire in XVI Century*, Cambridge, 1940.

Peers, E. Allison, *Spain in Eclipse*, London, 1943.

Pitt-Rivers, J. A., *The People of the Sierra*, London, 1954.

Pritchett, V. S., *The Spanish Temper*, London, 1954.

Radcliffe-Brown, A. R., 'Social Sanctions', *Encyclopedia of Social Sciences*, New York, 1933; (and Forde, Daryll (Eds.), *African Systems of Kinship and Marriage*, O.U.P., 1950).

Redfield, R., *The Folk Culture of the Yucatan*, 1941; *Tepoztlan—a Mexican Village*, Chicago, 1950.

Sainz de Robles, Federico Carlos, *Historia y Estampas de la Villa de Madrid*, Madrid, 1949.

Schneider, Pierre, 'The Minimum Man', article in *The Listener*, December, 1955.

Simmel, Georg, 'Superiority and Subordination as Subject Matter of Sociology', *American Journal of Sociology*, 1896-97.

(de) Unamuno, Miguel, *Obras Completas*, Madrid, 1950.

(del) Valle-Inclán, Ramon, *Flor de Santidad*, Madrid, 1920.

Veblen, Thorstein, *The Theory of a Leisure Class*, New York, 1899.

Vergara y Martín, Gabriel María, *Provincia de Segovia*, Madrid, 1900.

Warner, W. Lloyd and Lunt, Paul S., *The Status System of a Modern Community*, New Haven, 1942.

Young, Sir George, *The New Spain*, London, 1953.


OFFICIAL SOURCES AND NEWSPAPERS

*Archivo Histórico* (Biblioteca Nacional)—manuscripts.
*Anuario Estadístico de España*, 1957.
*Censo de Edificios y Viviendas*, 1950.
*Civil Code*, 1931.
*Guía de la Iglesia en España*, 1954.
*Heráldica Guía de la Sociedad*, 1956.
*15 Years of Spanish Culture 1938-1952*, edited by the Diplomatic Information Office, Madrid, 1952.
*Informaciones.*
*Hoja de Lunes.*

*A.B.C.*
*Ya.*
*Madrid.*
U.N.O., *Economic Survey of Europe*, Geneva, 1957.
U.N.E.S.C.O., E/ICEF/L642, 1954.
*The Universe.*
*The New York Times.*

# INDEX

# ABOUT THE AUTHOR

MICHAEL KENNY teaches in the Department of Anthropology at the Catholic University of America in Washington, D.C., and is Director of the Latin American Institute there. He is Editor of the *Anthropological Quarterly*.

Mr. Kenny, a native of England, studied at Oxford and the University of Zurich. He was a captain in the Indian Army during most of World War II, serving in the countries of the Near and Middle East. In the postwar period he traveled extensively in Europe and spent more than five years in Spain. There he was paid the singular honor "to be made a member of the fraternity of the village I studied . . . by a people who accepted me in spite of being a foreigner—a rare bird for them—with warmth and affection."

He is currently writing a sequel to *A Spanish Tapestry* which is a firsthand account of the problems concerned with cultural assimiliation of twentieth-century Spanish immigrants in Cuba and Mexico.